THE

PARENT'S GUIDE:

CONTAINING THE

DISEASES OF INFANCY AND CHILDHOOD

AND THEIR

HOMŒOPATHIC TREATMENT.

TO WHICH IS ADDED A TREATISE ON

THE METHOD OF REARING CHILDREN FROM THEIR EARLIEST INFANCY;

COMPRISING THE ESSENTIAL BRANCHES OF

MORAL AND PHYSICAL EDUCATION.

BY J. LAURIE, M. D.,

LICENTIATE OF THE ROYAL COLLEGE OF SURGEONS, EDINBURGH; GRADUATE OF THE HOMŒOPATHIC MEDICAL COLLEGE OF PENNSYLVANIA, ETC.

EDITED, WITH ADDITIONS,

BY WALTER WILLIAMSON, M. D.,

PROFESSOR OF MATERIA MEDICA AND THERAPEUTICS IN THE HOMŒOPATHIC MEDICAL COLLEGE OF PENNSYLVANIA.

PHILADELPHIA:
PUBLISHED BY RADEMACHER & SHEEK, 239 ARCH ST.
NEW YORK: WM. RADDE.—BOSTON: OTIS CLAPP.—ST. LOUIS: J. G. WESSELHŒFT.—PITTSBURGH: J. G. BACKOFEN.—CHICAGO: D. S. SMITH, M. D.—NEW ORLEANS: D. R. LUYTIES, M. D.
1854.

Stereotyped by G. Charles. Printed by King & Baird.

PREFACE.

This work has been suggested, firstly, by the acknowledged assistance which may be rendered in the domestic management of young families, by simple directions as to general treatment in all ordinary forms of the more common diseases of childhood; and, secondly, by the peculiar applicability of the medicines administered according to the Homœopathic rule to the cases of young children. The reasons of this special aptitude are obvious, and have been too frequently commented upon elsewhere, by the Author, to require recapitulation. There were already other works in circulation, embracing the same sphere, and emanating from disciples of the old school of medicine, but there was, hitherto, no Homœopathic publication which was confined exclusively to the treatment of infancy, and in which the medical directions had been combined with those relating to moral and physical education.

It is the opinion of the author that these departments in the rearing of children should be sedulously united, in order that they may, invariably, be conducted in conformity to each other, for reasons which he has taken the liberty of explaining in the body of this work. And, prompted by this persuasion, he has essayed to produce a treatise containing regulations by which all the branches of regimen and tutelage are made conformable. The author feels, likewise, that while great service may be rendered by works of this kind, some mischief may also be imputed to them, unless care be taken to warn parents against the error of trusting too much to their own judgment in the treatment of dangerous diseases, lest serious complications be induced, which, by timely professional advice, might, possibly, have easily been averted. He has, accordingly, been careful to announce this caution, and to repeat it constantly, in speaking of particular symptoms and morbid manifestations which are ever to be looked upon with suspicion.

Lastly, whilst he has, in some few instances, entered somewhat minutely into the treatment of the various phases of the malady under consideration, he has, at the same time, been at great pains to avoid anything approaching to intricacy and difficulty, by striving to reduce every suggestion and regulation to the simplest form, in so far as it was practicable to do so in conformity with the Homœopathic principle.

The author, therefore, trusts that the work may appear to the public as intelligible and rudimental as he sincerely desired and endeavored to render it.

J. LAURIE.

CONTENTS.

PART I.

CHAPTER I.

OF THE NURSING OF INFANTS.

CHAPTER II.

OF ARTIFICIAL FEEDING AND WEANING.

CHAPTER III.

OF THE GENERAL TREATMENT OF CHILDREN FROM THE PERIOD OF WEANING TO THAT OF EDUCATION, PROPERLY SO CALLED.

PART II.

OF PHYSICAL EDUCATION, AS TENDING TO THE MENTAL AND MORAL DEVELOPMENT.

PART III.

CHAPTER I.

OF MENTAL AND MORAL EDUCATION.

CHAPTER II.

OF THE DISTRIBUTION OF EMPLOYMENT DURING THE COURSE OF EDUCATION, AND ADMONITORY REGIMEN.

PART IV.

OF TEMPERAMENTS—THE MOST COMMON COMPLAINTS OF CHILDREN—AND THEIR TREATMENT IN ORDINARY CASES.

CASUALTIES AND DISORDERS CONCOMITANT WITH BIRTH, OR SHORTLY SUCCEEDING IT.

FEVER. ERUPTIVE FEVERS.

CONSTITUTIONAL AFFECTIONS.

CUTANEOUS DISEASES.

APPENDIX.

THE PARENT'S GUIDE.

PRELIMINARY REMARKS.

INASMUCH as infancy, with its helplessness and delicacy, must necessarily be the first stage of existence, and as the first fostering of a child is that which requires the greatest care and attention, I am led to believe that a work of the nature which I now offer for the direction and assistance of parents may not be found superfluous. It is not but there have been many very useful publications of the kind produced under the auspices of able members of the Faculty, but that I differ most essentially in many important points from the Allopaths,*—in our treatment of infants and children, as well as of adults.

I have, therefore, determined to divide my stric-

* A term employed to designate the practitioners of the old system of medicine.

tures on the subject into four branches, and to classify my advice to young mothers in particular, as follows.

FIRST—I would treat of the infant from its birth to the period of consciousness, or rather of perception, including nursing and its attendants.

SECONDLY—The development of the physical faculties and functions of the body should be suggested for the careful consideration of my readers.

THIRDLY—I should have to detain them a considerable time on the moral tutelage and mental development of infancy, premising that these should be simultaneous and similar.

Thus the second and third portions of my treatise would, in fact, include education and training, properly so called, in all their departments.

FOURTHLY—I shall have to dwell upon temperaments; the susceptibility of children to certain maladies, and the manner in which these maladies should be dealt with.

Thus the fourth portion of my work will be more essentially hygienic than any of the others.

It may be urged, that it is no part of a medical man's science to enter into a dissertation on moral or mental training; but, as I must be my own apologist for the present, I must beg to assert that it is so, and upon this ground, amongst others:—The animal or physical portion of human nature being generally the most dominant, especially in infancy, it is only by the anatomical study of the human frame that the organic construction can be justly comprehended or appreciated, and the whole moral and mental superstructure being dependent upon this organic construction, it is most important that no mistake should be made during infancy as to its capabilities and aptitudes. It is in this, indeed, that the fatal errors which, in after life, appear in the character of maturity, are made; for, paradoxical as it may seem, there is barely a human organization which, by proper treatment during the progress of its formation, may not be fashioned to good, as well as left to run to seed for evil.

There is another great question in the treatment

of infancy which, in my opinion, is not allowed to have sufficient weight, or is overbalanced by custom or fashion. It is, that the artificial state of society is allowed to distort even the cradle of infancies. A great deal less of Art and a great deal more Nature might vastly assist the embryo composition which is made a toy of, and, like most toys, spoilt in the playing with.

At the same time, it should be remarked that the affectation of letting Nature provide her own appliances may be carried to as pernicious an extent in the other direction.

PART I.

CHAPTER I.

OF THE NURSING OF INFANTS.

THE foregoing preliminary remarks have brought me to the first stage of my subject, and I will at once proceed to deal with it methodically.

At the birth, and for a very considerable period afterwards, it is palpable that the infant is thoroughly helpless, and entirely at the mercy of those in whose charge it remains. It is obvious also that it has barely any means of making its want or its sufferings understood. It is therefore of paramount importance that at this stage it should be submitted to a regular and methodical course of treatment, and that every precaution should be suggested and taken to prevent prejudice.

During the period of suckling, which averages at from nine to twelve months, but which sometimes extends injuriously to eighteen and twenty-four, there are double precautions to be adopted: first, precautions to guard against a scanty, unwholesome, or insufficient supply of milk; and, secondly, with the child, as to the frequency of suckling at various stages of growth.

Be it understood, however, that the period of suckling must, in all instances, be regulated by the casual circumstances of the case, under many of which the advice and direction of a medical man will indicate the judicious term.

Almost every case has, in truth, its identical circumstances of constitution, of accident, or of situation.

But for the more exact and explicit direction of parents, I will divide the care of an infant into two sections,—those of external and internal attention. In treating of external precautions, it were impossible to lay too much stress upon the observance of proper ventilation and the structure of the apartments destined for the purposes of a Nursery, and most especially in towns; for, be it observed, that too little importance has hitherto been attached to this most essential of requisites.

Houses are constructed for what is termed convenience and accommodation, that is, for the apportionment of as many rooms as possible in the smallest conceivable space; but, whereas appearances must ever be maintained, there is not commonly any such stint of pitch and space in the receiving portions of the establishment; thus, whilst the drawing-room must be some fourteen feet in height, the nursery, on the second or third floor, is allowed a scanty eight or nine feet, and often less.

Added to this, the too solicitous mother or nurse, over careful of herself or her charge, is ever loath to afford a free access of fresh air into the apartment.

To avoid the chance of some phantom cold or cough, a fever is sedulously cultivated.

Why is there less casualty amongst the brutes in their earliest stage of life than amongst human beings?

If a farmer were to raise his cattle as some matrons do their children, he would have but few to bring to market.

The most important of necessaries is air, whose pure chemical properties are essential to sustain vitality, and if that air be foul, or re-inspired after its rejection from the lungs, it does not possess those properties so necessary to life, but others which are more or less fatal to it. This brings me to another portion of the same question, which, after centuries counted by Epidemic and Endemic diseases, is at last beginning to dawn upon the world as something that should be. I allude to proper draining, and the careful prevention or removal of fetid odours and rank miasma. These two questions are of almost as much importance to humanity in all its other stages as in infancy. Half a century ago it might have been a matter of great difficulty to provide for the constant cleanliness of a house in London. But since the facilities for drainage have been so vastly multiplied, and the constant supply of water, great or small, has been rendered so much a part of every house, it is a mere act of wanton carelessness, or perhaps worse, to allow of anything like a cesspool, or foul pipe, uncleansed by a current of water, in or about any house. It is not unworthy of notice and censure, however, that the humane measure recently proposed for the better removal of all such pollutions of a healthy atmosphere should have met with such chicanery of opposition at every turn.

During the period of suckling there is a double evil inflicted upon the infant by mischiefs of this kind, inasmuch as it must not be forgotten that, first of all, the infant is individually affected by them; and, secondly, it is again affected by the prejudice suffered by the mother.

Treatment of Children at a Birth.

Immediately upon the delivery, every child should be carefully washed with tepid water, wrapped in its linen, and laid to sleep.

In the dressing, some care should be taken not to confine the limbs too much, as the old prejudice still prevails in some places that infants cannot be too closely swaddled. This is a very grievous error, as it is one which directly insults at Nature.

The free action of the limbs is indispensable to the free circulation of the blood, and, by a parity of reasoning and of reasons, to the free operation of the lungs and of all the vital organs.

No sleep can be genuine and really invigorating unless the body be relieved of everything that can oppress and bind it. Why otherwise should not persons of maturer years find as much refreshment from sleeping dressed as undressed? This allusion will be felt; it is commonplace, but it is apposite, and there are few who will not have had some occasion to experience its point.

The infant then should be left asleep for some hours, from three to five, according to circumstances, and if the mother be competent to suckle it herself, should then be put to the breast.

In the generality of cases there will not be a sufficiency of breast milk for several days, to afford the infant sustenance, and the want must be supplied by having recourse to the "*bottle*" as hereinafter described. There are some cases in which women are competent, from the moment of delivery, to afford an ample supply of milk, but they are the minority, and in *first confinements* they are very rare indeed. Circumstances, and the appetite of the child, must indicate its requirements for the period of ten or fifteen days after birth, and from that period general directions will be found elsewhere in this chapter.

And it should be remarked generally, that peculiar circumstances, showing that the course of treatment did not positively agree with the infant, should be the guide of the mother as to any alteration in the frequency of feeding.

One thing I would very strongly urge upon the attention of every young mother, which is, not to allow her child (unless coerced to do so by necessity) to suckle more from one nipple than from the other. As the being more frequently held in one position when the frame is so easily moulded and fashioned may induce a variety of distortions.

I would also entreat mothers generally to hold their children well up to the breast, and not to bend the body down to the mouth of the child, and, for the more natural observance of this rule, I would recommend the breast to be offered always either in an erect or recumbent position, as in the former in particular it will be more convenient to raise the child.

It is the habit, which, if it be not indolent, is

careless, of feeding the infant from the lap, which induces the method of bending over it.

With respect to the method of affording the proper rest to an infant newly born, it should be remarked, that after the first sleep the inclination of the child will indicate its necessities. For some weeks, at least, it will sleep continually, only waking to be nursed. Although the earlier it is broken of seeking the breast in the night the better.

After the lapse of the first few weeks, there will be longer intervals of wakefulness, and less frequent but longer durations of sleep. After the first two months it will become imperative to induce, if possible, regular periods of sleeping; at night, in the middle of the day, and, if needful, early in the evening, but for not more than three hours in the course of the day, as a greater indulgence at that time may be apt to render the nights more restless. The apartment should be darkened during the sleep, and a little time allowed to elapse between feeding and sleeping. The mother's observation will become the best index of the proportion of sleep which her child requires, for as with the nursing, &c., this will vary according to constitution and state of body.

A newly-born child has not sufficient power of generating heat, especially during sleep, to be consigned to a separate resting-place, and as this deficiency of indigenous caloric must for a certain period be conveyed to it from some other body in order to maintain a sufficient activity of circulation, and, by a complication and combination of pulmonary and hydraulic action, a sufficient oxygenation of the blood, it is needful that for a month or six weeks after birth every child should either sleep in the same bed with its mother, or with its nurse, or lie in the arms, or in close contiguity to the one or the other. No heat can be imparted to it which will have as beneficial an effect as the animal heat of its species.

After the expiration of the term prescribed, however, or otherwise according to peculiar circumstances, the child may be left to sleep in its little bed or cradle separately, provided care be taken that the temperature of the apartment be not too much lowered, (say about what is called temperate,) and that the bed itself be not exposed to a direct current of air of another temperature.

I must not be understood to recommend coddling, over-covering, and close apartments; because, as may have been gathered from my foregoing remarks, I am beyond measure averse to them, and look upon them as the bane and destruction of infancy. I would have a curent of air constantly passing freshly through the room, if possible, by means of ventilators, open doors, &c., when the weather is too cold to admit of a window continually unclosed; but I would not have the body of the child exposed to the direct action of any such draughts as might be thus occasioned. Above all things, the head and face should be constantly uncovered, in order that the breathing may be free and fresh, and the coverlets should be in plenty to encourage proper warmth without being of sufficient weight to oppress or confine the limbs, or so closely fastened as to bind them down.

I cannot say I agree at all in the common notion that a feather bed is necessary to young children, nor do I imagine anything of the kind to be as wholesome as a good sound French wool mattress. It is far more essential to attend to the thorough sweetness and cleanliness of the bedding, which can be attained by repeated exposure to the air, and being kept very dry, than to its excessive softness. As regards the warmth induced and sustained by a feather bed, I am very much inclined to the notion that there is something in it which does not thoroughly contribute to wholesome rest.

Precautions to be taken by the Mother.

There are many personal precautions to be taken by the mother to secure a plentiful and wholesome supply of milk, and amongst these, perhaps the first is to partake of regular exercise as soon as she is able to do so. Never omitting the daily walk, still careful not to exceed her strength and expose herself to suffer from fatigue.

The free use of water, also, is amongst the essentials for a nursing mother. The skin cannot be kept too clean and pure.

The diet should be as plain as may be, partaking of mixed kinds, but very generally nothing in the shape of made dishes, or, more particularly, highly-seasoned viands. She should sedulously avoid fermented liquors, unless deficient in vigour, and even then they should be of as little stimulating a nature as possible, and not taken in greater quantities than had been her custom before confinement.

All surprise or excitement, whether for good or evil, should be avoided.

By observing these rules, and paying great attention to the general bodily health, a mother of capable constitution (for there are many who should never attempt to nurse), will always find herself able to supply ample nourishment to her child.

During the first week or two after delivery, the frequency in offering the breast to the infant must depend almost wholly upon the child's own desire and inclination. But after the expiration of the first stage, the administration of the milk should become as regular as possible at certain stated intervals, say from two to four hours according to appetite; and this routine should be most rigidly adhered to during the remainder of the month or six weeks after birth, for the strengthening and toning of the stomach, and the avoiding of craving and gnawing pain (which renders every infant fretful, and consequently feverish,) depend wholly upon the strictest regularity.

Again, after the brief term pointed out for this course, it becomes most essential to the mother, and, consequently, to the child, to cease offering the breast for some hours during the nights. This, it will be observed, can be effected by giving the last meal when the mother retires to rest, say about 11 o'clock at night, and the next about 5 in the morning; the mother will thus have her nocturnal rest comparatively undisturbed, and the child will, after a very few days, become perfectly habituated to the change. The greatest mistake which can be made is to forego these rules for the purpose of quieting a child, because *irregularity* only deranges the stomach, and thereby renders the infant daily more fretful.

After from six to eight months the first teeth will have appeared, and then the treatment of the child may begin to be varied, although this should be done as gradually as possible; because, if the child should hitherto have been healthy and thriving, it might have nothing immediately to gain from the change.

But, at the same time, seven or eight months of exclusive nursing may drain a very strong constitution, and the mischief of protracting the course any longer may become too serious to be overlooked.

It is, moreover, very easy to begin by administering good cows' milk, a little diluted, and proceeding to select the lightest and most nourishing of farinaceous diets (premising that they should not be the least of a greasy character,) in small but increasing quantities, as the mother's breast is more and more withheld.

It should not be out of place at this juncture to add that those who, from circumstances, whether of compulsory employment or pleasure-seeking, are unable or unwilling to perform the duties of a nurse, except by fits and starts, and to observe the simple regulations as to diet, as herein laid down, should as an obligation, abstain from undertaking these duties at all, in common justice and humanity. Of the expedients, as substitutes for their nurture, I shall have to speak hereafter, and therefore I shall not at this moment detain the reader with them.

It will not unfrequently occur, that, although the mother is in other respects in sound health, there will not be a sufficient supply of milk for the sustenance of her child. In such a case as this, rather than submit the infant to a half-artificial and half-natural regimen, it would, generally, be advisable either to intrust it entirely to a wet nurse, selected with great care, or to feed it at once from the bottle. Diluted cows' milk (about $\frac{2}{3}$ of water to $\frac{1}{3}$ of good milk), with a little sugar, being the best substitute for that of the mother.

Most women who do not marry or have children before they have attained somewhat ripened years, are apt to be deficient in their supply, either from the first few weeks after delivery, or, at all events, after the lapse of a month or two; and in such cases they should by no means persist in nursing their children, inasmuch as they are weakening their own constitution on the one hand, and hazarding the health, if not the life, of the child on the other.

The ordinary rule with women is, that their MONTHLY INDISPOSITIONS will be entirely suspended during the period of their nursing; but cases to the contrary are by no means unfrequent, and when they occur the mother should generally abstain from offering the breast to her child during their continuance. Should the return of this affection only occur after from eight to twelve months, it will not be difficult to understand that a wet nurse, and the hazard attached to the choice of one, may be avoided altogether, inasmuch as the child at that age will be quite sufficiently advanced (if of a healthy frame) to be submitted to artificial feeding, or, in fact, to be weaned; and if not of a healthy habit, would, in all probability, gain something by the change.

It is necessary, however, whilst advising the mother to withhold the breast during the monthly periods, to point out a method of encouraging and preserving a flow of milk, which can be effected by simply drawing it off at about the stated hours that the child (if nursed) should have been suckling. And with relation to the substitute which must be provided for the child in the interim —as that will only be of a few days' duration— it would be best to resort to the "Bottle," and a mixture of milk, water, and sugar, as directed under the head of "*Artificial Feeding,*" with this reservation that the proportions of milk and water be accommodated to the age of the child as hereafter mentioned,

Tight Lacing injurious to the Nursing Breast.

Whilst engaged upon the subject of nursing, I cannot refrain from calling the attention of all young women, and especially of those who are married or likely to marry, and become mothers, to the extreme injuries which they sustain from the practice of *tight lacing.*

First of all they render themselves subject to danger in delivery, or, if safely acquitted of that operation, still they frequently become unable to afford the natural sustenance to their children. The nipples of the breast become very frequently incapable of affording a sufficient passage for the milk; and it is in consequence necessary to hand the child over to a wet nurse, and immediately to dry up the milk of the breasts.

To most women it would no doubt be exceedingly painful to be withheld from performing their maternal offices, and therefore the caution is by no means to be disregarded.

There are some women who should never be suffered to take upon themselves the office of nurses to their own children, inasmuch as they are constitutionally incapable of performing this office beneficially. Such, for instance, are those who are afflicted with any hereditary disease, or a tendency to pulmonary or scrofulous complaints; because not only will their milk be impure, insufficient, or inferior in power and quality, but they will be apt to sink under the drain caused by the nursing. Those, also, who are of the most acute sensibility and are alive to every little excitement,—who are startled at trifles,—or whose intense anxiety works upon their nerves to the point of constantly suggesting some ill which is accruing, or likely to accrue, to their child, should wholly abstain from attempting to nurse it.

The delicate state of mothers for some time after delivery, be it observed, is not unlikely to induce symptoms of this nature if they have had the least tendency to them beforehand; and as soon as they betray themselves they should become the signal for abandoning the charge.

With respect to the former cases of hereditary weakness or complaints, it should not be overlooked that children of such parents have already an aptitude for the same disorders engendered with their blood, and that these disorders will almost inevitably be confirmed or superinduced if the mothers should persist in nursing their infants under such circumstances.

Without any apparent cause it will sometimes be found that the mother is not sufficiently robust to nurse her own child, a fact which will soon be betrayed by certain symptoms attendant upon her suckling, such as a drawing through the body and from the spine, whilst the child is at the breast, and a dizzy, faint sensation immediately after it.

Whenever this should occur there is no safe

course but to abandon the attempt, for its continuance will only engender more serious and even dangerous affections. The symptoms which usually follow those recited, are pains in the head, irregularity and astringency of the bowels, want of spirits, faintness, cough, palpitation, and so on.

There are, nevertheless, some cases in which the first symptoms may be allayed and overcome by seasonable advice and judicious employment of medicines.

OF WET NURSES.

It has frequently occurred in the foregoing suggestions that I have had occasion to appeal from the mother to the wet nurse; it is, therefore, incumbent upon me to give some directions for the selection of persons to fulfil that important office in a household.

The first inquiry which should be made, in my opinion, is as to moral character, for no person is adapted as a wet nurse who is not, above all things, cleanly, sober, good tempered, and well conducted, It is also desirable that she should be accustomed to the management of infants, fond of them, and gentle in her treatment.

The general state of bodily health is the next point to be considered, for it is paramount in the wet nurse as in the mother, that she should be sufficiently robust and healthy to perform her duties sufficiently. The breath, above all things, should be sweet, and the appearance of the mouth wholesome; the breasts firm, full, and of a good colour; the skin very clean, healthy, and free from any surfeit or humour; and her own child healthy and robust, and bearing all the appearances of thriving upon her nurture.

Again, the date of her delivery should, as nearly as possible, tally with that of the mother whose infant she is about to take into nursing, because the breast-milk varies very materially with the age of the child, and becomes more and more heavy as the child advances in age, being then too powerful for a new-born infant, as the milk of a woman newly delivered would be too poor in quality for a child of two, three, or four months old.

In addition to the external signs of the fitness or unfitness of a nurse, the choice ought to be regulated by the quality of her milk, which point can be best determined by a professional man. The direction of a medical attendant, who has made the treatment of *females* his exclusive or especial study,* will, moreover, be frequently necessary in

* This is not the author's case; but, as the well-being of naturally-reared children, during the first months of their existence, is so inseparably connected with an unexceptionable con-

the selection of a *wet nurse,* for many other reasons; and, therefore, any hints which are afforded in this work should not lead persons to depend entirely upon their own judgment and discrimination in this important matter.

Great attention should be paid to the nature of her diet, and a strict inquiry made as to her habitual kind of living, because she cannot but be prejudiced in her capabilities by a change; and, as it is not unfrequent for wet nurses to make a holiday-time when they go out nursing, and cram themselves to excess because varieties of meats and drinks are within their reach, a careful watch should be kept over them in this respect. They have it ever ready to say that good eating and drinking assist them in their capacity as nurses, and that a considerable quantity of malt liquor is, above all things, needed by them. The excuse is plausible, and, sad to say, is too often successful; but the practice of humouring them in *all* their inclinations cannot be too strongly deprecated.

The truth is, as has before been stated with respect to the mothers, that the plainer a good substantial diet can be, and the better and the nearer it can be assimilated with the habit of the person, the

dition of the mother or wet nurse, he could not avoid making some cursory observations on the above and other subjects, more correctly belonging to the province of the obstetric practitioner.

more likely is it to yield her good milk. As for stimulants and fermented liquors, they are all more or less objectionable, and should, consequently (excepting perhaps in the instances analogous to those I referred to when treating of *nursing mothers*,) be forbidden.

The same precautions should be observed by the wet nurse, as previously indicated for the mother, as to daily and regular walking exercise, careful washing and cleansing of the skin, regular and early hours, and so forth. The latter injunctions also need considerable attention with respect to nurses, inasmuch as there are very few who are *too* cleanly in their person, and they are almost invariably indolent and lazy. With reference to diet, for those who can afford to keep a kind of separate establishment, I should strongly recommend a table peculiar to the nursery, and great care that nothing should be smuggled to it which was not gratuitously allowed.

I would also add that it should, where there is a selection, be a sufficient reason to reject a nurse, that she was herself suckling a first child; for, in the first place, it is not uncommon for a deficiency of milk to attend the first delivery; and, secondly, a young mother is more in need of advice and assistance over her first child, than she is competent to afford them to others.

On the other hand, there is almost as much inconvenience attendant upon having a woman too far advanced in years as a wet nurse, inasmuch as she is very often deficient of an adequate supply for her own child.

In cases where the mother is unwilling to intrust her infant to the chances of a wet nurse, and unable to suckle it herself, she must needs have recourse to the bottle, as the best artificial means of affording nourishment to the child, great care being taken not to overload the stomach at one time, but to adopt frequency rather than quantity in feeding. Nothing will sooner derange the stomach of a new-born child than to cram it, or allow it to glut itself.

A mixture of about one proportion of good fresh milk to two of water,* sweetened, if possible, with beet-root sugar, or otherwise with the finest loaf sugar, will be the best representation of breast milk. The water should have been well boiled, but the mixture should be given lukewarm.

On no account should the same be given twice from the bottle, but a fresh supply prepared for every feeding.

* The water added should be boiling; and the temperature at which the food ought to be given should be the same as that of the mother's milk, viz. at 96° to 98°.

CHAPTER II.

OF ARTIFICIAL FEEDING AND WEANING.

I HAVE now arrived at the period in my treatise in which I must call the particular attention of the reader to the question of "ARTIFICIAL FEEDING."

And not only shall I dilate upon this topic as the *successive course of treatment to breast nursing*, but also as its substitute.

It has been sufficiently shown in my foregoing remarks, that there are very many instances in which the mother is *constitutionally* unable to nurse her own child; many also in which she *accidentally* becomes so from casual debility or sickness; and many more in which she is so by *habit.*

It is not, therefore, only at the period of weaning and subsequently, that *artificial feeding* is needful in the nursery, but very frequently from the day of birth.

It is not unnatural that an anxious mother, finding herself incompetent to perform the duties and offices of her tender capacity, should yet be loath to intrust a child into hireling hands for nurture. There is, and too often with just reason, a secret loathing and uneasiness respecting some possible imperfection in the wet nurse, and whenever this should chance to be felt with unusual intensity, rather than submit the mother to a restless anxiety on this score, it is perhaps better to recommend recourse to absolutely artificial means.

The nearest representative to breast milk has already been detailed,* but it should perhaps be added that the mixture prepared for the bottle should not be persisted in in certain given proportions, irrespective of the condition and wants of the infant. After the first fortnight has expired, for instance, the addition of about ⅙ of milk may be recommended (which should in all cases be quite fresh, and in hot weather should be carefully guarded from its effect), and after the lapse of a month or six weeks after birth, the proportion of milk to the water may be as 3 to 1, and so on.

It should also be understood that cows' milk does not in all cases agree with children, when asses' milk may be tried.

Instances are not wanting of the very successful trial of asses' milk† for infants who have pined away upon the milk of the cow, and therefore should

* Page 33.

† The proportions of asses' milk and water should, at first, be equal parts; after the fifth or sixth month the milk may be given undiluted.

the latter, after a week's trial, be found to disagree with the child, no time should be lost in procuring the other.

The most common symptoms of an indigesti bility in the milk, are gripings, great flatulence, and difficult, though liquid and greenish, or curd-like motions—sometimes also, these last will be hard and dry, a very evident sign of derangement.

Some children, from the day of their birth, reject all milk, and equally refuse the breast and the substitutes.* In such cases the use of the farinaceous food may be advised, of which mention is hereafter made,† as much *liquefied* as possible; in fact, having no consistency. For children of five or six months old and upwards, it may be prepared as follows; Mix, thoroughly, a tablespoonful of the powder with a tablespoonful of pure cold milk; pour thereon half a pint of boiling water, stirring constantly; then boil the mixture for eight minutes, slightly sweeten with a small quantity of loaf sugar, and add a few grains of salt.

Weak barley-water may also be given, or *thin* grit gruel, arrow-root, or ground rice, well boiled in water, and seasoned with a very little sugar and salt; fixing upon that which suits best, and ad-

* This intolerance of milk may, sometimes, be readily overcome by means of medicine. See page 183.

† Page 42.

hering to it as long as it appears to agree. An excess in the *quantity* is, however, a much more frequent source of disturbance than a faultiness in the quality of the food. Milk, when it can be had pure, is always to be preferred to other kinds of food; it should not, therefore, be discarded without sufficient reason. Sometimes it may be made to agree by altering the proportions of the milk and water; and when that fails, the medicinal means, already referred to, should be tried before the milk of the cow or ass is laid aside. Although I confess myself opposed to the expedient, weak veal and beef-tea and snail-broth have been suggested by some.* The last is perhaps the most likely to be beneficial.

In using the bottle, it is not unfrequent, as just stated, that the proportions must be changed to suit the stomach, more or less milk and sugar being given. Nevertheless, great care should be taken lest the cause of ailing, if any, be mistaken, and lest the food be varied without sufficient ground. Again, therefore, it may be enjoined as of a paramount consequence that the quantity should be moderate at each feed-

* It is only when infants become soft, flabby, and otherwise ill-conditioned, that animal broths may be resorted to, combined, in general, with an equal quantity of thin barley or grit gruel, &c.

ing, and that, if needful, the repetition should be more or less frequent. The worst of all injuries which can be inflicted upon the stomach of an infant respecting its food, is by overloading it.

No occasion should be taken to allay peevishness by feeding out of regular hours, as this will inevitably increase the cause, and consequently the effect eventually. For, in nine cases out of ten the irritability of an infant arises from derangement of the stomach.

In general there can be no harm in following the same rules in the use of the bottle as have been before set forth relative to breast feeding, and which it is consequently unnecessary to recapitulate.

But, in particular, the attention of the reader may be recalled to the question of *night* feeding, and reminded of the strict observance of the same regulation. The sooner a child can be got into the habit of taking from five to six, or even seven or eight hours of unbroken rest the better.

It is therefore advisable, after ten or fifteen days from the birth, to train an infant to forego the *one* or *two* meals (if I may so call them) which would fall nearest to the middle of the night. Thus, then, would it be advisable to commence and proceed with the application of the "*bottle.*"

The same stages and gradations, the same observance of quantity in repetition, should hold as when the mother nurses at the breast, ever premising that care should be taken to accommodate the feeding to the necessities and peculiarities of the child. It may be taken as a general rule, that where an infant is robust and healthy, the flesh being full and sound, and the mouth and gums of a healthy colour, with an absence of peevish irritability, it is thriving upon its food, and changes should not be made except in the regular course prescribed for breast nursing.

Before proceeding further with ARTIFICIAL FEEDING, it may be as well, at this place, to caution mothers against the administration of *solids* to children before the first teeth appear, and indicate that the child is arrived at a proper degree of maturity for their adoption. In fact liquid food should be adhered to exclusively for the same period as the breast would be persevered in under other circumstances. The stomach of a child under six, seven, or sometimes eight months old, is generally incapable of properly digesting solid food, and it is not at all unfrequent that great derangement of the functions is induced by such a method of nourishment.

Upon the appearance of the first teeth, which, on the average, occurs about the seventh month, whether the infant has been raised "by hand" or not, the treatment becomes much the same, alternating the breast or bottle with some delicate farinaceous food (of which hereafter,) gradually increasing the solid, and diminishing the liquid, and thus, by imperceptible steps, weaning the child.

Upon the first trial of solid food it should be confined in its administration to once in twenty-four hours, and that in a very small quantity; after the lapse of a week or ten days, repeat it twice, and after a month or six weeks, three times, with the proviso that, in all cases, great attention be paid to the motions, the bodily health, and the temper of the infant, in order to ascertain if in anything the method disagrees with it, and might be altered for the better.

There is one thing to which there is not sufficient importance attributed in artificial feeding, which is the position of the child. Infants are frequently fed by hand upon the mother's or nurse's knee, with the head hanging backward, and the middle of the body alone sustained by its resting place. Such a method may, on some unlucky occasion, cause suffocation, and will invariably impede the regular reception of food. The head of a child, whilst feeding, should always be raised slightly on the arm or pillow, and the position be as much as possible one of comfort. A short time* after the child has completed its meal, it should be hushed gently to rest, for there is nothing which better facilitates an easy and comfortable course of digestion than the infantine "siesta." In very hot weather the repose may be prolonged.

After the lapse of six or seven months from the birth, or, more properly, when the first teeth have appeared, the diet of every child should become of a more solid character, and the addition of a variety of preparations, will become necessary.

Still, however, a strict observance of the rules as to frequency, quantity, and posture is enjoined, and still the casual circumstances attendant upon the constitution and bodily health of the child, to which the mother will have become accustomed,

* "It is true, that during the first month, the infant sleeps immediately on leaving the breast, and no evil consequences ensue; but it must be borne in mind, that it takes but little at a time, and the tenuity of the milk is at that time wisely adapted to its delicate digestion; but as the secretion becomes richer, and suited to the increasing power of those organs, it is injurious to put the child asleep immediately after a full meal; his rest is then restless and disturbed, from the process of digestion being interfered with, more particularly when nurses endeavour to force nature, by resorting to the baneful practice of prolonged and violent rocking."—*Homœopathic Domestic Medicine, art.* SLEEP.

and with the peculiarities of which she will doubtless be intimate, must be her guide.

Amongst the most valuable of diets for infants I should reckon baked wheaten flour, sago, and arrow-root,* but neither should be given without having been carefully prepared for the purpose.

It should be remarked that, in most cases of indisposition amongst infants, particularly in those in which they are afflicted with the common ailments usually prevalent amongst young children, every mother should be slow to exhibit medicine: it should only be resorted to when strictly required.

It is very customary to administer calomel, castor oil, jalap, rhubarb, and magnesia, and other drugs, for every little derangement of stomach and irregularity of motion, and still more, perhaps, to resort to narcotics, to lull the griping so frequent amongst infants.

Nothing can be more erroneous, and nothing more likely to set the germ of future disorder than such a course. The flatulence, looseness, or costiveness, so prevalent in the earliest stages of infancy, more frequently arise from diet, want of air, or irregularity, which may produce a derangement

* A farinaceous compound, of a very nutritious and wholesome description, which has been denominated "HECKER'S Farina," may be had at the Homœopathic Pharmacy, 239, Arch street, Philadelphia.

of stomach, than from any other cause; and, in almost all such cases, may be cured by a careful attention to these particulars, and by such changes as may be thought necessary. The exhibition of medicine on all occasions induces a morbid state of the stomach, which is not afterwards so easily corrected. The ill which it was sought to remove thus becomes more and more aggravated, until it assumes a really serious aspect, and compels the medical man to resort to expedients which he is ever loath to apply in cases where Nature, left alone, is the best of doctors as of nurses. It is not that, under our principle of medicine, any medical preparation would be used or suffered, which, in its quantity, could affect the constitution prejudicially, but that we prefer when possible, abstaining from medical methods at all in dealing with infants.

And now, it might not be irrelevant to observe, that, where Nature is not sufficiently powerful to overcome the obstacle which causes derangement, and medicine becomes absolutely necessary, the Homœopathic remedies have peculiar advantages for infant organization. The membranes and tissues which line or surround the organs of life, yet tender and susceptible, are far too keenly alive to the action of artificial powers, to sustain uninjured the raking of drugs poured wholesale into the body, and mingled to combat each other where they ought, if at all, to operate singly, and in integrity. In more advanced stages of life, a patient may not, perhaps, unfrequently escape unscathed from the effects of the most violent drugs, owing to the maturity of the various parts which perform the functions of the body—owing to their sturdiness in rejecting and excluding the hurtful impressions of a deleterious foreign power,—but in early infancy it is far otherwise, and the use of drugs at all, in their crude or unattenuated form, too often engenders something which should not be.

As I am here treating of the method of dealing with children apart from medical resources, and as I shall hereafter have occasion to give a few details as to the simplest and most useful remedies for some of the more prevalent diseases of infancy and childhood, I shall not here enter further into that department, but content myself with repeating my injunction against the too trivial and constant exhibition of medicine of any kind in the strongest and most unequivocal terms.

In most cases, attend closely to the diet, the cleanliness, the ventilation of the nursery and its inhabitants, and do not spare the out-door exercise, and you may generally be successful in overcoming the little affections which

"Infancy is heir to."

Of Weaning.

I come now to that important epoch in the life of every human being, designated as the period of WEANING.

If WEANING be attempted all of a sudden, it is not uncommonly attended with a considerable temporary derangement of the system, but by pursuing the course which I have already indicated, of WEANING, as it were, by degrees, the change may be made so imperceptible as to be without any prejudicial effect, even for a time.

The age at which the infant should be finally withheld from the breast will, of course, depend upon circumstances, such as the supply and quality of the milk, and the health and strength both of mother and child. Most mothers are able to nourish their infants satisfactorily from the breast for, at least, five or six weeks; but if the supply of milk is ample, and its quality unexceptionable, children thrive better if they are fed exclusively from the breast for three or four months. In all cases the change of diet should be effected, if possible, by gradation, and by commencing to discontinue the breast at night.

The average date of *final* weaning will be found to be about the ninth or tenth month, after which, in the great majority of cases, if not all, the mother should desist from the tender duty of nursing Instances are not wanting of suckling being continued until eighteen, or even twenty-four months, but whereas no good is conferred on the child, and very serious mischief may accrue to the mother, nursing should not be persevered in after about the ninth month.

After the sixth month a gradual change should, in general, be made to farinaceous food; and when the grinding teeth have made their appearance, but particularly if the child, at the same time, grows rapidly, or if it is of a lymphatic temperament, with soft flabby flesh, the diet may partake yet more of the solid quality; but so long as the child looks healthy, and presents a satisfactory muscular development when fed on milk, farinaceous food and light soup or broth, there can be no necessity for an alteration. I confess myself opposed to the too early adoption of absolute animal diet; and as the period of teething is subject to such a variety of ailments amongst infants, and is especially attended with so constant a disposition to fever, I should conceive this to be a sufficient reason for being slow and cautious in attempting a change to highly-concentrated diet, requiring considerable powers of digestion, without very strong and sufficient grounds.

CHAPTER III.

OF THE GENERAL TREATMENT OF CHILDREN FROM THE PERIOD OF WEANING TO THAT OF EDUCATION, PROPERLY SO CALLED.

Of Rest.

THE subject matter of the forthcoming chapter should, to be explicit, be divided into the following sections—that of rest, that of cleanliness, that of air, occupation and exercise, in so far as the last two can be applicable, and that of diet and clothing, these being the greatest essentials to the maintenance of a child's health. Under the head of rest I shall, to avoid further subdivision, include regularity of habits.

It will, perhaps, be incumbent upon me to anticipate a little of what would properly come within the subsequent department, which has been appropriated to moral training as a part of education. As there is no question but that, at this early stage of childhood, that is, from the second to about the fifth year, a parent may begin to sow the seed which shall later germinate in the character.

In treating of the method of inducing sound

and wholesome sleep, or, in other words, beneficial REST, the subject will be a continuation of the directions which have hitherto been given in my former chapters, and there will perhaps be little to add to those former instructions, for the simple reason that sleep is one of those requirements of humanity of which Nature is ever the best indicatrix.

It must not, however, be lost sight of, that in sickness as in health, in the former for restoration and in the latter for preservation, the thorough ventilation of the chamber is one of the first desiderata, which, with cleanliness, may be ranked as amongst the most essential of points.

The observance of regular and early hours may also be reckoned in the same class of essentials, for nothing is more prejudicial, both to mind and body, than irregularity in this particular, or a habit of protracting the day through half the night, and carrying the night half through the ensuing day. I have frequently heard children, subjected to this practice, complain of faintness upon rising, and observed a lack of appetite amongst them at the first meal, which entirely originated in the unnatural transposition of the two sections of the twenty-four hours.

The use of feather beds and very soft pillows is, also, as unnecessary as I might say it is unnatural, even if it be not very detrimental to the physical vigour of the frame. And after all, these appliances of luxury will never be required or sought for in after life if the child has not been constantly accustomed to them. Like many other foibles, it is merely a matter of habit to desire their use. Similarly ought the use of the nightcap to be reprehended, for what should make the head require more than its natural covering at night than in the day (when unexposed), it is difficult to conceive. Even the use of head covering in the open air is acquired by habit. There are many thousands who do without it in colder and less genial climates than this. And, moreover, there are some instances extant of children who, from philosophical reasons of the parents, have done very well without it in this country, although brought up to a sphere in which the best of covering was to be obtained, and was considered indispensable. As to the use of a bandage for the head at night, it is worse than useless, it is a great error.

Let me add, that where houses are sufficiently roomy, and it is not absolutely necessary to huddle half a dozen children into the same chamber, I look upon the practice as most reprehensible. And also as that without much additional cost the proper conveniences may be erected in every house, it is a sad pity that impure vessels should be suffered in a nursery; or that any of the conveniences referred to should be constructed without the provision of an ample supply of water on every floor.

It should be taken as a general rule with young children, that the absence of sound and healthy sleep and a nightly restlessness, are indications of indisposition, and they should ever be closely attended to as such. Infants, and children even beyond infancy, can but very rarely be subject to a moral or mental uneasiness to predominate over the physical requirements, and, consequently, it may be considered as a symptom of physical derangement that these natural pronenesses are interrupted.

Sleeplessness in children will, apart from dentition, generally arise from a febrile affection originating in the stomach, or in the effects of cold, and it is by dealing with it as such that it will be best overcome.

There can never be any harm upon the first manifestation of this affection, in moderating the diet and allowing less of solid in its proportions, and in withholding anything like stimulants, as tea or coffee, and certainly wine and all fermented liquors, if at this early age they have been allowed —a thing which should not be.

Any continuance or aggravation of febrile symptoms had better be checked by recourse to medical aid, because the incipient stages of many of the illnesses to which children are peculiarly subject manifest themselves so similarly that it would be difficult for an unpractised observer to discriminate between them. (See also article DENTITION.)

Of Cleanliness.

I now come to the second section of this chapter, in which I have undertaken to give some directions as to the method, not only of keeping children cleanly during the months or years of dependence, but also of habituating and training them to such habits for after life.

The first necessity of an infant, at the birth, as has been before shown, is to be thoroughly washed, a necessity which accrues daily during the whole course of existence.

It is very requisite that all the orifices of the body should be kept thoroughly clean, being well washed and bathed at least once a day, and, if required, oftener; and also that the skin should be preserved free from the slightest taint from transpiration or dirt, which can only be effected by careful washing and immersion. In the first period of infancy the immersion should not be hazarded in quite cold water, but in that of a moderate temperature (from 85 to 95 Fahrenheit).

If the water be too hot it will create too great a relaxation of the skin, and instead of producing a glow will leave the child chilly and susceptible of taking cold. On the other hand, for some weeks after birth, if the water be too cold, the child, in all probability, will not have an adequate power of generating heat to produce the reaction which should take place in drying.

Quite cold water should be used as soon as it safely can be, because the reaction and glow which succeed immersion will be more decided, so that on each successive day the temperature of the water may be lowered until it can be used quite cold, provided always there be no bodily indisposition which requires the contrary. But the washing and bathing should, in all instances, be an operation of very short duration, expeditiously completed, and followed by brisk friction with soft towels and flannel, for the purpose of drying, and accompanied also with something of advantage by the gentle use of the flesh-brush.

This method of accomplishing the bathing and drying will invariably produce the warm glow on the skin which is so conducive to health, and which is generally so sure an index of the wholesome effect of the bath.

Even at a very early age the open air bath may be used with very beneficial effect in fine weather, and it should be a part of the education of every child of robust health (females not even excepted) to learn to swim as soon as the fourth or fifth year is attained. Heterodox as this doctrine may seem, especially as regards girls, in pleading guilty to the *apparent* want of delicacy in the suggestion, I must insist, that so many remarkable instances of its paramount advantage might be quoted, that they not only overcome, but shame the "*mauvaise honte*," if not prudery, which affects to blush at the recommendation.

To mention no other advantage which can be derived from swimming, it is of no mean importance to encourage a strenuous muscular action during the bath, and it greatly facilitates the thorough cleansing of the body. But, apart from this, who will pretend to assert, that swimming is anything like a useless accomplishment? Are there any circumstances in life in which it may not become the safeguard against the fatal consequences of an accident?

In many parts of Europe, even, not to mention the islands of the Pacific, and elsewhere, it is as common for women as for men to swim.

It is just as easy to teach a girl to swim as a boy, and the girl is always as apt a scholar, a proof that it is not inconsistent with the faculties and powers provided by Nature; and this universal mother made quite as perfect a provision for the female as the male.

If this branch of education be commenced, as I have directed, from the earliest years, there will be no difficulty in it. Every child will take to it as naturally as to any other physical exercise. But the same proviso must be made as with respect to everything else in the treatment of young children. Have a care that they are not constitutionally incapacitated, or that the casual derangement of the bodily health does not indicate another kind of treatment. And, above all things be very careful how you deal with a child of a highly nervous, timid, and susceptible temperament,—constitutions which it is impossible to trifle with, with impunity. It is in forcing upon children that which does not simply go against the whim or inclination, but also works upon some moral or physical weakness, that the greatest mischiefs are brought about. Lead, but do not drive; because, by the latter course, you will permanently injure the tone of the temper—you will irritate the nerves, and you will induce a perpetual loathing for what might have become congenial after a time, and might have been of the greatest advantage to both the principles of the system in subsequent periods of life.

The great art in dealing with children, is to introduce them by habit to what is most conducive to their well-being, and to render everything they have to do or to bear a matter of gratification and not of repulsive obligation. All the virtues of humanity take their rise in these little cares of childhood, and all the vices which afflict society may be traced to the injudicious observance of them or to their omission. The human organism in its worst phases and developments may be modified and subdued for good, and the most perfect construction may be rendered inoperative against the animal propensities, and be overcome by evil.

From the first moment that perception dawns upon the infant mind, the child is susceptible of good or evil impressions, and should be dealt with as a creature gifted with superior faculties. From that instant its moral existence has commenced, and from the same moment it should be fashioned after the better models. I would therefore have parents, who for many years are the responsible guardians of the character of their child, beware how they abuse the high responsibility which they have incurred in becoming parents.

Of Air and Exercise.

Sufficient has already been said of the require ments of infancy, as regards fresh air, not to require much recapitulation on that score; but there are a few things respecting exercise, the times and methods of administering it, and so forth, to which it will be necessary to call the attention of all parents.

In the early stages of infancy great care must be taken as to the posture of children, when rocked or dandled, and when carried about, as a great deal depends upon this. Until the age of three or four, and sometimes six or seven months, the spine has not enough of consistency and strength to sustain the frame erect, and, consequently, so long as a child sinks forward when held up, it should not be placed in such an attitude that the principal burthen of the body rests upon the lower vertebræ of the back. The spine and head should invariably be well sustained by the arm of the mother or nurse. With this precaution an infant should always be carried about the apartment, if not out of doors, several times in the course of a day, and gently rocked in the arms, or on the knee, but without jolting or rough tossing. The mere swinging backwards and forwards in this manner is a species of exercise which is as necessary as it is gratifying to the child, and which is usually as pleasing to the mother.

The weather permitting, no day should pass without the regular airing, although it may be advisable to abstain from exposing any child to cold and nipping winds. And on no occasion should the face and mouth be so muffled up as to obstruct a free inspiration of the atmosphere. It is very erroneous to imagine that affections of the lungs arise from a free, habitual access of external air, on the contrary, when they do not arise from constitutional predisposition, they are much more likely to arise from the mistaken attempt to exclude it at all times.

Respecting EXERCISE:—Besides the appropriate and beneficial rocking produced by slow lateral movement as the infant reclines in the nurse's lap, it should, when sufficiently strong to roll about by itself (in such a place and position that a fall is impossible,) be allowed to indulge freely in its gambols. These little recreations expand the limbs, relieve the joints, and greatly assist in the muscular development of the system.

There is no harm either in permitting children to crawl about the room; they will commence to do so as soon as they can manage to move from place to place in this manner. But any attempt to induce precocious use of the legs and feet is liable to be followed by pernicious results. Far from being beneficial, it is a great disadvantage to children to walk too early; for it conduces much to produce weak and falling ankles, knock- and bow-knees. and other little deformities of construction, if not far worse evils, by the mistaken system of hurrying on the capacity and inclination for walking.

Eschew all your BABY JUMPERS, and your leading-strings, and such absurdities, if you wish your children to be erect in their carriage, and to walk with ease and grace in after-life. All these artificial contrivances to effect the purpose are mistakes.

The injunction which should be observed is brief and simple enough.—*Let your child learn to walk of its own accord.*

When this first feat of childhood has been ac complished, allow the child for some time the usual apartment alone in which to indulge in independent exercise; having first taken every precaution that there be no china ornaments, gewgaws, looking-glasses, knives, or other obnoxious implements within reach, and no articles of furniture which may be easily overturned. When sufficient strength is attained (weather permitting), it were as well to begin the daily walk out of doors, commencing with a quarter of an hour, and increasing the length of time as strength is gained, until the child enjoys open-air exercise for at least one fourth portion of the daylight.

Modifications as to time must, of course, be made according to the physical energy and vigour of the child; because over-fatigue may be as prejudicial as the lassitude produced by too sedentary and confined a life. So long as there is no absolute occupation, it were well if the mind were engrossed by the little excitements forthcoming from constant exercise abroad in the manner which has been indicated; and this suggestion may be accepted as the general rule. But, as there will be ample occasion in the ensuing part of my work to dilate further on this topic, it will not be requisite that it should be pursued further into detail at present.

Occupation.

With reference to the occupations to be provided for early infancy, it may not be improper to premise by stating that they should be as light and little irksome as possible. There is no great advantage, however, in rendering them frivolous and unproductive of any moral or mental effect. There is a common adage, that "all work and no play makes Jack a dull boy." But as a great philosopher was ever urging, we should define terms before we deduce reasoning from them. What is work? and what is play? Does it not appear that this depends more upon the method of providing the employment than upon the nature of the occupation? Might not building card houses and trundling hoops be made *work* (in the popular sense of the word) by the manner in which they are recommended, or suggested; whilst some light handicraft, which is popularly looked upon as *work*, might become, with proper management, a constant source of enjoyment? There is no doubt but that for the first three, four, or five years very few children would be competent for, or could be trusted with implements for any such occupation as is hinted at: and so long as this is the case, their toys may be as useful, if well selected, as any other medium of employment.

As guide for the selection of *amusements*, it were as well to choose such as partake more of the gymnastic or athletic, than of the sedentary character. Puzzles and devices of that kind are anything but desirable resources with very young children, as they tend to concentrate the energies too much upon the mental portion of the system; whereas, the animal powers, being the first in the field, are the first which should be exercised, leaving the mind to ripen by degrees, and to assume its predominance in due course. For the first few years of existence the development of the reflective faculties is exceedingly slow, and should by no means be forced. And for this reason, any occupation which racks them, especially with a child of very susceptible and nervous temperament, which is usually accompanied by more acuteness, will have the effect of galling the master-passion, self-love, and thus embittering and irritating the temper.

Another little hint might be afforded, which will not be found without its good effects if acted upon. And it is this: in those cases in which the parents have leisure hours, they cannot do better than join their children in their trifling amusements, so as mildly, yet firmly, to curb any occasional outbursts of passion or ill-humour, as much as possible without wounding or irritating the child. This, very few nurses have patience to do; and fewer still feel sufficient of real affection and kindliness towards their charges to trouble themselves to observe.

The said method is accompanied by another advantage:—that an observant parent can catch every opportunity for inculcating a sound principle out of the most trivial circumstance, without damping the redundant buoyancy of youth. And this rule is more particularly important where there are several young children in the nursery;

because the parent will have constant opportunities of detecting in their intercourse the varieties and inconsistencies of character (if they exist), and repeated occasions to enjoin the observance of due decorum and propriety, an affectionate and protecting regard on the part of the elder, a confiding and grateful respect on that of the younger, and a kind and gentle consideration of the boy for the girl—all points of paramount moral importance. Great caution is needed in reproof; great moderation, mingled with firmness, in punishment; a moderate appreciation of merit; and a calm rejection of the contrary. Above all things, parents should guard themselves against the loss of their equanimity; and should preserve, as much as possible, an even unruffled tenor of temper towards their children, and avoid betraying uneasiness or irascibility amongst them. The example is the most operative of all means of instruction amongst the young; and unfortunately, they are too often more quick at the mimickry of a weakness than at the imitation of a sterling quality. Besides the moral to be gathered from these particulars, they have all far more effect upon the physical functions than is usually attributed to them; for febrile affection is so easily induced in infancy, and is known in all stages of life to exercise so powerful an influence on the frame, that the bodily health may be sapped by ever-recurring irregularities of the above description before the parent dreams of such a consequence.

In dealing with children in the respects above mentioned, over-severity is one great mistake, carelessness or inattention is another: the one soon weans the child from due and affectionate regard, and makes it look upon the parent as an object of dread; the other allows this regard to perish for lack of fostering. The child that never sees its parents but to be chided learns to wish for their absence:—the child that rarely sees them at all, or that is rarely noticed by them, seeks the caress, which Nature prompts it to look for at their hands, from others, and loves those who tender it accordingly. The natural attachment between parent and child cannot be too sedulously fostered and stimulated. It is one of the mainsprings of pure moral aspiration; for inasmuch as affection well directed is the groundwork of all the virtues, it is by encouraging the first and most tender impulse of Nature that the character is to be moulded aright. Be it observed that this principle of affection, or love, or yearning, or whatever it be termed, must rest somewhere. The human being is a parasite, and cannot subsist alone; his nature is to coil about some other and support himself there, and as this parasitic inclination is well or ill disposed, the determination of the character will be good or evil. And can art suggest a better prop for the social adhesion of a child than that which Nature so pre-eminently indicates in the parent? Society is the state of Nature:—solitude, though seemingly attractive, plausible, and preferable, in the morbid imagination of the dreamer, is impossible. What if the heart, desolate in the world, looks forth upon the inanimate creation, and associates itself with a tree or a flower, or a cavern, or the bounding surface of the endless ocean? If there be secret converse between that heart and those inanimate things, it constitutes a society peculiar to itself, from the lack of that which might have been more consistent with its own organism. No: solitude is nowhere in the world but in the withered hopes, the blasted affections, the distorted mind, or the churlish and hopeless abstraction of a misguided, and consequently wretched, existence. It is to these, and to the heartburnings and remorse which cling to ill-regulated conduct, that you expose your children, whose happiness should have been your own, when you forego or pervert the high privilege of conferring upon their infancy a sound principle of conduct, of training them to a good precedent, and of inculcating by practice the purity of an exemplary precept.

Of Diet.

The diet of young children, as has been shown throughout, should be one of the chief objects of the assiduous attention of all parents. There is no point, perhaps, in which error is likely to arise so easily from mistaken kindness as in this. It is too much the custom with parents, in their treatment of infants, to fancy that feeding is the universal panacea of all their ills. The least symptom of frowardness, peevishness, or irritability is to be allayed by food. And as children advance a few years in life, there is too little restriction put upon the natural inclination to eat so long as food is before them. Very few children know when they have eaten a sufficiency, especially if the dishes placed before them be gratifying to the palate: as is, unfortunately, the case with too many adults, they very rarely measure the quantity which they swallow by the necessity for sustenance. But it has already been constantly urged that, of all things which tend to derange the digestive system and to weaken the proper operation of the functions, there is nothing which so seriously produces those effects, as the overloading the stomach of a child, particularly with heavy and solid food.

Hitherto the earlier kinds of diet have alone

been referred to; but I shall now proceed to continue this subject during the period of childhood generally, setting no particular limit as to age.

Having abandoned the suckling-bottle and the pap bowl, the child emerges from sheer infant feeding to the more mixed and general diet to which it will become accustomed. Broths and light vegetable soups, plain rice, sago–, or bread-puddings, thick milk, made preferably of *baked flour*, and so forth, still varying by gradation, and not on a sudden from the liquid to the predominating solid form of diet. It is very essential, however, in this progress of the dietary system, to observe the useful and invariable rule, that, in the case of children, frequency of feeding is highly preferable to quantity. A child should, generally, eat four or perhaps five times a day—first, very soon after rising; and last, a considerable time before rest (say an hour and a half). The long period which elapses between the last meal in the evening and the first in the morning produces a sensation of sinking and exhaustion, and renders it very necessary that, previous to any exertion, the frame should be revived by food.

At the morning meal, it were as well, if milk agree with the child, to adhere to that as the best of liquids, toasted bread, or soaked bread, or biscuit being added to supply solidity. Tea, coffee, greasy or spiced chocolate, are anything but desirable articles of food. At the same time, it is not to be understood that feeding entirely upon one thing is peculiarly beneficial, because it is generally by the variety of simple and wholesome diet that the healthy action of the various functions is best promoted. Rich dishes and compounds, consisting of numbers of stimulating ingredients, are, however, to be carefully avoided; for, apart from the ill effects of such a system of diet upon the body, the same demoralization may be attributed to it as to any other course of sensual indulgence. A pampered appetite, whether it be for gluttony or crapulence, is ever the same in its effect. Besides, it were well if it were ever remembered, that wealth, with her accompaniments of luxury, circumstance, ease and comfort, is not immutable. And it is very essential to inculcate practically, from the earliest age, that fortuitous circumstances may oppress with unforeseen calamities and privations those who seemed most beyond their reach

Want of the attendants of splendour will be no privation where they have not been made habitual; whereas, the want of them may be as great a privation to those who have been accustomed to look for them, as the want of the common necessaries of life to another.

Of the varieties of diet peculiarly adapted to the

treatment of particular constitutions, there will hereafter be occasion to speak in the Fourth Part of my work; and therefore, without entering into directions on that score, at present it will be sufficient to refer the reader to the forthcoming chapter on CONSTITUTIONAL TENDENCIES.

But there is another injunction with respect to diet, of a more general character, which is of no mean importance to the physical as well as moral powers, the latter being always more or less affected by the condition of the former. It is not universally known, or, at all events, practically evinced, that diet should vary very materially with the changes of temperature, in the same way that it must vary with climate.

There is a notorious fact in the natural history of every species, which is, that the same frame cannot thrive upon the identical food in a tropical as in a temperate zone? Why, then, should not the same reasoning be good, of different seasons in the same climate? But, apart from any analogical reasoning of this kind, it is mere matter of experience, that, whereas in the colder seasons the frame requires a greater supply of food, and that of a more generous kind, to aid it in the generation of animal heat alone, than in the warmer periods of the year, when it requires to be relieved of superfluous caloric or to be allowed to radiate faster than it engenders. Amongst adults the inclination to eat is commonly less at such periods, and the lack of inclination may lead them to observe the rule insensibly. But children in the first place, have that inclination more constantly; and in the next place, do not possess sufficient of reason to moderate it. They eat or cram because things which please them are offered to them. The digestion, as an inevitable consequence, becomes thereby debilitated, and serious derangement of the functions ensues.

According to the season, it were always as well to lighten, and to moderate, as to render more generous and increase the diet. And, as Nature has provided an additional variety of food in the vegetable kingdom for the warmer season, it is, generally speaking, advisable to adopt the hint, by affording a predominance to vegetable diet at that period of the year, observing certain reservations as to constitution, hereafter suggested.* Fruit perfectly ripe, in moderation, is wholesome in its proper season, and ought, therefore, likewise to form a portion of the allotted diet.

Another mischief, which must carefully be guarded against, is the habit of eating very fast, or of "*bolting*" the food, as it is called. When once

* See Part IV.

a child is gifted with teeth, it possesses them for some purpose. That purpose is mastication, without which the digestion is either obstructed altogether or rendered too sluggish in its operetion to disperse the sustenance derived from food through the frame, and to reject the spurious portions as fast as the body requires it.

Some children acquire the trick of swallowing their food without proper mastication from a greedy habit, which has not been checked at its first manifestation. With others, again, it is engendered by a constant craving, arising out of an unhealthy condition of the stomach. In the latter case, this habit only increases the ill, and in the former it generally produces it. So that, whether the consequence of a weakness of body or of a young vice, it is equally injurious.

Another rule, to which more importance should be attached, than at first sight appears, relates to the improper *interspersion* (if it may be so called) of food. For instance a child has meat, vegetables and bread placed before it; and it is not uncommon for the young feeder to attack the meat with voracity, leaving the vegetables and bread untouched. This ought to be early corrected; and it is the easiest thing in the world to accustom children to partake of each, mouthful for mouthful as it were—a method which greatly contributes to the easy and healthy operation of the digestive organs, and tends, perhaps, as much as anything to subdue the uneven and craving appetite above alluded to.

Again, a sufficiency, though by no means a superfluity, of fluid should be taken at every meal —another assistant of digestion which is often not adequately attended to.

Manners at Table.

Without departing from the proper subject-matter of this chapter, it appears that some notice might be taken of the MANNERS OF CHILDREN AT TABLE. It cannot be too often repeated, that out of these insignificant little points arise the most important consequences; and good-breeding, if it be not a virtue, verges so nearly upon it, that it should be accepted as one ingredient of virtue at the least.

There is no reason why, because feeding is entirely the business of the animal part of the system, it should be too much subjected to the disposition of the brute. Intellectuality is rarely of any avail unless it succeed in ruling man, even where it has no participation in his occupation. And intelligence is indeed reduced in its sphere if it cannot attend the human being wheresoever he may range or in whatever he may do. But in this, as in all other matters, the animal inclinations will generally predominate unless they be subdued and rendered rather the servants than the tyrants of the mental and moral faculties from the earliest youth. Cleanliness, patience, order, decorum, and the like, should be enjoined at table as soon as the child is accustomed to be placed at it. The habit of scrambling after any favorite service, of screaming spontaneous remarks, or demanding, without propriety, whatever shall chance to appear gratifying, of interrupting conversation, or of wanting whatever is being served to some one else or is most scanty, and similar vagaries, should be checked at the first onset. It may be a mere suggestion, but somehow or other it seems as if the jealous disposition of a child might as soon be detected at the board as anywhere; and if so, the suggestion may not prove useless in facilitating the subjugation of this insidious and mischievous passion.

Elsewhere there will arise an occasion for me to lay some stress upon the usefulness of training male children to pay deference to the gentler sex. And as in point of moral and social virtue this is amongst the first of vehicles, there can be no need of apology in anticipating a little upon the design of this work, and in impressing this feature of treatment strongly upon the parent whilst dealing with a subject with which the first opportunities for inculcating the rule will inevitably be connected. The mainspring of civilization is centred in the fairer portion of the creation, and not only do honour, generosity, and propriety, dictate a true regard for the weaker sex, but it is the observance of this regard—which the Divinity, for great and good purposes, has implanted in the more ascendant sex—that softens down the ruggedness of the world, cements and polishes society, and renders the intercourse of mankind conducive to the reciprocal benefits and the welfare of every community. Among very young children no better occasion can be taken to impress this preference upon them than when at table, at which time they will usually be brought together, and when they are frequently not over nice in betraying their selfish inclinations. Thus, although it may appear to the rugged philosopher but a mere act of superficial courtesy to pass the service on until all who are entitled to preference at table are served, it will often be found in after-life to have produced a rooted respect for the *bienséances* of society, and to have been one of the many agents, under tutelage, which have assisted in removing the coarseness of the natural character.

It is, doubtless, true, that these remarks apply almost solely to the circumstances of the wealthy;

but there is a similar philosophy, comparative in its degrees and appliances, which is good in all grades; and as it is as sweet to be heard and appreciated in the cottage as in the palace, and as there is frequently more earnest attention in the former, the suggestion would not be without its use amongst any class in which the repetition of it may introduce the practice. The reason for which many of my remarks are more directly addressed to the rich than to the poor is, that the former are doubly to blame if they overlook questions of importance in the education of their children—they have no excuse for the omission; whereas those whose whole time is employed by toil, relieved only by sufficient time to rest and eat, have barely the leisure to pay minute attention to particulars of the kind. It is not therefore to say, however, that a well-disciplined character would not be as useful, as productive of happy results, and as commendable amongst the poor as amongst the rich. Goodness, in whatever condition of life it be planted, must ever have its sphere. It is only consistent with the eternal principles of justice that it should.

Of Clothing.

The lighter and looser the clothing can be, without exposure, the better. The confinement of the limbs, and the restriction of the joints, are highly prejudicial to the free circulation of the blood, and conducive to many deformities (if they may be so called) of the body. Every part of the frame should be left at liberty for the fullest action. Not to digress again, it should be remembered that the use of stays with young girls is apt to become exceedingly injurious. It has frequently been urged, and with great justice, that the adoption of this artificial support at all is not only unnecessary, and the use of it induced by habit, but very serious and sometimes fatal in its consequences. It is evidently a mere whim of fashion, inasmuch as the many thousands on the face of the globe who support themselves very well without them would be just as subject to the necessity, if it existed, as those who adopt them from the custom of society. It is by no means true, physiologically or anatomically, that the frame of womankind is too fragile to sustain itself without artificial support. And this excuse so often urged in favour of the fashion, becomes too much the pretext for an excess in the tightness with which this part of female dress is fitted on, until it is suffered to destroy the regularity of the proportions, and actually to impede the operation of most of the vital organs. The heart, the lungs, and the liver, are stripped of the efficacy of these safeguards with which Nature has provided them, when the bones, which constitute the protection, are forced from their proper places, to occupy part of the space assigned to the functions which they were constructed to defend.

With respect to texture of dress, the finest descriptions of woollen may, on the whole, be preferable to any. But woollen textures must be very smooth and fine indeed, otherwise they are apt to be too irritating, especially to the tender skins of children. The rivalry between fine cotton and fine linen leads, after all, to no very essential distinction. If, on the one hand, the linen be purer, and in many respects cleaner, the cotton, on the other hand, is softer, and better suited to a very young and tender skin; but neither the one nor the other possess the merit of the *fine woollen.** The last may now be procured with as smooth a surface as any calico, and thus the greatest objection is done away with.

Again, the clothing should never be heavier than need be, and particularly the covering of the

* On this subject of clothing, see the Introductory Remarks to the Domestic Medicine. In that work, the author took occasion to object strongly to coarse woollens, such as the common flannels, and so forth. The objection does not, however, hold good as regards very fine textures, which, on the whole, are preferable to cotton or linen.

head. It is very much the custom to invest young children with heavy hats and feathers, and articles of that kind. And whether the costume be in good or bad taste, which it is not my business to discuss, as a question of utility and advantage it is a great mistake. The head especially should be very lightly covered. With respect to *under clothing*, it is by no means prudent to draw a distinction between the seasons. The difference should consist in the *outer covering*. For, for example, if flannel be worn next to the skin in the winter, and be found necessary or become habitual in that season, it is really far more necessary in the summer, when the changes and transitions of temperature are greater. And, moreover, far from being productive of inconvenience from heat, it is more likely to lessen it, by facilitating radiation, or, otherwise, because it is a better conductor. The difference of colour in the outer clothing is often more essential than the difference of texture, that is to say in bright weather.

It has transpired in the course of this work that in some respects, what is termed the hardening system,* pursued with *reason* and *moderation*, (and otherwise nothing can be a greater mistake,) may

* The author has, in his DOMESTIC MEDICINE, passed severe strictures upon the excess of this method; but he must not be understood to recommend the other extreme.

be extremely beneficial, and that, to say the least of it, it is far better than the method of coddling children. One remark on this point should have place here, which is, that although the skin may be rendered more or less obdurate and insensible to temperature, the blood cannot be altered in quality by any experiments in lessening clothing, and *vice versâ*;—a caution as to notion of materially changing the constitution by external means, and by stripping the body of the due amount of clothing which it requires for protection.

But, at the same time, the absurd fashion of muffling children in wrappings of every variety of shape and texture, is as likely to be prejudicial as it is ludicrous. The more especially are the wearers likely to be injured by this over care, when the garments are so constructed as to confine the joints, particularly about the shoulders. There should be abundant scope for the expansion of the chest and the free motion of the arms. In fact, the limbs should in all respects be left unrestricted by the clothing.

There is unfortunately as much indulgence in the fantastical devices of fashion and of seasons amongst the children of the upper classes as amongst the adults,—fantastical devices, which too frequently forego the essential for the appearance. But it should not be forgotten, that, what may not conduce to injury in an adult, may be very seriously prejudicial to a child. Wherefore the requirements of health, ease, and comfort should have a double preponderance in the treatment of the latter.

It were not improper to suggest, as a method for the construction of the clothing of children, that it should be so effected as to afford every facility for active, athletic, and gymnastic exercises —*to cover, but not to bind.*

Thus both of the more serious objections of confinement and exposure would be effectually removed.

PART II.

OF PHYSICAL EDUCATION, AS TENDING TO MENTAL AND MORAL DEVELOPMENT.

It is the spirit of humble but well-intentioned recommendation that every one should embark in a treatise upon the education of childhood; and it is certainly with some degree of diffidence that the most experienced in the arts of training and tutelage should claim for their own peculiar method the titular distinction of the best. With these reservations, which are due to the subject, let me, however, intimate at the outset that the reason why, in most instances, a very great portion of the regulative system in such matters should emanate from scientific and professional sources, is that, as has been already repeatedly shown in this work, much of the efficacy of education must depend upon the constitutional aptitude to the system of training. What will suit one frame and one development of faculties will by no means suit another, in the same manner, as the old adage has it, that "what is food for one may be poison for another."

But, previous to entering into the detail of any system of training, it is necessary to classify the faculties in some method, so as to deal with 'the subject a little more systematically.

Let us premise, therefore, that PERCEPTION is the first among the orders of mental and moral powers which is brought into active operation, and that REFLECTION is only of subsequent development.

But both these are compound terms, and imply combinations of faculties, in which there are various gradations of progress, and to which appertain various degrees of intensity.

These gradations of progress and degrees of intensity are manifested at various stages by the use of the senses, or organs of sense and expression.

Again, we must premise that *knowledge*, or *learning*, are never intuitive, whereas OBSERVATION is so—*observation* being the offspring of a peculiar combination of the *perceptive faculties*. With PERCEPTION, then, let us begin—and, taking it in its simplest state of activity, trace the first period of education to the epoch of its dawn.

As far as any agency brought to bear upon it is concerned, the parent must look entirely to its manifestation, because if it be unmanifested by any outward sign it is yet dormant.

The infant first displays the activity of such faculties in expressions of glee or pain, caused by the appearance of external things. The chuckle, the stare, or the sudden alarm, are, doubtless, expressions of pleasure, wonder, or pain; and without considering abstrusely whether the effect arises from a simple or complex idea, originating in the external cause, it should be dealt with according to the manifestation of that effect.

Thus, that which is unnecessary, and causes evident discomfiture, and conjures disagreeable ideas to the child, should be avoided, as likely to exercise a prejudicial effect upon the temper, where reflection is yet inactive, and consequently, the powers of judgment and discrimination, and the faculty of reasoning are not present to correct any misimpression to which the child is subject. Never expose what you wish to accustom an infant to, to dread, loathing, or distrust. There will ever afterwards be a predisposition to the same impressions, and almost a horror, quite as causeless, perhaps, but equally powerful in its repulsive agency on the mind.

So long as the PERCEPTIVE FACULTIES continue to be the predominant organs in active development, the tuition must necessarily be one of example almost solely. Precepts will make but little impression: they will be heard, and perhaps repeated from memory, but without much importance being attached to them. But whatever of external circumstance, is conveyed by PERCEPTION to the senses and to the intellect, will make a rooted and lasting impression. The eye will catch an attitude, a shape, air, antic, or a feat, which will almost invariably induce an attempt at imitation. The ear will listen to forms of expression, and prompt the tongue to repeat them. The manner will be quickly conveyed to the imitative intelligence of the child. The demeanour, the temper, and general habits will grow into general habits with the younger scion. And, in things which gratify the senses whilst they satisfy the demands of a natural instinct, such as feeding and the like, the impression imbibed from observation will be doubly strong. Upon the first appearance of bad habits, a mere sign of disapproval will serve to check them, whilst care in withholding the examples which have suggested them will provide against their reacquisition. But when they have, by long continuance, become part of the habitual conduct there will be the greatest difficulty in controverting them.

Moreover, children are, by instinct, apt to be very jealous of the attentions and caresses of their parents, so that it is most needful to observe the strictest impartiality where there are two or more of an approximate age. Nothing will more rapidly tend to embitter the temper of the neglected child or children, and to alienate their affection, not only from the parent, but from their brothers and sisters also, as any distinction made by the parents between them.

It were as well, too, for the purpose of aiding in subduing the propensities, and elevating the supremacy of thc moral sentiments, *to inculcate very early, and to continue to instil into the male child a kind of venerative and ideal esteem for the weaker sex;*—accustom every boy to treat that sex with *tender respect*—to deal more gently by it than by his own—to feel that there is a reverential admiration due to it, which will grow upon him with maturer years, and, as a consequence, teach him properly to comprehend and appreciate woman, and lead him to place her in that high position in the social scale to which she is so justly entitled.

Nothing is more degrading to humanity, and nothing more summarily dishonours the purity of the heart, which pollutes itself to pollute, and to be again polluted, than the ascendancy of the animal propensities. And if it be imagined that these propensities only eke out of the character in a more advanced stage of life, it is an error which cannot be too sternly exposed.

The first faculties are animal, and partake of that character alone, inasmuch as the first faculties are little more than instinctive, and if they be allowed to outweigh the sense of wrong, which is innate in human kind, (perhaps in all kinds,) they will grow great and powerful in the subjugation of the counterbalancing power.

It is in the earliest germ that these defects are to be dealt with; in after life they will have become inveterate and indomitable.

It may even be suggested that attention might with advantage be paid to the organic developments of the head, whilst closely watching the manifestations of the character, and treating the child as nearly as can be, so as to modify one defect without arousing another, and in general by exciting the sentiments of benevolence, veneration and their like, whilst the PERCEPTIVE FACULTIES are carefully directed upon good models, and the exercise of the reflective (as soon as they shall become active) is encouraged into fruitful operation.

The prominent features of virtue and vice are ever easy of distinction to parents who really watch with earnestness over the progress of their child; and, from the earliest age of perception, they each propound their unalterable evidences, and exhibit themselves, at first, under those unsophisticated and undissembled phases natural to the first simplicity of childhood.

It is then that the evil should be subdued and the good fostered, before vice has learnt to mask itself in the garb of virtue and to appear like what it should be, and not like what it is. And it is because defects so soon find the means to cover their deformity with subtle craft, that the first period of infancy should be marked at every turn.

The method of correction in cases of evil propensities should be moderate, insensible, and, if possible, imperceptible to the child itself. The sources of temptation, should, on this account, be removed from reach and contact without remark, and without any apparent design. Because it is dangerous to appear to thwart a hankering, and it is even dangerous to betray that it has attracted attention, inasmuch as what was almost innocently done before, will, with some tempers, be perversely and eagerly pursued afterwards. And this pursuit will engender one of the most noxious of vicious tendencies, the *desire of concealment*—an evil which cannot be too carefully guarded against.

Of Spoilt Children.

Having thus far treated of children generally, as regards their *natural defects*, it will be necessary to dwell upon another gradation—to wit, what may be termed *acquisitive defects.*

The vicious inclinations to which allusion is made, under this denomination, are those which grow out of errors in management and education, and may be divided into two broad sections, those which accrue from *over-indulgence*, and those which are consequent upon *over-severity.*

Those who betray the former propensities are well known by the denomination of *spoilt children.*

It has already transpired that there are two very great errors in the management of children—excess either of severity or of indulgence, nor is it easy to determine which of the two produces the most baneful effects upon the character, so equal is the rivalry betwixt them on that score. But the *spoilt child* is, in one remarkable particular, inferior to the *alienated child*, which is that whereas the latter has usually learned to cater for himself, and is consequently, as it were, prepared to struggle with the world, the other is incapacitated and helpless, and unadapted to any independent action. When parents, therefore, spoil their children by over-indulgence, they first of all make them the plagues of the household, and the standing nuisances of every body that is introduced there; and, secondly, they leave them, perhaps, to be the playthings and vic tims of a world which is jealous, cruel, and vindictive, enough to revel in their torture- They expose all the fine qualities of resolution, determination, courage, and firmness to be relaxed by disuse, or, by never being allowed an occasion for exertion, they suffer the moral convictions of the soul to be subdued by gratified appetites, they expose the temper to be soured by every little cross-purpose which may chance to thwart a whim, and they allow the mental and physical powers to remain so long in disuse, that they cease at last to be capable of development. It should be remembered that of what may be useful to a man, nothing of knowledge is too little for a great mind—nothing that is good is too mean. The hands were provided to execute what the brain was devised to conceive. The great lesson, therefore, that is early to be inculcated, is, that nothing can be procured without some self-exertion. Let it appear, as it were, to the child as if he had earned whatever gratifications were conceded, and thus constitute a species of mutual obligation between parent and child, which will become the chief agent in moulding the character.

Over-severity—Alienated Children.

It has already been intimated of *over-severity* that, far from being productive of good moral effects, it cramps the development of the faculties, damps the buoyant ardour of youth, so essential to manliness and enterprise, embitters the temper and alienates the affection; and, although it may effect one good, which is to teach the child to act and contrive for himself, it teaches him, at the same time, to do so too much irrespective of the parents' wish and judgment, and too much in positive contradiction to both. It induces a habit of harbouring secret designs, of being jealous of the parents' watchfulness, of evading supervision, and of concealing his actions and his motives. Moreover, with children who do not possess sufficient determination of character to trust exclusively to their own resources and judgments, the constant habit of finding fault, and of never praising merit, puzzles them, and produces too great a confusion between the faults and the merits. They become at a loss to distinguish when they have really done well, and hence grow careless of well-doing, and reckless of ill-doing. Eulogy properly bestowed is a powerful preservative of good, and consequently no mean arm against evil.

An affected reserve and austerity towards children is as dangerous as it is mistaken. There are but few instances in which children have been educated upon the recluse principle, which have not terminated with some very mischievous tendencies of character. A proper liberty of thought and action is more likely to induce reflection, and teach the folly of certain habits and certain pursuits, than the most arbitrary confinement or exclusion from them. Under this system they will be invariably sought after, and will possess a peculiar charm; with a little more freedom in the attainment of them, they will generally appear what they are, disgusting or revolting.

This remark applies equally to religious, moral, or physical discipline. The disciplinarian who makes his rules, rules of iron, will have them broken, when the mind or frame is strong enough to break the chain. The good, and not the ill, becomes hideous and assumes deformity, and the mind and body alike shudder at the injunctions, against which Nature has learnt to revolt. It is barely a matter suited to a work of this kind, to enter into the method of religious education of children, and it is far too delicate and elevated a subject to be lightly handled. Besides, almost every parent has a peculiar religious bias or prejudice, or conviction, and it is an arrogant assumption rashly to impugn and condemn the motives which actuate him: but, without making any direct observation as to method, it may be suggested to parents as advisable, not to force very serious subjects upon children too early, and rather to content themselves with inculcating pure morality, consistent with the maxims of true religion, without troubling the child with the origin of and reasons for belief or conduct. Let reason assume her inquiries on these topics as she grows old enough and strong enough to enter into them. The religious duties should not be made troublesome, but, on the contrary, consoling, comforting, and grateful, and the memory should not be dosed with empty repetitions: they mean nothing, and lead to nothing but to mockery.

With reference to mental discipline, have a care that the mind is sufficiently strong and matured to bear it. Begin gently, and do not force on too fast where the occupation is irksome, tedious, and unfruitful. Whenever the mind is glutted, it has not only received the superfluous in vain, but all that it has received is annulled in the same way. It is a profitable recipient only of as much as it can bear and digest, when no more is artificially crammed into it; but when crammed, it is a *profitable recipient of nothing—or, possibly, rather worse than nothing, because its powers are impaired without any accession of knowledge.*

Your systematic and perfect *grounding* (it should be grinding) of very young children, in the rudiments of everything which they are intended to learn perfectly, may be very economical, in as far as it tends to complete a pseudo-education very early, but it is not only far from tending to a perfect and sound education, but it vastly deteriorates the natural capacities, and lessens greatly the ultimate value of what has been taught, besides being seriously prejudicial in many instances to the vitality and organic construction of the frame. Precocious learning is the curse and not the blessing of childhood; and the *severe discipline* with which it is necessarily accompanied by no means heightens the moral qualities, as is fancied, but renders them obtuse and insensible. Keen sensibility will be goaded by this method, till, by goading, it grows callous. Dull apprehension and susceptibility will be rendered duller, or acrid and irritable, and will pass from acrimony and irritability to sullen stupidity.

For the same reasons, excessive severity in punishment does permanent injury to the character: obstinacy, moroseness, contradiction, and the like, are induced by it, and the wrong doer only becomes hardened in wrong, and not amended. If you inflict too much of mental suffering, you may induce nervous incapacity—if you inflict corporal suffering, you may do great injury to the bodily health. *The true method of punishing with efficacy, or without prejudice, is to do so as much as possible by withholding enjoyment, not by inflicting pain.* No course of penance, either, should be continued too long—no offence, however grievous, allowed to appear unforgiven, if not unforgotten; because, besides the detrimental state of mental suspense and anxiety, in which a child is kept by such a method, you are infringing one of the first maxims of pure morality, and setting the example of its infringement. By precept and practice inculcate the axiom, "*forgive, that it may be forgiven unto you.*"

There is reason for not detaining the reader too long here with the subject, inasmuch as it must necessarily be again introduced under the head of *Admonitory Education.* Let us, therefore, proceed with *Over-severity in physical discipline.* This also, in early childhood, does both moral and physical injury. A mere child does not readily understand or appreciate the advantage of, or the necessity for, laborious occupation; and although in no respect is the excess of severity in discipline, in this particular, likely to become so noxious as in the two former, still there is no particular advantage in inducing a loathing for the employment. Moreover, with some constitutions, and with natural debilities, it may become injurious to the bodily health and to the organic construction. For example, let us suppose the occupation to be engraving, or any other which is very trying to the sight, it would barely be judicious to compel its continuance whilst the eyes were becoming daily impaired by it; the sight might utterly and irretrievably be lost, as has, indeed, been very repeatedly the case, before the parent could be brought to believe that the occupation was not congenial to the physical construction of the frame.

Otherwise, as will hereafter appear, it seems established beyond contradiction that, for the first five or six, or even eight years of life, the occupation should be wholly, or almost wholly, of a physical character: well selected, and enjoined with judgment and precaution, it is the best groundwork of education. Not all the books in Europe combined can afford a young mind one half the useful information, as far as any retentive power is concerned, that can be gathered from mechanical device and mechanical ingenuity. These things speak for themselves in natural facts; the others reason to show what these exhibit,— and sometimes reason more towards their unshowing, or, at all events, towards their mystification. A solid in figures and a solid in fact are the same in calculation, but very different to the first apprehension. Still the pursuit of the more mechanical occupations should be directed with precaution and moderation, and over-fatigue, or the exhaustion of any particular organ of sense or muscular power, avoided as much as possible.

The Duties, and their Inculcation.

Now come we to the great centre upon which the whole of the well-being of individuals as of communities depends—as that upon which morality, social, transcendental, and speculative, are and must be founded.

Mankind have been so fashioned and disposed by the Creator that there must be a reciprocal communion between them; and this reciprocal communion is manifested in the duties which one man thus owes to another—duties whose observance is, therefore, imperative for his own well-being, and upon which communities, polities, laws, societies, and nations must be organized, and by which, and which alone, they can subsist. The justest system of legislation and government, and the most conducive to national happiness and prosperity, is that which as closely as possible assumes and follows the Christian duties as its text. The inculcation of those duties, and of the general principles which enunciate them, is, therefore, the first office of a parent towards his child; and whilst it is the first and the best, it is the noblest and greatest: for the goodness of the child cannot but reflect a portion at least of its lustre upon the parent who awoke and fostered it. And, in passing, it may not be amiss to remark, whilst genius and learning have so long been toiling to produce the evidences of Christianity, that the best of all evidences is the internal evidence of pure moral and sound social doctrine; for there is not one iota of the relative duties of man towards man, which is not explicitly, clearly, and simply enunciated in the Gospels in that parental spirit of affection, compassion, and remonstrance, which may most surely achieve the happiness of the human race.

First and foremost amongst these duties, and indeed embodying the whole code of obligation, is *that of doing to another what one would wish to have done to one's self.* In early infancy, especially where there are several children of an approximate age and of constant companionship, so many opportunities will occur of inculcating a deferential preference to one another, that it becomes the more easy to root the principle in them; and where the training is well conducted, the practice will so frequently become the source of genuine self-gratification, that its very pleasure will secure adhesion to it: it is the antidote, as it is the reverse, of the worst and darkest passions of human nature—vengefulness, malignity, hatred, jealousy, deep selfishness, and the like. It should, moreover, be constantly remembered, in dealing with the human character, that it possesses one dominant, overweening, but necessary passion, *self-love*, and, therefore, in controverting any mischievous tendencies of disposition, (which, too, may not unfrequently have their source in this master passion,) that the surest way of effecting a cure is to endeavour to wean over that very passion from wrong, and to enlist it for good purposes. Thus there should ever be some suppositive *reward* or *punishment* for good or evil. Mankind unfortunately require some internal or external incentive to *do* good, although they *know* and *feel* it well; whereas they are prone by weakness to do wrong, although they are rarely deceived by its specious aspect, however they may be willing to close their eyes upon the truth.

It is easily conceived how the duty of doing to others as we would be done by involves the whole of the terrestrial obligations of mankind, but yet it involves subordinate branches of duty, of which it is necessary to take some particular and individual notice.

The Six Social Duties.

First amongst these may be ranked the *duty of the child towards the parent*;—secondly, the duty of a child towards its nearest of kin: which are obligations that Nature has rendered incumbent on consanguinity;—thirdly, the duties of the *younger towards the elder:* reverence for age was ranked high amongst the Spartan virtues;—fourthly, the duties of the master towards the servant, the superior towards the inferior, and *vice versâ*;—fifthly, the duties of wealth towards poverty, and *vice versâ*; —and, lastly, though not least, the duties towards the community—the duties to one's country.

The early inculcation of these social obligations being alone capable of fashioning a good child, a good brother, a good master or servant, a good proprietor or tenant, a good citizen, and in fact a GOOD MAN, can alone conduce to a happy and prosperous state of society, and consequently to a happy and prosperous existence. It is incumbent upon every father of a family to do his own part towards ameliorating the condition of his race, and assisting in the organization of a better social state. Vice, crime, destitution, and misery, though too sadly and inseparably bound to humanity, are, in great measure, attributable to faulty tutelage in childhood.

Legislators and statesmen are too apt to overlook this immense fact, in squeezing out the small instalment for the consummation of a happy community. Let them lay it to their hearts, and remember occasionally that the sweets, the profits, the flattery, and the ascendency of office are not unaccompanied with high and noble moral obligations to the people for whom they act,—and to human kind in general—obligations indeed, which, overlooked or unheeded, degrade them sadly from their high estate, and make them indirectly guilty of the hideous atrocities which defame and afflict the populace. A vigilant police, an apt, brave, and determined soldiery, or even a flourishing trade, immeasurable wealth, and an ample exchequer, if these be ever at hand, are not the only appliances which they have to provide for the public safety and the public welfare. It is by no means to the credit of statesmanship that it should have so long delayed to turn its attention to public education, and perhaps but little more worthy of eulogy that it should have set so erroneously and meanly about it even now.

Duty towards the Parent.

But, to return, let us proceed with the first of the six duties. The errors of over-indulgence and over-severity which have already been noticed, are, more than anything else in the treatment of children, likely to lead them to forget, neglect, or despise the obligations which are due to their parents; and, as there can be no more gnawing affliction than is suffered by the parent from such forgetfulness, neglect, or contempt, no care should be foregone in securing the observance of these duties by the temperate and judicious treatment of childhood.

The duties of a child towards his parents may be summed up in the words Love, Honour, Reverence, and Obedience.

Of Obedience.

But obedience is subject, it must be remembered, to modification, and may, in particular circumstances, be vice or crime; abject submission to improper injunctions is an idolatry, not a genuine ministry or service.

In order to inculcate a wholesome, genuine, and virtuous submission, the first care must be with the parent: even the ordinary directions of everyday occurrence should not be given hastily, or without due deliberation. Here, as in all other respects in the tutelage of infancy, the parent must keep strict guard over his own temper, must learn and subdue his own infirmities, and must have a care to understand the temperament, moral and physical, of the child with whom he is dealing.

Of Love.

Love is natural to mankind; all created beings must love something, and, if nothing else, themselves,—the last direction of love is a vice, and one which can only be provided against by directing the affection elsewhere. But, although love is natural to man, it is not natural to him to love one fellow-creature more than another; he has only a peculiar aptitude and inclination to love his parents, because they are the first on whom his eyes are cast at their earliest awakening, and because they are the first by whom he is loved, cherished, nurtured, and caressed. It is, therefore, an error, to suppose that it is the *natural right and privilege* of parentage to be loved by its offspring; but inasmuch as the alienation of the offspring is a great calamity to both relations, and inasmuch, moreover, as there is an inherent *predisposition* in the child to vest the depth of its affection in the parents, it is the interest of the parent, as it is his duty to encourage, maintain, and cherish that affection; for, it is through predilection and by attachment that the injunctions of the parent will come with double and sweetened effect upon the child.

It is not uncommon for parents to reproach their children when they betray a coldness and want of duty towards them; but they should first search their own memory and reflection, and ascertain whether in anything they have foregone the tenderness which they owed to the age and temperament of their children; and they should, perhaps, also remember that tenderness and care and nurture are rather *duties* incumbent, as *duties*, upon the parents than the children, inasmuch as the latter are guiltless of their own existence, and the former have incurred these offices as *duties*, in consenting to become parents. These offices will thereafter *become duties, and imperative duties*, in the children, by reciprocity, and in gratitude for the gentle observance extended to themselves.

Thus the parent must, in some manner, earn the affection of the child, and engross it. The primary duty is in the parent; the secondary, reciprocal and inductive duty, is in the child. *Power and ascendency, in all their phases, in human nature, are too apt to assert rights which are not their own, and to forget the obligations which are the foundation of their privileges*, and therefore I lay particular emphasis on these distinctions of position. Power and ascendency, in all their phases, have their relative circumstances to learn.

Honour and Reverence.

The honour of the parent is the honour of the child, and *vice versâ.* A good, just, and tender parent is entitled to honour from the child; but even this is only an *inductive duty* in the latter:—and yet it is almost an obligation on the child to shield and preserve the honour of the parent when the latter has allowed it to be tarnished. The age, experience, knowledge, and social relation of the parent towards the child entitle the former to honour and reverence in a peculiar degree, from their particular combination in his person; for as each may claim its share of distinctive respect separately, their combination in one person multiplies the claim.

In the inculcation of these duties, as, indeed, of all others, the example of the parent should be carefully guarded of whatever is obnoxious to either honour or reverence. For, if they be claimed by parentage indiscriminately for good and evil, the principle of morality with which they are associated is relaxed,—and the habit of respecting infirmities would certainly be sufficient to induce them; but, on the other hand, their due and careful inculcation, by precept and example, will greatly heighten the sense of pure morality, and form one of the keystones of the fairest of social virtues.

The Duties of Consanguinity.

The duties of consanguinity are affection, protection, and so forth; or, more properly, they are the general duties to one's neighbour, (to mankind), heightened by peculiar and close relations. It is necessarily reserved that they are in a way duties to merit, and not to demerit: because the latter changes the aspect of all duties, and, to a certain extent, abrogates the vestment of obligations that they may become vested elsewhere. It should also be remarked that there is a very essential point gained by their inculcation, which is, that the broad principle of the reciprocal duties of mankind is involved in them, is inculcated with them, and that this is the first and simplest method of expounding the great social doctrine.

The Duties of the Younger towards the Elder.

Age, which is supposed to be accompanied by experience, matured reflection, moderated passions, knowledge, and their dependent acquirements, is clearly entitled to respect and veneration on these grounds; and, in teaching children a proper decorum towards persons of more advanced years, it must, *primâ facie*, be taken for granted that these merits have been acquired, whereby a respect for the merits is justly inculcated. At all events, a mere child is barely a competent judge on the subject, and it is the duty of the parent to prevent association with those in whom some such merits do not exist. At a little riper age, youth may be allowed to discriminate, and to exercise some discretion and judgment on these matters, as such discretionary exercise of judgment is wholesome; and under such circumstances the rule becomes, like all others, subject to its exceptions.

But, on the other hand, the exposition of good examples of age, for the respect and veneration of youth, is calculated to moderate the impetuosity, to calm the excited passions, to form the judgment by reflection, to inculcate self-control, to silence dogmatism (so common amongst precocious children), to subdue overweening conceit, to abash pride and arrogance, to induce method, industry, application, firmness, resolution, forbearance, and endurance, and to overcome the self-willedness which is so baneful in itself and in its effects.

The Duties of the Master towards the Servant, the Superior towards the Inferior, &c. &c.

The remaining of the six social duties, according to the foregoing subdivision, it is true, appertain rather to maturity than to childhood, but they are, nevertheless, of necessary inculcation in youth, inasmuch as the only method of securing the observance of moral duties is to impress them strongly upon the mind in youth, and to allow them to grow up with the character, so to speak.

The duties of superior and inferior, of employer and employed, are not, like the others, of general application, they are offices resulting from circumstantial and casual relations and intercourse, but they are none the less an essential portion of the moral code; for the circumstances in which they originate must occur, on the one hand or the other, throughout the existence of all mankind.

First, in addressing those who, by circumstances, are placed in a superior condition of life, and in command, it may be suggested, that not only should they be careful to impress upon their children the following precepts, but that they should be very guarded of infringing them themselves.

As all mankind are liable to error, it is incumbent upon the superior to bear and to forbear; for he will hope to obtain such grace of those who, again, are above *him*.

Arbitrary dictation, overbearing arrogance, pride, undue affectation of superiority, and the like, are not only indecorous, but are acts of injustice. Every one, however mean his casual position in life, is entitled to the same individual consideration of his merits and his services.

Leniency, good humour, polite address, and the like, are not so very onerous as duties that anything should preclude the title of the inferior to look for them. It is no uncommon thing, in households, for children to be constantly seeing and hearing the dependents treated like so many animals of an inferior caste; and it is no more uncommon for children to be suffered to assume the like tone towards them. Nothing can be more reprehensible in itself. Not only is it unbecoming, but far from asserting a genuine superiority, it is, on the contrary, extremely derogatory to authority; and, whilst it is thus both reprehensible, unbecoming, and derogatory, it renders the child, so habituated, incapable of the restraint and control which the usages and necessities of the world will require of him from some other.

To those whose circumstances place them in an inferior position in society, whether menial or not, it might be urged that, although employment with them is necessity, and is therefore (in some shape or other) perhaps the birthright of every dependent person, yet, in engaging in any particular occupation, they assent to a tacit contract, by which they bind themselves to be just and honest towards the employer, and to afford his own views, wishes, or even caprices, every consideration in their power. They are not, therefore, to consider themselves aggrieved by every little trifle, but to offer the same margin to the superior as they themselves expect at his hands. Obedience to every reasonable injunction is part of what they undertake to fulfil; an industrious and honest performance of the toil which they have assumed as their own; an unmurmuring and cheerful disposition to yield an obligation when they have the opportunity, without waiting to consider whether what they are about to execute can be demanded as a right at their hands.

In this country, I must say, these regulations cannot be too strongly impressed upon the young; for, to refer more particularly to an individual class, who attend upon the households and the luxuries of wealth, there is barely any order of society more pampered or more fantastical than that of household servants. They are apt to fancy themselves ill-used when Mr. A. does not afford them the comforts or luxuries conceded to them previously by Mr. B.; to imagine that nothing can be expected of them but a certain particular occupation, and that if they are simply asked to do something else they are insulted and oppressed;

they give themselves ten times more airs and graces than their employers; and, in the midst of it all, they are as obsequious as they are vain and insincere.

In these relations a good master is a superior who is not too easily found, and should not be too lightly provoked; and a good servant is an invaluable treasure, which should be preserved and adapted with all reasonable precaution, and with some exercise of self-possession. How important, is it not, to both classes that their infancy should be trained according to their respective capacities? *Teach the child who appears born to command how to forbear, and to obey, if need be; and teach him who seems less fortunate in his fortuitous position, to obey and endure, that he may be capable of commanding if he be called to do so.*

The Duties of Wealth towards Poverty, &c. &c.

The laws of this country show indeed that the duties of wealth towards poverty are *partially* appreciated and understood, but no more. Indigence is entitled to a far more valuable free gift than just necessary sustenance at the hands of Property,—it is entitled to CONSIDERATION. Labour makes property, and without it property is nothing.

It is not my intention to diverge into the

economy and relative rights and privileges of property and labour, but merely to hint at the propriety of an early inculcation of the duty which the former owes to the latter.

The obligation, on the other hand, of indigence is to guard, protect, and assist in guarding and protecting, the property from which it derives subsistence. These mutual obligations, be it observed, are essentially obligations of interest, involving the well-being of each and of both, as well as of duty; and therefore each class should be early trained to afford them the consideration which they deserve.

The Duties to One's Country.

Every citizen owes certain duties to the country, of whose polity he is a subject. He owes it his energies, his influence, his power, and so forth, to defend the rights, privileges, and immunities which it confers upon him and upon his fellow-citizens.

In speaking upon proper submission to parents, it has before been stated that *passive obedience and abject submission* are, *under special circumstances*, vices, and not virtues. It is the same in political as in social and domestic life. But it is due to the country in which any man is a member of the community, either to subscribe to the will and inclination of the majority of the people; or, in renouncing allegiance to that order of things, to withdraw from it rather than to disturb it.

It is due to one's country to use one's talents to the best advantage in endeavouring to ameliorate what is wrong or to preserve what is good:—to defend it alike against internal and external violence and oppression, and to treat the community as one vast family, of which one may be a member.

Under well-constituted governments the people (majority) have the power of announcing their convictions, and, those once announced, it is the duty of the minority, to assent to the declaration; otherwise society would ever be in turmoil.

Where there exists a palpable wrong, it is the duty of the citizen to discover its origin, and, upon conviction, to strive for the conviction of others by all fair and just means. But he is by no means inconsiderately to *suppose* his own persuasions to be those of the majority, or his proposed remedial measures to be infallible, and to act upon them as such.

In inculcating what may be termed political morality (although it is quite as much social) in children, the habit of assuming some hero too near one's own time as a model, is very apt to engender partisanship and other mischievous inclinations; it were therefore as well if the examples and illustrations were sought for in antiquity, or in some personage of recognised and universally respected memory.

Moreover, some care is necessary in separating what is crime from what bears the glow of virtue, for barbarism was far too much addicted to making crime accessory to the great deeds of heroic and patriotic prowess.

Be it further remarked, with reference to abject submission to any established power, whether good or bad, that it may be the very reverse of the obligation due to one's country, inasmuch as the duty is one which is owed to mankind, to our fellow-creatures in general, and to their welfare—and the will of the potentate is very frequently that of mere individual gratification and selfish desire. On the other hand, as already intimated, we must not allow ourselves to be beguiled by the glowing term of patriot, into mistaking an atrocity for a good action. Cold-blooded guilt remains guilt, by whatever charming appellation it may be designated.

According to my own ideas, and with due submission to the opinions, the prejudices, or the convictions of others, it is upon some such principle as this, that children should be taught to observe the obligations which they owe to the country of their parentage and their home.

PART III.

CHAPTER I.

OF MENTAL AND MORAL EDUCATION.

It were useless as it were superfluous to enter into the vast and intricate details of the vices and the virtues of humanity; and, for the purposes of this work, it will be sufficient to indicate generally under this head, that VIRTUE is the observance of the MORAL DUTIES (as herein before detailed), and that VICE is the omission of them, or the adoption of a reverse course of conduct.

We come now to the period when education may first become physical, and secondly, mental as well as moral. These I will take leave to term the *tutelage of occupation*, in opposition to the former education of *precept and example.*

Tutelage of Occupation.

By way of preamble, it may be remarked, that the two branches of education, comprised under this term, tend as greatly to a perfect moral development as the others, if, at their own stage, and in the proper periods of life, they be not, indeed, far more powerful agents.

Whether the occupation be purely mental or purely physical, it will, to a certain extent, engross the mind; and, for the efficacy of a moral education, it is above all things necessary, that the attention of the faculties in activity, whether *perceptive* or reflective, should be engrossed by something.

In IDLENESS may be detected the root of many of the most fatal vices and weaknesses. The mind, running to seed in its own way, without previously perfecting its germination, expansion, and bloom, produces but an imperfect, if not unnatural and cankered fruit. Better far be occupied with innocent (or, more properly, *innocuous*) pleasures and amusements, than not be occupied at all. The lozel, of whatever denomination, is invariably a vicious and bad man. Whilst he gradually grows into the habit of clothing employment in repulsive vestures, he accustoms himself not only to heap vituperation or ridicule, or both, upon industry itself, but what is worse still, upon the virtues which spring from it. He taunts industry with the term of slave, whilst he himself is the abject slave of his own folly: he jeers at sobriety as churlish abstinence; in fact, he occupies his listless idleness in finding terms of reproach, scorn, and ridicule, to cast upon everything which contributes to the goodness and happiness of mankind. Far from being happy himself, with fiendish malignity he endeavours to allure others into his own weary existence, by glozing it over with the apparent charms which it possesses; and, in constant *ennui*, he struggles with his time, as if to choke it, and lives and dies in this weary contest with what he finds, at last, should have been the dearest and most valuable companion to him.

Assuming it to be established, that some occupation is necessary, as the medium of mental and moral education, it becomes a question as to what that occupation should be. And, for the determination of this question, it might be more explicit to establish a kind of general scale of ages, taking the average of temperaments as a standard (and peculiar constitutions and organizations of course excepted), and to assign to each stage a relative proportion of physical and mental occupation.

Stages of Youth.

The first period, then, may extend from three to six years old;—the second, from six to ten years;—the third, from ten to twelve;—the fourth, from twelve to fifteen;—and the fifth and last, from fifteen to the termination of the educational courses.

During the first stage there is but very little development, physical or mental; during the second, the physical advancement is rapid, but the mental little more than perceptible; during the third, the mental faculties begin to ripen, and to gain upon the ascendancy of the physical powers; during the fourth, they are even capable of taking the lead; and, during the fifth, they become matured, and may be made highly predominant.

In conformity with these gradations of advancement, therefore, and in strict unison with the organic developments, the method of training should be, from first to last, conducted. Besides this, there is much reason to suggest that some consideration should be had of the probable sphere of life in which the pupil is likely to move, as to what are to become his probable occupations, and as to the likelihood of a preponderance of mental or physical exercise.

It will occur in the course of my remarks upon this subject that there will be occasion for animadversion on the system of Public Education, as that is perhaps of the most importance to society at large. It is a sad fact that the tutelage of the lower orders in public and charitable establishments, now that they are at last somewhat better endowed, should, in the particulars to which I have just referred, be, in my humble opinion, conducted upon so erroneous and mischievous a principle as it is. Far from instructing the people in useful arts, and in trades or occupations, which are likely to lead to a comfortable subsistence, all the time is usually lost in drumming vain sectarian dogmas, which, at best, are scarcely understood by the teacher (if by any one else), into the heads of so many ploughboys or reaping girls. Empty collections of words and sentences are attempted to be driven into the memory of a hundred parish children, who attach little or no sense to them. except the idea of punishment, if they are not perfect in their parrot performance.

It is, unfortunately, the same with all the places of instruction, whether of one persuasion or another.

It is not to be understood that because a ploughboy is a ploughboy, he must always be a ploughboy. There is no intention of closing higher attainments against him, and compelling his mind, of whatever capacity, to remain in perpetual and boorish serfdom. But there are ages, in the first place, in which, as has already been intimated, the occupations should, in all children of whatever grade, be wholly physical; others again, in which the physical employments should certainly predominate; and in no instance does it appear established by experience that book-work should be adopted at an earlier period than the sixth or seventh year. Secondly, without debarring the peasant from higher learning, or the artisan from historical, literary, or other attainments, it appears, nevertheless, that the first instruction offered to him should be consistent with his own sphere, and that the direction of the teacher (if he had any) should guide him in selecting those amongst his pupils who were capable of greater things.

For this purpose it is also necessary that the teachers should be well selected and carefully tested as to competency; but the so-called model seminaries of this country are not the real sources wherein to search for the requisite capacities and the more important qualities. The system now adopted of training teachers to instruct upon one cramped, narrowed, bigoted, system, and often upon that alone, is more likely to incapacitate the teacher, and to deprive him of the free exercise of his judgment than otherwise.

To continue, however, with the education of children: during the first and second periods, in which their stages of advancement have been divided, they should be accustomed to manual exercises, the use of implements adapted to the trade with which they are most associated, the best methods of husbandry, and the like. Whilst in the higher orders of society, there would be no harm in allowing every child to make a selection of some particular occupation, whether carpentering, gardening, or what not; and confining him during these two stages to such physical occupations, and to athletic and gymnastic exercises. All those who are likely to become proprietors or holders of land, might be most consistently instructed in agriculture, horticulture, and the like; those who are, or may be, designed for a maritime career might, without detriment, turn their hands to ship construction in miniature; those who are likely to be connected with town and house property would not lose by a little practical knowledge of architecture in its various departments.

And whilst this course is pursued, the first desideratum should never be lost sight of—that of rendering the selected occupation at once agreeable, and, in so far as is possible, useful.

It is a very great encouragement to a child to see that his work is not wasted, that it turns to something; in fact, to believe that he has accomplished something which may obtain consideration. And, moreover, the surest way to discover any latent ingenuity, tact, or capability in children, is to offer them the means of developing them, and to gratify them by adopting their work, however trivial. They grow disheartened, and disgusted, if what they do, and what seems perfect to their young eyes, either escapes notice altogether, or is cast aside, repudiated, or sneered at as *imperfect and useless.* A sensitive child feels the sting at the heart, and turns sick and dejected, and nurses the chagrin till it worms into the character and sours the temper; and, worse than all, in its future moral consequences, till he dreads to undertake any thing, lest a gibe, a sneer, or heartless ridicule assail him in his conscious achievements. Fan the little glow of self-complacency with which a child surveys his earliest work. It is an innocent vanity which will perish in his next performance, and so on to infinity, and one, too, which will prompt him to attempt, and urge him on to accomplish.

It may be said that there never, yet, was the first sample of mechanism, art, or other undertaking, which, whilst it incipiently flushed the tyro with aspiring triumph, did not disgust him after future attempts, and urge him to accomplish more perfect productions. Thus, vanity, to a certain extent, and well controlled, may not only be harmless and *suicidal* (as it ever is), but will even be a powerful motive to improvement.

The truth of this theory was eminently exemplified in that most masterly of educational establishments, HOFWYL,* so justly celebrated throughout Europe. The true philosophy of learning to teach and teaching, and the sure method of effecting high moral, physical, and mental developments, has been practically established by the successful experiment there so long continued; and the principle deduced from this experience, and upon which the essay was chiefly founded, is embodied in the regulations which have been offered in the course of these chapters.

In brief, it is this:—*Allow the merits, weaknesses, inclinations, faculties, and so forth, of all children every opportunity of betraying and manifesting themselves, and then conduct the education accordingly.*

On the contrary, the method in common practice is briefly this:—*To establish a certain routine of tuition, which, like the code of two ancient nations, is immutable; and then to attempt to fashion all the varieties of capacity, temperaments, and character upon this one infallible, unswerving, and unalterable rule.*

Can any thing be more vain, more erroneous, or more absurd? and can any thing be more unjust and cruel?

And yet the very men who sagely propound such a magnificent system, would be the first to

* Near Berne, in Switzerland.

ridicule the idea of forming a menagerie containing every animal on the discovered surface of the globe, and adapting them to one uniform system of treatment. NOAH'S ARK is the only instance *on record* of an approximate success; whilst the HAPPY FAMILY is certainly a case of circumscribed attempt.

It is observed also, that there is an analogy in the cases, insomuch as there is an endless variety in the organism of the human race, far exceeding that of any other species, and resembling rather the concentration of a variety of creatures. There is but one step from genius to idiotcy. The same parents, even, may engender children of the most contrasted mental, physical, and moral construction.

Herein it is that the founders of systems, particularly of education, err:—they form a *beau ideal* of their own, founded rather upon themselves than their neighbours, and adapted, no doubt, to all who are precisely of the same temperament, but to no one else. The truth is, that every system upon which education is to be unswervingly conducted is false; that Nature must, in each instance, indicate her own system; and that the soundest of all systems is, therefore, a *methodical absence of systematic rule*, except in those matters in which all are alike, or nearly so, as, for instance, in the progress of developments before mentioned. Even here there are many exceptions; and, therefore, it must be carefully taken into consideration that circumstances should modify generalities. There is one particular in which, nevertheless, explicitness is not inconsistent with the position now asserted, to wit, with respect to the *several stages of advancement.* The only essential in which they differ is in the periods, and of these the parent or teacher will have abundant opportunities of judging.

Having attained the *third stage* of progress, a child may be submitted to mental exercises, beginning, doubtless, by means of the first implements, the ALPHABET and the PEN. The course of study may, for the first year or two, be advantageously confined to the simplest material, and to a very short period in each day, beginning with half an hour, and not exceeding two hours within that term.

Arithmetic, History, and Natural History should perhaps be the first studies entered into,—avoiding everything which savours of abstruseness or perplexity, and shunning dogmatic teaching. Amongst other things very commonly adopted as the medium of instruction, and very popular with masters, there is one which is anything but commendable or useful, that is, the habit of making children learn by heart. It answers no commendable purpose, and abstracts the mind too much from the matter to vest all the attention in the sounds, rhythms, and words.

Grammar also, as it is usually taught, comes under the same category. Grammar is a science which can only be well learnt and understood by habit and by reading, and which is never perfected by dinning a certain set of rules into the ears of very young children. They learn, to be sure, that there are such rules, and that, according to those rules, such and such a construction is right, and such another is wrong, but they very rarely acquire by this means the method of applying the rules correctly, or of turning them to any account. The use of grammatical knowledge is, after all, only to induce a correct, ready, and precise method of writing or speaking, and these are so necessarily induced by habit, and not by grammatical rules, that the grammar rule ought only to be learnt after its practical application is acquired and understood. In fact, it is reading and writing which more properly teach good grammar, and not good grammar which teaches the art of reading and writing correctly.

In the study of history it is very requisite to avoid confusing the young pupil with a multitude of punctilious dates. Chronology is very important as an accessory to history, but does not the least affect its bearing in moral tuition; and as the earlier periods of general history, in the popular method of teaching it, ramble over a vast portion of the globe, and, from lack of particulars, crowd a great number of events, each of which identifies an epoch, into a very narrow space, it is of cogent importance that the first studies of general history should only be cursory.

Abridgements of historical works are only of real service to one who is more advanced, and is familiar with the particular national details, for the purpose of collating and condensing his reading. It is then, also, that chronological accuracy begins to tell to advantage; before, it only serves to muddle the pupil.

Having acquired one summary view of universal history, the pupil might commence reading the particular histories of every nation which has figured in the progress of civilization, and which has exercised an important control over the condition of mankind. Still the doses of study should be few and far between, and, moreover, never of long duration, or ever suffered to weary the pupil. For the great end of all reading is, that it shall be digested: in other words, that the mind, by not being damped in its energies, shall ponder upon the matter which it has gathered, and cast it somewhat into shape. It is very common to place such books as *Keightley's Outlines of General History* into the hands of beginners, with the false idea that, without much labour, they can thus become pretty well acquainted with the general course of events. But, in the first place, as has been urged, the events are necessarily so huddled together, and placed so little in juxtaposition, that it becomes a labour even to a tolerable historian, much more to a child, who knows nothing whatever of his subject, to understand them; and, in the second place, these kind of historical works are totally destitute of anything like moral instruction—they are nothing more than chronological tables.

Another thing it were as well to submit to the careful attention of the reader respecting the earlier departments of education, which is the impropriety of the still very general custom of devoting years to the almost exclusive and imperfect teaching of the dead languages. And, independently of the objurgations just offered to this all engrossing study of the Greek and Roman writings, another, and still more palpable, objection is to be found in the circumstance that many of these works (those of Ovid, for instance) are wholly perversive of delicacy of sentiment, and highly obnoxious to pure morality. Much mischief is thus liable to accrue to the pupil with some taste for classic acquirement, by having his propensities flushed and excited by the laxity of ideas which he gathers therein.

Besides the mischiefs, then, which thus accrue from early classical study, as it is called, such a course of reading but too generally leads to nothing. We live in an utilitarian age, and education should be consistent with the spirit of the time. The cultivation of the taste and the elegancies of mental acquirements are the polish which may be sought and acquired, when more essential information has been attained.

Moreover, such attainments are only calculated for a very limited proportion of society. The laborious or industrious classes must handle the spade, guide the plough, toil at the loom, serve the counter, labour at the desk, or pursue a hundred other productive avocations; and the dicta of Cicero or the subtle rules of Aristotle will boot them but little at their work.

Children should, before all things, be tutored in the rudiments of the arts and sciences of civilization, and of every-day application; and it is still so far inconsistent with this system to pursue the present method of education, that, even in what are called the liberal professions, for the attainment of which classical knowledge is made the scale of ascent, that kind of knowledge has comparatively become quite obsolete, and there remains but little vestige of its use in practice. Be it understood that it is not here intended to contemn learning: learning is doubtless a most noble qualification, but it is not of popular application; and, noble as it is, if erroneously instilled, it too often warps the understanding. After the utilitarian education is completed, if the pupil has a bent that way, and time, leisure, and opportunity to indulge the inclination, it becomes a worthy and beneficial pursuit; but otherwise, worthy as it may be, it is anything but beneficial.

Before instruction in the dead languages, therefore, if elegant acquirements be the object, the course of reading might more profitably be sought amongst the many eminent writers of our own country, or of modern and living tongues. There is a vast fund of pure morality to be gathered from this latter class of English writers, and the taste might well be formed upon worse models.

Languages.

With respect to other European languages, we have made some progress of late years, owing to the rapidity and frequency of international communication; and there can be no doubt but that the study of contemporary languages is extremely useful, if not almost necessary, in our time. It might not, therefore, be unprofitable to place this course of study next in importance to those before recommended. The knowledge of French, German, Italian, and Spanish in particular, and especially the first two, will be turned to account in every situation of life, in every art or handicraft, and in every science. It is a piece of stupid dogmatism, and not a worthy national pride, to despise that which owes its discovery to a foreigner, and a dogmatism which is fortunately growing into severe contempt.

One nation is, *primâ facie*, as likely to produce an eminently useful discovery as another, and it is nothing less than stupid folly to avoid or despise anything which may be turned to account because it is imported, and not indigenous. It is frequently by comparing the productions of one nation with those of another that perfection is attained. It is by combining the efforts of genius that art and science are consummated.

If less time were devoted in childhood to the study of what is totally obsolete, and can become of no social service, there would be more left to apply to studies such as those from which great social advantages may be gained.

Whether the study of contemporary languages be confined to the materials of useful art or science or not, it will inevitably become serviceable, nor do I conceive, if the pupil has an inclination to study Schiller, or Corneille, or Tasso or Cervantes, that he should be debarred from access to them; but still I would not have him crammed against his inclination with the productions of the higher, or imaginative, order of literature. The knowledge of other languages will afford him facilities for the mastery of all the other studies. The study of history, before recommanded as so highly essential, will owe more than is readily imagined to the familiar acquaintance with two or three, or more European languages.

With respect to the manner of teaching them, it should be borne in mind that, in early years, children have a peculiar aptitude for the acceptation of sounds, and that they possess, for that reason amongst others, a ready and intuitive power of learning dialects; and, in the second place, it may be remarked generally, that far too great stress is laid on grammatical rules, which, for reasons before recited, are oftentimes quite unavailing to the student. Young children must necessarily trust more to the senses and the perceptive organs than to those of reflection, and whilst they cannot sufficiently abstract the intellect to dive into the reasons of things, they very readily catch them, such as they are.

It is not to say that we need launch into the extremes of a phonetic system, because it seems obvious enough that that rather puzzles than assists, but merely allow the pupil to be rather subject to phonetic than to didactic influence.

Mathematics.

Having passed from HISTORY to LANGUAGES, we will now turn our attention to another most essential branch of science.

Let us consider the study of Mathematics as amongst the useful departments of learning. They may be simple or abstruse—they may be complicated or wrought in single integrity—and may, in a measure, be as usefully adapted to the meanest and most narrow understanding, as to the most commanding and comprehensive intellect. MATHEMATICS are, therefore, the science of all men: the commodity which can come ill to none, and to none prove unserviceable; of every-day use and application in the world, down to the most trifling handicraft, they may, at the same time, be the constant toil, or recreation of the sage in his closet. A Columbus or a carpenter are equally subject to the laws which they inculcate, and derive their knowledge from them as a common source. The builder who indulges what he calls his taste upon a suburban villa, would be as much puzzled without their aid as Sir Isaac Newton might possibly have found himself in solving the binomial theorem.

The study of mathematics, however, should not be too early adopted, inasmuch as it necessarily depends upon a powerful exercise of the reflective faculties. It were as well, in the generality of cases, even, if the rudiments of this science were not taught before the age of from twelve to fourteen years.

Mathematics are not, like languages, a study of the senses; and whereas the latter may be commenced with the first articulation, the former must be slowly adopted, after the superior mental powers become somewhat developed, and manifest some signs of activity. When, however, this study has been judiciously commenced, it may, and will, if the capacity exists, be rapidly pursued. The study of mathematics has, of late years, been most abundantly engrossed for engineering purposes. It may be adapted to facilitate any trade or handicraft, as the accessory to architecture, dynamics, chemistry, and, in fact, all the useful arts; and when in course of study, this science possesses the peculiar recommendation of adapting the mind for the reception of others, whilst, at the same time, it forms a portion of every one of them.

Geography.

Next in rank to mathematics, we might be allowed to suggest Geography. It is never useless to know something of the relative positions of places and countries, nor is it superfluous to possess some knowledge of climate, productions, people, manners, and so forth. Even setting aside all other advantages derivable from this kind of information, he were a bigot, indeed, and an ignorant one, too, who would aver, in the pride of his semi-ideal civilization, that he could gather nothing worth knowing or having, even from the savage. Apart from such considerations, a knowledge of geography may become highly useful to any individual at any time. It is an information of every-day requirement; and yet how few there are who know any thing of their own country, much less of others. It is true that a new social condition, arising out of the mastership of mechanical art, has certainly forced this knowledge even upon the most ignorant, by experience, as it were: but this very fact renders the early acquirement of it the more essential to every man. It should moreover, be observed, as of LANGUAGES, that it is more the acquisition of the perceptive than of the reflective mental power, and is therefore capable of far earlier inculcation than the former science of mathematics.

Geography can best be taught to a child by means of his eyes: a map placed before him shows him at once the relative disposition of lands and zones. But in the teaching of this science, as well as of others, there appears to be a very prevalent and serious error; it is that of making children learn chapters of a geographical compendium by heart. Humbly conceiving this practice to be prejudicial in all cases and for all purposes, I venture to suggest the propriety of its discontinuance.

If the child be left to learn by means of his senses, and not of artificial cramming, he will form a just and accurate idea of his subject, and it will remain in his mind; if, on the other hand, it be forced into him by sheer repetition, he will remember nothing but the words, and those only for a short time.

CHAPTER II.

OF THE DISTRIBUTION OF EMPLOYMENT DURING THE COURSE OF EDUCATION, AND ADMONITORY REGIMEN.

It has already been mentioned that a great deal depends upon the proper distribution of occupations; and, for the purpose of drawing a more distinct line between the gradations of advancement and capability, a kind of scale of ages had been constructed.

A very general and popular method of teaching is to submit children, of three years old, at once to a course of mental tuition. They are taught to read and write, and are crammed with the rudiments of every thing, before they are capable of understanding the application of any of them; besides which, no distinction, as to the length of time which is to be devoted to this species of study, is made between the child of three years old and one of twelve. It is too often just as common to confine a mere infant all day over its parrot learning, as it is to require the same application of a child of far more advanced development; and it is vainly imagined that such confinement and such early application are alone capable of producing the finished scholar, and to produce such a prodigy.

It could be clearly shown, by example, that far from having gained any thing by this system, not only is all that has been superficially and artificially attained lost, but, moreover, it carries with it a great deal of the pristine vigour and energy which the natural intelligence originally possessed. The mind becomes, so to speak, sodden before it is matured, and, instead of being rendered capable of any thing, is deprived of all capability.

This error, which is one of mistaken zeal, has, however, so thorough a conventional footing in the majority of modern nurseries and schoolrooms, that it is very difficult to persuade parents that it is an error.

Most people, now as of old, had rather be "*wrong with the world than right with philosophy*," even if they go so far as to admit that they are wrong at all. But it is an error which will sooner or later work serious evil in the degeneracy of nations, unless it be counteracted, and which may, perhaps, have to work its own cure in a somewhat inconvenient manner.

In the first epoch of mental education, which need not commence before the fifth or sixth year, an hour or two a day is ample time to devote to occupations of that kind, and this course may be most advantageously pursued for two years.

If the child be placed in such circumstances as to preclude the necessity of manual labour, the rest of its time should be occupied in athletic and gymnastic exercise, and in open-air occupations—such as running, leaping, and the like; but in all circumstances it were as well if the attention were directed to some useful manual occupation, such as gardening or agriculture. Employments of this kind are exceedingly healthy, and tend greatly to invigorate the frame and the mind together, and to render the pupil robust and vigorous; whilst, at the same time, they heighten the moral aspirations, and elevate the understanding.* When the muscular powers have attained sufficient development, the use of implements of husbandry or of mechanical trades, may conveniently be taught. The Germans have a peculiar fashion of apprenticing all their children to some trade, with the object of enabling them to produce the little presents which celebrate the advent of a new year from their own handiwork; and it is not without example that more than one aristocratic student of Heidelberg has before now found the means of subsistence in the trade which he thus learnt as a plaything. This is no mean lesson to the Englishman, who piques himself upon his utilitarian system of education. The plan might be adopted without derogation to the solemn aspect of learning, and, certainly, without tarnishing the frivolous pursuits of vice, at our own Universities.

Apart from the usefulness of such attainments, in cases of need, there is the everlasting moral of "*Belisarius begging*," which inculcates itself with the acquirements ; a moral which all should learn betimes, that they be not too rudely taught it

* This is the method adopted at the celebrated college of Hofwyl, near Berne, in Switzerland, and which has proved so successful in its issue.

perforce; a moral, too, which may serve to subdue the arrogance of pomp and circumstance, and bestow upon our gifted nation one thing, which it sadly wants, a fellow-feeling for misery. The sympathies may be awakened by the simplest incidents and the most trivial occupations, and, as there is no people where egotism and deep selfishness are carried to such excess amongst individuals as in England, it is no work of supererogation to suggest some means of arousing them.

It should not escape notice that in England alone, for I believe this could not occur elsewhere in Europe, the sublimest genius might perish in the streets, unfed, unclothed, and unhoused, for lack of the means and the opportunity of making itself known and recognized; and this may, in a great measure, be attributed to the faulty system of education, whereby the instruction in useful occupations is wholly overlooked. Thus, so many are left with vast capacity, pre-eminent talent, but without a field for their exercise. We might well forgive ourselves, if we could show that from all this system of book-learning a high order of taste was cultivated, and an elevated cast of intelligence dispersed amongst the population; if we could so much as aver that we had a pure and noble contemporary literature, or that, if there were such, we should number any readers; but as we cannot do or show either of these things, we are unpardonable.

Having, therefore, pursued the course above recommended for two years with the pupil in his first stage of education, the time devoted to sedentary occupations might safely be doubled, the remainder of the day still being employed in invigorating exercises or employment.

Whilst the proportion of mental occupation is increased, the material may gradually be rendered more scientific, and thus the reflective faculties called into play as they ripen and develope themselves, without being forced into premature activity. For instance, the geographical study, which commenced with the atlas, may, by degrees, be carried to higher philosophical and literary inquiry, whilst the geometrical problem, at first confined to actual representative figures, may become a matter of numerical calculation.

In this stage, however, it would still be preferable to confine the occupations to useful attainments, excluding the dead languages, or classical acquirements, from the pale of early education; for it may be averred that it is not until the combination of perceptive and reflective faculties is sufficiently matured to form a fixed and defined taste, that letters, as letters only, can advantageously be admitted as a portion of every-day study.

A thousand circumstances may transpire, even in the early stages of life, to render such acquirements useless to the pupil; whilst the time which has been vainly exhausted in their superficial and repulsive attainment, might have been beneficially devoted to the useful arts or sciences.

Emerging from this stage of educational course, the pupil may be submitted to redoubled mental labour, and consequent decrease of physical occupation; that is, where no circumstances transpire to render the completion of a good, elegant education abortive, or to divert the tutelage into more productive channels at once.

Even at this period, however, it is my humble but firm conviction, that the dead languages are not only a superfluous and useless, but also an injurious study. The course of reading may, nevertheless, become more and more abstruse and scientific as the reflective organs ripen and gain the ascendency.

We have now ventured to provide for mental exercise in the proportion of one third of the whole day, or rather, twenty-four hours, beginning with two hours at the utmost, and doubling that at the second and again at the third stages, thus obtaining a maximum of eight hours a day; and supposing that eight hours more be allowed for rest, which is a very fair proportion, we have eight left, or another third for refreshment and active recreation. The rule is of course made for robust and healthy children, because sickness is subject to no rules of the kind, and the state of health must indicate the capability for mental or bodily exertions in such cases. But, admitting that the pupil is robust, healthy, and capable of such regimen, the third of the twenty-four hours thus apportioned for study should be the maximum set apart for such purposes during the whole course of education.

It is quite enough for young people, with the best capabilities and the most buoyant energies, to be confined to close mental occupation for one third of their time; and everything beyond that, if it does no harm, does no good. The only gradations after that consist in the intensity of the application, or, in other words, in the abstruseness of the reading.

Natural and experimental philosophy, the higher branches of mechanics and dynamics, the grateful and interesting study of analytical and experimental chemistry, astronomy, in so far as it is explanatory of natural phenomena, now come within the sphere of the pupil. The philosophical and jurisprudential readings of history and the particular code which regulates the community of which he is a member, with its origin and pro gress, should also become subjects of serious consideration; although, during this stage, these sciences should still be confined to their simplest and incipient guise. The historical reading, in particular, should be dilated and particularised, whilst, at the same time, it was being collated and condensed by the resource before suggested. The mathematical studies may range a little higher, according to the capability and progress of the pupil, and the study of languages become more scientific and grammatical.

At this stage, also, the inculcation of grammatical rules, to which, at a former period, an objec-jection had been raised, may be commenced, as it will materially assist the pupil thus far advanced.

At the next stage of advancement, whilst the study of the natural and useful sciences is being actively pursued, the dead languages may become a subordinate portion of the material for completing a polished education. But even now they should only be adopted with a very careful selection of works; and with this reservation, that they be mere accessories to the supererogatory portion of tuition, rather than be made an essential part of education.

Here, again, may the principal burthen of occupation be centered in the higher order of the natural sciences, in which the pupil should by this time have attained some proficiency. A deeper and yet more abstruse study of history and jurisprudence, and the first class of mathematical calculations, may also come within his reach.

If, indeed, metaphysical study should at any time be admitted within the pale of the educational courses, it might be suffered to commence at this fourth stage; but my impression is, that metaphysical lore is rather an exercise of the imagination, than properly within the region of necessary learning.

Sound metaphysical principles certainly exercise a most powerful control over the grosser passions of humanity, and tend greatly to enlarge the understanding and expand the mind.

Nevertheless, I am inclined to think, that the less this species of learning is encouraged the better, until, at least, the education has, for some time, been devoted to the physical sciences and their glaring experimental evidences and truths; since, after such training, the pupil might gather confidence enough to think for himself on metaphysics, and not place a blind reliance on the dogmatic teaching of others.

It hardly needs recapitulation, that the hours of confinement to book study should by no means be forcibly increased, even with those of the most elastic minds, beyond the prescribed limit of eight hours a day; because, amongst other reasons, the mental and moral faculties are so dependent upon the physical functions of the frame, that, if the latter are disorganized or debilitated by too sedentary a course of life, or by too close an application, the former will inevitably suffer. The physical energies should in all cases be carefully sustained by the occupations and exercises heretofore indicated.

Having thus attained the fifth stage of education, this period may, with an advanced and well-regulated pupil, become one almost of self-teaching; and the higher orders of refined literature may freely be admitted within the pale of materials, whether in the living or dead languages. There are, unfortunately, but comparatively few conditions and circumstances in life, in which this stage is not entirely foregone for more productive industrial occupations; and, consequently, there are but few who are ever able to attain the sphere of elegant and finished scholars. But, as these are, after all, but the gilded ornaments which heighten the splendour of society, we may console ourselves with the reflection, that, as society is constituted, we can do without a majority of them.

Admonitory Regimen.

We now approach another of the essential branches of education, which forms a distinct and important department. I refer to what has been denominated as the ADMONITORY REGIMEN, or, in other words, the regulation of rewards and punishments. The natural frailty of humanity, and the necessity also of working upon and adapting the passions to good purposes, render this a very paramount question. The best of children will sometimes incur punishment, and should suffer it; and the worst will occasionally earn reward, and should obtain it accordingly.

I have already alluded to two very mischievous errors in this branch of treatment—over-indulgence and over-severity—and have taken it upon me to enunciate as a rule in punishment, that it should consist rather in the privation of enjoyment, than in the infliction of pain.

It need only, therefore, be repeated, that, with the youngest as with the eldest of pupils, the incentives to industry and good actions should never be withheld, nor those merits allowed to perish for want of notice; and that, in punishing generally, we should be most careful to induce no worse failing by the method of dealing with that which incurs present punishment, and also to avoid any physical injury, however momentary. Both errors may have lasting and pernicious consequences.

Corporal Punishment.

Corporal punishment, I therefore conceive to be clearly an error, if it be no worse. Of late years, the application of this resource has, with very good reason, fallen into general disuse; although it is still resorted to by some.

The ROD or CAT can never, I opine, produce more perfect scholars or more obedient and exemplary pupils; and it certainly has the effect of counteracting to a great degree the refinement, delicacy, and polish which should and do spring from good education. It is a remnant of barbarism, and ought to be utterly excluded from every sphere of civilized society.

Besides this very great moral objection to the system, we have also another: that, in many cases, corporal punishment has been applied where the pupil was already labouring under a mental or physical incapacity, or both, and thus became a double victim. In such a case, the incapacity, of whatever kind, is only heightened by the remedy.

Close Confinement.

Close confinement, thought not open to the objection of suscitating the natural harshness and coarseness of the grosser portion of the human character, is none the less subject to the same strictures on other grounds.

You may set a robust youth to dig, by way of punishment, if you please, consistently with the power and endurance of his frame, because thereby you are affording him a healthy and useful occupation; but if you condemn him to be closely confined for any length of time, depriving him of the air and exercise which are essential to his physical constitution, you run great risk of inducing some serious malady.

Another evil, as in the case of the ROD, may arise from close confinement, which is, that, supposing the pupil to be of a highly susceptible and nervous temperament, it would inevitably work upon the mind, so as to render that also incapable of regular exertion and application.

The same may in general be said of the system of enforcing IMPOSITIONS and the like, by way of punishment, for if these be really complied with and completed, they may be guilty of the same mischief; and if they are evaded, they are only the agents of a lax morality.

Thus in all cases, it may be held far more safe and preferable to inflict the punishment (which it is not the less expedient should attend every misdeed, in proportion to its magnitude and importance), either by subjecting the pupil to a wholesome and useful physical occupation, adapted to his constitution and strength, or to subject him merely to appropriate expostulation and to the process of foregoing all his enjoyments, recreations and relaxations for a given time.

It were, moreover, advisable that a strong distinction were drawn between the mental and physical and the moral wrongs of omission or commission. The latter are ever the most to be dreaded, and should ever be painted in the darker hue, and subjected to the severer regimen. And lastly, the term of punishment should extend only to reasonable limits, in order that the resolutions be not damped, quelled, or made callous; that the sense of shame be not (as it too often is) converted to one of mere sullen acrimony; and that its compunctions may have occasion to enjoin reformation, and not its sting, to goad to repetition and inveteracy.

Rewards.

The method adopted at the College of Hofwyl, to which allusion has heretofore been made, consisted in holding forth rewards for every thing that was recommended to the pupil. Learning had its prizes; art had its prizes; agriculture and handicrafts had their prizes; horticulture had its prizes;

and the gymnastic and athletic exercises, such as running, leaping, archery, skating, swimming, and military discipline, were encouraged in the same way. Without dwelling very long upon this article, I would humbly suggest some such system for every place of education. It is, perhaps, not too well to *over-excite* emulation amongst mankind; yet it is necessary to call it *judiciously* into play, for the purpose of improvement, which will and can make no progress without it.

Finally, in the sense that it has been contended, no wrong should be allowed to escape some punishment or counteracting power, no meritorious trait or act should be suffered to pass unnoticed or unrewarded.

PART IV.

OF TEMPERAMENTS—THE MOST COMMON COMPLAINTS OF CHILDREN, AND THEIR TREATMENT IN ORDINARY CASES.

Characteristics of Constitutional Tendency and Temperament.

In treating the indispositions, maladies, and weaknesses of children, as of adults, it is very essential to ascertain distinctly and to be guided by the peculiar caste of constitution and temperament of each particular patient, and the degree of virus, or taint, inherent in such temperament; and not only so, from the various general degrees of susceptibility which accompany these differences and modifications of constitution, but because, amongst the ingredients of our Pharmacopœia,* we have frequently many, of which the operation would effect the same end, but which are each adapted to some particular phase of temperament,

* A book with rules for the composition of medicines.

preferably to any other, or perhaps to one only. Thus, then, in giving general directions for the exhibition of medicine, we sometimes appear to confuse the reader with the multiplicity of our prescriptions for the same complaint, unless he happen to be aware of the peculiar applicability of each medicament to some distinct tenor of temperament, or unless he happen to cast his eye upon the list of medicines most recommended for each shade of complexion.

It is my object in this section to give a general outline of the various phases of constitution, and to attach to the description of each such a list of medicines, in order that the reader may be able to refer back from my subsequent prescriptions (amongst which there will necessarily be many remedies for the same malady) to the summary catalogue contained under the head of each particular temperament to assist in guiding his selection in the case of any particular patient.

The varieties of temperament may be generally and briefly included under the following heads: the LYMPHATIC, the SANGUINE, the BILIOUS, the MELANCHOLIC, the NERVOUS, the CHOLERIC (which partakes of the characteristics of the bilious, melancholic and sanguine), the PHLEGMATIC, (which is the reverse of the former), and the ADYNAMIC, which is akin to the LYMPHATIC.*

The constitution and habit of body peculiar to the *lymphatic* subject may be generally described as lax. The predominant features are languor and indolence, roundness, bulkiness, softness, want of strong expression, a fair, but dead complexion, and inanimate eye. The circulation is slow and dull, the passions are lethargic, and the brain is inactive; and with some subordinate distinctions, the same may be said of the *phlegmatic* and *adynamic*. Those which usually mark the *sanguine* subject are, rapid and strong circulation, fulness, energy and strength. The muscular and cerebral systems are vigorous and active, the skin is soft, the complexion fair and florid, the eyes bright and blue, and the hair of a bright auburn yellow or red.

The *bilious* subject is characterised by a strong and frequent pulsation, a dark or swarthy complexion, with effective and well-marked lineaments

* The above subdivisions of temperaments have been adopted for practical purposes. The following are the four, *primitive* and natural temperaments, commonly recognised by modern physiologists: the *bilious*, the *lymphatic* (or *pituitous*), the *sanguine*, and the *nervous*. These are frequently met with in a mixed form, as, for instance, a combination of the bilious and nervous, the sanguine and lymphatic, and the nervous and lymphatic.

and a countenance expressive of great energy of character; a moderate fulness, but firmness of flesh; violent passions, and the like.

The *melancholic* temperament is distinguishable by a firmness of fibre, accompanied by a dryness and meagerness of frame; scanty secretions; an arid cutaneous system; a brown complexion; gloomy, saturnine, meditative look; obstruction in the digestive operations, of a congestive tendency. It is a modification of the bilious temperament, without its predominant and characteristic energy; the imagination vivid, but all things are seen through a dismal medium; the pulse is hard, slow and contracted; the functions of the nervous system are usually deranged; and the disposition is sombre, suspicious, and meditative.

The peculiar characteristics of the *nervous* subject are, attenuation of the muscular system; fine, thin hair and skin; predominance of the cerebral system, and, in fact, of the whole nervous system; rapidity of movement, intense susceptibility and excitability, want of decision, and the like.

The *choleric* constitution is marked by a swarthy and yellowish complexion, dark hair, and a firm but arid muscular system; great susceptibility of the biliary organs, which renders the patient peculiarly subject to bilious disorders, and to give a tone of bilious affection to every complaint; superabundance of bile; and a tendency to inflammatory complaints. In many essential respects the bilious and choleric temperaments are identical; but the latter, like the melancholic, is a modification of the former, with more similarity in some particulars to the last of the three. It possesses, moreover, great affinity, in some respects, to the sanguine temperament.

The *phlegmatic* subject is to be identified by many of the characteristics of the lymphatic, without necessarily being so destitute of the impulses to action or of perseverance in action. There is, however, a want of tension in the fibres and muscular system, and a tendency to copious lymphatic secretions. The phlegmatic subject is very tardy of excitement.

The *adynamic* constitution, whilst it partakes also of many of the features of the lymphatic, may be characterized by the scantiness of secretions, as well as by their copiousness. It is equally marked by over-elation and over-depression; and, unlike the lymphatic, is not slow to excitement, but quickly susceptible of it, for good or ill. There is, in this species of constitution, a striking want of strength and endurance, and a weak pulsation.

LYMPHATIC TEMPERAMENT. *Remedies for selec-*

*tion from the prescriptions.** *Merc.*, *Sulph.*, *Calc.*, *Puls.*, *China*, *Ars.*, *Bella.*, *Hyos.*, *Phosph.*, *Hell.*, *Dulc.*, *Sep.*, *Ant.*, *Carb. v.*, *Arn.*, *Sil.*, &c. &c.

DIET.† Generous and solid; a predominance of animal food; little or no vegetable; very little fluid or liquid; when artificial drinks are necessary, they should be rather of a generous than stimulating nature.

SANGUINE TEMPERAMENT. *Remedies.* *Acon.*, *Arn.*, *Bella.*, *Calc.*, *Hep.*, *Merc.*, *Cham.*, *Nux v.*, *Bry.*, *Lach.*, *Phos.*, *Ars.*, &c. &c.

DIET. Plain and simple; no made dishes, unless light; equal admixture of animal and vegetable, or even preponderance of the latter; unstimulating liquids; milk diet.

BILIOUS TEMPERAMENT. *Remedies.* *Acon.*, *Bry.*, *Nux v.*, *Cham.*, *Ars.*, *Arn.*, *China*, *Sulph.*, &c. &c.

DIET. Generally low; small proportion of ani-

* As has already been observed, it is to be understood, that the temperament of the patient must only serve as an auxiliary guide in the selection of a remedy. In cases where, from the similarity in the given directions, it is difficult to discriminate between two or more remedies, the temperament will often regulate the choice.

† The short dietetic rules given under the head of each temperament, are subject to modification in many cases, but particularly in morbid states of the system.

mal food; green vegetables only; small proportion of fruit, and none with kernels; abstinence from all stimulating liquors, comfits, made dishes, and spices.

MELANCHOLY TEMPERAMENT. *Remedies. Nux v., Lach., Sulph., Staph., Veratr., China,, Natr., Phosph., Viol. odor., Ars., Bry., Sil., Puls., Sep.*, &c., &c.

DIET. Very similar to that recommended for the bilious temperament; abstinence in general from strong acids and stimulants; and precaution against milk diet may be added to the previous regulations.

NERVOUS TEMPERAMENT. *Remedies. Acon., Coffea, Bry., Cham., Nux v., Sep., Lach., Ac. nitr., Cocc., Ambra, Ars., China, Cup., Ign., Phosph.*, &c., &c.

DIET. Almost wholly animal, very plain, but very generous, without being stimulating; meat eaten rather underdone; very small proportion of liquids, and those unstimulating.

CHOLERIC TEMPERAMENT. *Remedies.* When of affinity to the *bilious*, it is subject to the same regulations as that variety; and when to the sanguine or nervous, the regimen should be accommodated to those phases of constitution.

DIET. The same remark holds as to diet, as with regard to remedies.

PHLEGMATIC TEMPERAMENT. *Remedies. Puls., Ac. phos., Sep., Ars., Hell., Bella., Sil., Sulph., Nat. m., Euph.*, &c., &c.

DIET. Similar to that recommended for the lymphatic subject, with this difference, that fluids need not be so strictly avoided.

ADYNAMIC TEMPERAMENT. *Remedies. Ars., Sulph., Calc., Phosph., Phosph. a., Carb. v., Nux. v., China, Lach., Merc., Natr. m., Staph., Sep., Veratr., Sil., Ant. c., Arn.*, &c., &c.

DIET. Similar to that recommended for the nervous subject.

The Homœopathic treatment and remedies are peculiarly well adapted to the management of young children. Amongst other things, one of the most constant inconveniences of Allopathic* remedies is, frequently, their nauseous and bulky character, by which great difficulty occurs in their efficacious administration. Again, the delicate condition of the membranes and fibres of the frame renders them far too susceptible of the action of large doses of powerful drugs to admit of their being uninjured by such means.

* The medicines employed in the old method of treatment.

Both of these objections are wholly set aside by the Homœopathic method of exhibiting remedies; for, in the first place, they are without smell or taste; and, in the second, they are of so minute and delicate proportions as to render their judicious employment only operative for good.

There are too many ingredients of the commonest use in the Allopathic pharmacy, by which the most serious consequences are liable to be engendered, either by an over-dose or by their prolonged administration. Moreover, it is by no means an unusual occurrence that the indisposition against which they have been prescribed may indeed be removed, but not unfrequently to be supplanted by more or less permanent derangement induced by their unduly powerful and pernicious operation. The simple use of aperients alone, and the favorite practice of purging, not to speak of the employment of strong tonics, etc., are only too often quite sufficient, ultimately, to induce obstinate derangement of the digestive functions, and the system at large. Our pharmacopœia* has wholly avoided these shoals. We repudiate not only the large and hurtful doses of the ingredients themselves, together with the popular, yet often futile, method of attempting to modify their ef-

* A book containing rules for the preparation of medicines.

fects, or to correct and mitigate their extreme action, but also the mode of preparation.

Previous to giving any directions relative to the peculiar treatment of any complaint, it should be premised that parents must by no means suffer works of this kind to be the substitute of medical advice for their children, in the graver or more occult kinds of cases, because it is always imperative to be prompt in dealing with infants, but to trust to these directions only in the less important instances, in the disorders which have striking and identifying symptoms and manifestations, pending the arrival of a professional practitioner, and in the daily casualties and accidents which may occur, and which cannot be mistaken.

CASUALTIES AND DISORDERS CONCOMITANT WITH BIRTH, OR SHORTLY SUCCEEDING IT.

When labour has been unusually protracted, and of difficult completion, various mechanical injuries, of more or less importance, are not unfrequently inflicted on the child.

Tumours and Contusions.

Tumours are very frequently occasioned about the head and other parts of the body, as also contusions from undue pressure. In most instances, these casualties will not be attended with any danger, but they are in the department of the surgeon, and should be dealt with by professional hands alone. Where inflammation is induced, the consequences may become serious, unless great care be taken to subdue the irritation.

A lotion composed of about six drops of tincture of ARNICA to a wine-glassful of pure water, together with the internal administration of one globule of the same remedy, is generally the surest and safest of remedies. In default of success with ARNICA, RHUS TOXICODENDRON may be resorted to; or, in some cases, CALENDULA. (See art. WOUNDS.) The features are not commonly much distorted on delivery, but they will generally resume their shape spontaneously.

Swelling of the Head

The head of the infant at the birth is invariably more or less swollen, and this swelling usually subsides of itself. If it should last, one globule of ARNICA, as before, will materially assist the removal; or, in case of longer duration, the lotion. Sometimes there is considerable tumour of the *fontanel* (or larger mould,) which is more serious than the former description of swelling, but which is rarely alarming. If it continue more than a day or two, one globule of RHUS TOXICODENDRON should be administered: or, when the fontanel is too long in closing, the same quantity of CALCAREA CARBONICA, repeated twice or thrice if required, at intervals of a week. SULPHUR and SILICEA are sometimes requisite in protracted cases.

Ruptures.

The birth of children is not unfrequently accompanied by ruptures, in the form of protrusion of the intestines at the navel, and other parts, in the form of a swelling, which, at the first-named and by far the most frequent locality, varies in size from a hazel-nut to a walnut, and is distinguished by its becoming increased in size when the infant coughs or cries, and by its capability of being reduced by gentle pressure.

But as these are essentially surgical cases, it is perhaps useless to dilate much upon them here. Suffice it to say that, in cases of protrusion at the navel, stout plasters and light bandages are the only external resources with infants; there are no trusses of sufficiently delicate pressure to be used with new-born children.

The internal employment of *Nux v.*, one globule every four or five days, for three or four times, will materially facilitate the cure in ordinary cases.

Jaundice.

A yellow discoloration of the skin and eyes is a frequent manifestation in new-born infants; but, generally speaking, this is of but little import, and will pass off of itself when the secretion of the bile becomes better balanced with the requirements of the digestive organs.

In cases in which it lasts more than a few days, one globule of *Mercurius* may be given, and repeated after an interval of forty-eight hours.

The worst of resources in cases of jaundice, whether in new born infants, or children more advanced in age, is the administration of aperients. It is by the too great frequency of exhibiting purgatives that confirmed jaundice is very frequently induced, and that its constant return is rendered common.

In some instances jaundice, in a very young child, may arise from natural obstructions in the biliary duct, in which cases there is but rarely any successful treatment.

In the subsequent period of childhood, the symptoms of jaundice may be described as yellow, of various shades, first appearing in the eyes, and soon extending over the whole surface of the skin. It is attended by hard whitish motions, and deep orange-coloured secretions of water occasionally;

also, a sense of pressure and distension, or other uneasiness, is complained of in the region of the liver; and there is much irregularity of digestion.

Sometimes even the perspiration will tinge the linen of the patient.

The principal sources from which jaundice may originate are,—disordered state of the liver, prolonged indigestion, poisonous substances, over-fatigue, cold, great mental excitements, the habit of constantly taking drastic purgatives or emetics, obstructions in the biliary ducts (sometimes from worms, gallstones, and the like).

Too sedentary or irregular a method of living are amongst the most common exciting causes.

This disease is not unfrequently intermittent, and, in many cases, it will recur at stated seasons for some years after it has been once had.

With careful treatment jaundice is ordinarily by no means a dangerous complaint, but it may lead to a variety of organic derangements from want of care.

The most prominent specific remedy for this disorder is MERCURIUS; but if, as is not unfrequently the case, the patient has suffered from the effects of this mineral in large and frequently repeated doses under the old mode of treatment, or when the affection assumes an intermittent form, or has been excited by over-exertion, accompanied by profuse sweating, CINCHONA is preferable. When it originates from mental excitement, (such as a fit of passion,) or from a chill, CHAMOMILLA may be looked upon as the most efficacious remedy; or, when attended with *costiveness*, or alternate costiveness and looseness of the bowels, NUX VOMICA is to be preferred. The last remedy is also the first in efficacy in cases where the complaint arises from sedentary habits.

When the attack has been excited by rich, indigestible food, and it is attended with great lassitude, chilliness, and restlessness, especially towards evening, we should administer PULSATILLA, or *Pulsatilla* and *Ipecac.* alternately every four hours, until improvement results, or some other remedy is called for by a change of symptoms, if vomiting ensues. ACONITUM is sometimes required where febrile symptoms supervene.

Should the symptoms not yield to the use of one or more of the foregoing, *Sulphur* may be resorted to, and, if it fail to conquer the affection, professional advice must be sought.

ADMINISTRATION OF THE REMEDIES.—Four globules, in four dessert-spoonfuls of water, one dessert-spoonful of the solution every four hours,* in the course of the day.

Occasionally it may be found necessary to give

* See rules for repetition of the dose.

nearly the whole of the above-named remedies, either successively or otherwise. In such cases an interval of four days may be allowed between each remedy, if the attack is of a mild, though obstinate form. In those of a more urgent character, or when a decided change in the symptoms appears, with *well-marked* indications for the employment of a fresh remedy, the alteration may be made without delay.

The diet should be very plain, light, and unstimulating; veal or chicken broth, unfermented bread, baked apples, light vegetables, such as stewed lettuce, vegetable marrow, French beans. The drink should be chiefly water, or toast-and-water.

(*See* also *Derangement of the Stomach*, *Mental Emotions*, and *Bilious attacks*.)

Inflammation of the Eyes.

Amongst the most common casualties which befall newly-born children, we may include inflammation of the eyes (purulent ophthalmia.)

This disorder is by no means to be overlooked or thought too lightly of, inasmuch as, without attention, it may frequently terminate in blindness.

Various causes have been assigned as the origin of the complaint, such as cold, exposure to the light or to any kind of glare. In some cases, however, it appears to be of epidemic origin; whilst in others it is attributable to a constitutional state of the mother before delivery, or to contact with leucorrhœal matter, and sometimes from worse manifestations of parental disease. The affection usually displays itself at first by an inflammatory redness of the inner surface of the eyelids, which speedily extends to the ball of the eye, and is soon afterwards accompanied by a profuse secretion of matter. The eyes are usually quite closed, and are so sensitive to the light, that it is generally impossible to obtain a satisfactory examination of the eye. On separating the lids, a flow of matter ensues, and the inner lining of the lid exhibits a vivid red hue.

TREATMENT. · Upon the first discovery of inflammation, the better course is to administer one globule of ACONITE, repeating the dose after a lapse of eight hours. In the majority of cases, *Sulphur* will form the most appropriate remedy after *Aconite*. One globule of that remedy may, therefore, be administered twelve hours after the second dose of *Aconite*, and followed, after an interval of twenty-four hours, by another dose of the last-named medicament; and then again *Sulphur*, after the lapse of twelve hours. In other cases, *Pulsatilla*, *Rhus*, *Belladonna*, or *Calcarea*, &c., may be required; but, whenever the first-named remedies fail to produce a speedy improvement, professional aid should be sought without delay. Lukewarm water is the only lotion required, and should be dropped or injected between the lids several times a day when the secretion of matter is copious. A poultice is often serviceable when the lids adhere firmly together.

Red Gum.

Most children a few days after delivery, exhibit a reddish eruption or rash, in the form of red pimples, intermingled with a few red patches, about the face, neck, and hands, which is known by the name of RED GUM ; but which in no case is of very serious import, or requires special treatment. It is generally esteemed as a symptom of strong health and vigor in the child.

If the rash should continue to be thrown out for any length of time, or reappear more than once, which will occasionally occur, we may assist it by administering *Arnica montana*, one globule in the morning, and again at bedtime. Four or five days afterward, *Antimonium crudum* may be resorted to, if needful; and then *Sepia*, after a like interval. When there is considerable irritation, a globule of *Aconitum* may be given, and repeated in twelve hours.

Swelling of the Breasts in Infants.

All children, of either sex, are subject to the manifestation of these symptoms at the birth. The breast of every infant is charged with a kind of secretion, bearing some resemblance to milk; but it is very erroneous to attribute this to a species of disease, or to treat it as such, as is the common custom. The symptoms will disappear of themselves, if they are left alone; and the practice of pressing the breasts, to produce or to encourage a discharge, is not only useless, but is so far injurious, that it not unfrequently produces inflammation, and sometimes an abscess, which is really serious. Nurses should be strictly prohibited from resorting to their favorite expedient. When inflammatory symptoms have been excited by the wanton interference of the nurse or other ignorant persons, a weak lotion of *Arnica* (three drops of the mother tincture to an ordinary-sized wine-glassful of water) may be applied to the part three or four times a day. If matter has formed, one globule of *Hepar s.* may be given, and the dose repeated after twenty-four hours.

DISEASES OF THE DIGESTIVE ORGANS.

Inflammation of the Mouth.

This disorder almost invariably originates from a derangement of the digestive functions (mucous membrane.) It is, consequently, generally a mere symptom of other intestinal disorder. Cold, the use of irritating aperients, a want of care and cleanliness in feeding, or a too stimulating or otherwise unsuitable and indigestible diet, form the most frequent exciting causes.

SYMPTOMS. This complaint manifests itself by more or less redness, tumefaction, and heat of the coating (lining or mucous membrane) of the mouth and gums. It is usually accompanied by a parching of the tongue and lips, and not uncommonly by swelling and peeling of the lips. Sometimes, also, an eruption appears externally about the lips. The continuance of this disorder is also accompanied, in some cases, with dribbling, caused by a great accumulation of saliva in the mouth, when the infant is yet but a few months old.

When *Inflammation of the Mouth* takes place at the age of seven or eight months, it is generally accompanied by a good deal of fever; but, in younger infants, this is but very rarely the case.

When it is combined with considerable internal derangement, it may be of very serious import; but, otherwise, it does not indicate any very important evil, nor should it be allowed to give alarm.

TREATMENT. In simple cases, MERCURIUS is generally sufficient to effect a speedy cure, particularly when there is an excessive secretion and flow of saliva. To infants of a few weeks old, one globule may be given in the morning or in the evening, and repeated after an interval of twenty-four hours. For those of a more advanced age, three globules may be dissolved in four teaspoonsful of water, and a teaspoonful of the solution given every twelve hours.

If the symptoms do not improve after the lapse of four or five days, SULPHUR may be administered in the same manner as *Mercurius.*

When there is much acidity and excessive regurgitation of milk, NUX V. and PULSATILLA are useful—the former particularly in children of bilious, sanguine, or nervous temperament; the latter more especially in those of lymphatic constitution. *Nux v.* is, moreover, more appropriate when constipation accompanies the irritability of stomach; whereas *Pulsatilla* is, generally, to be preferred to that remedy, when the bowels are much relaxed. In administering either of the last-named remedies, one globule may be dissolved in four teaspoonsful of water, a teaspoonful every twelve hours. The medicine may be repeated in the same way, after an interval of two to four days, if the symptoms continue, although with diminished severity. A globule of ACONITE will act beneficially, either a few hours before or after the employment of any of the above remedies, if considerable febrile disturbance supervene.

Ulcerative Inflammation of the Mouth.

This disorder is, properly speaking, only an aggravated feature of the last, and is not unattended with danger, from the liability of the ulcerations to extend into the intestinal tube, and even the air-passages. The first manifestation of it is almost invariably in its former character, and unattended with ulceration; but mismanagement, want of care, an acrid state of body, and the consequent virulence or duration of simple inflammation, will often, if not generally, produce ulceration.

SYMPTOMS. The ulcers are but rarely multiplied, and in most cases there is but one large irregular sore, which is covered with a whitish-yellow slough, generally surrounded by considerable redness, and accompanied by much irritation in the whole mouth. The roof of the mouth, sometimes the tongue, but more frequently the insides of the cheeks, are the seats in which the ulcers appear.

TREATMENT. In mild cases, MERCURIUS is here also the most useful remedy. One globule may be given, and repeated after twelve hours. Two days afterwards, the same medicine may again be administered, if the symptoms remain stationary. In severe cases, with foulness of the breath, swollen, spongy-looking gums, and diarrhœa, accompanied by much straining, MERCURIUS is still the most appropriate remedy; but if no permanent improvement follow its employment, ACIDUM NITRICUM may be resorted to, and administered as recommended for *Mercurius*. When there is fetor of breath, with frequent efforts to vomit, great debility, and constipation, or scanty, discoloured, offensive stools, give one globule of NUX V., and repeat the dose in twelve hours; or, particularly with infants of eight or nine months old, dissolve two globules in four teaspoonsful of water, and give a teaspoonful of the solution every twelve hours. SULPHUR is often required to complete the cure after *Nux vomica*, and sometimes after *Mercurius*, and *Acidum nitricum* likewise. It may be exhibited in the same way as *Nux v.* When fever runs high, and there is, consequently, great restlessness, with heat of skin, and quick, full pulse, one globule of *Aconite* may be given, and repeated in the space of twelve hours; or it may be administered in alternation with the remedy otherwise indicated, allowing an interval of from eight to twelve hours between each medicine.

In children of two years of age and upwards, the following remedies are frequently required:

CARBO V. where the immoderate use of salt or salted diet, or unwholesome food is the cause of derangement, and when the gums swell excessively and bleed when touched or moved; also when the mouth is much heated, the teeth are loose, and the tongue very sore.

ARSENICUM should follow *Carbo*, if the ulceration remains unabated, and a burning heat is complained of in the gums. Or this remedy should be alternated every twelve hours with CHINA, if the gums appear purple or blackish, and present symptoms resembling gangrene.*

Whereas NUX VOMICA is preferable with children of a bilious temperament and choleric disposition and of meagre appearance or dark complexion, or with those who lead a very sedentary life. CAPSICUM will commonly be found more effective with those of a plethoric habit and phlegmatic temperament.

* Incipient mortification.

DULCAMARA will sometimes be found a useful remedy as consequent upon MERCURIUS, when the glands of the throat are enlarged and somewhat tender; and it may be adopted as the substitute of MERCURY where the primary cause is exposure to cold or damp, or the malady is very susceptible of cold or damp weather.

When, notwithstanding the employment of the above medicines, the ulcers are slow of healing, and the mouth, lips, and gums remain sore, and show no symptom of cicatrizing, SULPHUR may be prescribed; and if this remedy proves insufficient to establish the cure, medical advice should be sought.

ADMINISTRATION of the above medicines. Four globules, in six dessert-spoonfuls of water, one every twelve hours.

DIET. It is imperative that the food should be of the lightest and most wholesome kind during this disease, and that the patient should be taken into the fresh air daily. To children who have attained the proper age, an adequate proportion of vegetables should be given.

Aphthous Ulceration.

Aphthous ulceration, or what is commonly denominated THRUSH, is more frequently met with in children than the form of ulceration above described. The affection is characterized by the small, white, and circular appearance of the ulcer, which first presents itself in the form of round, white dots or specks, either widely scattered or occurring in clusters, according to the parts they occupy; being generally few in number, and isolated, or even single, when occupying the inside of the lips, the gums, or the tongue, but more numerous when situate on the inner surface of the cheeks. When in clusters, they often become confluent, and spread over the entire cavity of the mouth, and even, in severe cases, extend to the throat and throughout the alimentary canal. In these cases a thin white crust forms in a continuous coat over the ulcers, and, on being thrown off or detached, the ulcerated spots are exposed to view.

Considerable tumefaction of the glands often accompanies the severer varieties of the complaint, and the bowels are commonly more or less deranged, being either much confined or relaxed, and the motions unhealthy; acidity of stomach is also a frequent concomitant. In properly-reared children, the affection is seldom or never malignant or dangerous, although troublesome at times, from its protracted nature, or its tendency to repeated recurrence under favoring circumstances. It is almost exclusively amongst the ill-housed and ill-nourished children of the needy poor that the disease is liable to assume a serious aspect, by extending to the air-passages, or by assuming a malignant or gangrenous character. In the former case, hoarseness, oppressed or otherwise abnormal respiration, and cough, are the first indications which excite our alarm; in the latter, the livid hue of the surrounding parts, the soft, lacerated-looking margins, and the brown-coloured coating of the centre are the appearances to be dreaded. Prostration of strength ought always to give rise to apprehension. The greatest inconveniences which arise from the ordinary forms of the malady, are—firstly, the obstacles offered to the act of sucking or deglutition, and, secondly, the irritation and soreness which is generally communicated to the nipple of the mother, by contact with the inflamed and ulcerated mouth of the infant.

Want of sufficient attention to the temperature and ventilation of apartments, and to the cleanliness of the child itself, and of the bottle (when reared by hand) from which it is fed, combined with irregularity and excess, or want of care in the preparation of food, form the principal exciting causes of thrush (*aphthous ulceration*). It far more frequently occurs in children reared by hand, wholly or partially, than in those which are entirely suckled at the breast.

TREATMENT. In *slight* cases, a dose or two of MERCURIUS are generally sufficient to effect a speedy removal of aphthous ulceration. One globule may be given in the morning or in the evening, and repeated after an interval of twelve hours. Four days afterwards the medicine may again be administered in the same manner. This remedy may be employed with equal advantage, in such cases, as a lotion, by dissolving four or five globules in half a wineglassful of water, and gently applying it, twice a day, by means of a camel's hair brush. In severer forms of the affection with copious flow of saliva, diarrhœa, and straining; also when the ulcers (aphthæ) present a yellowish (bilious) appearance, *Mercurius* is still the most important medicament. If the aphthæ present an improved aspect under the use of this remedy, but the disturbance in the bowels continues with unabated vigour, and the secretions become more vitiated and very offensive. *Acidum sulphuricum* may be resorted to in the same way as described for the preceding remedy. When the derangement of the digestive functions is chiefly manifested by flatulence, regurgitation of food, and even vomiting of acid or of bilious matter, *Nux Vomica* and *Pulsatilla* are the most appropriate remedies. The former is, generally speaking, to be preferred when the bowels are constipated; the latter when they are more or less relaxed and discoloured. The administration of these may be conducted as follows: Dissolve two globules in four teaspoonfuls of water, and give a teaspoonful every twelve hours. If the infant cannot be made to swallow the liquid, a globule may be placed on the tongue in the morning, and again at bedtime, or *vice versâ.* Twenty-four hours afterwards, the medicine may be repeated, and again after an interval of forty-eight hours. And so on, lengthening the intervals as the improvement advances, before finally discontinuing the remedy. When the above-mentioned medicaments are insufficient to accomplish a cure in the forms of the complaint alluded to, SULPHUR will generally be required. And when there is great nocturnal restlessness, sleeplessness, with febrile symptoms, a globule of *Aconitum* may be given. Should the ulcers display the unhealthy aspect alluded to in the description of the disease, and the prostration of strength be great, *Arsenicum*, *Cinchona*, *Acidum nitricum*, &c., are the most serviceable remedial agents in the hands of the professional adviser.

DIET AND REGIMEN. The diet in children who are reared by the hand ought to be light and well prepared. The mouth of the infant should be gently, yet carefully, washed after meals; and if a suckling-bottle is employed, it ought to be thoroughly cleansed after use. Personal cleanliness, proper attention to ventilation, and regular exposure of the child to fresh air, must also be observed.

White Thrush.

It sometimes occurs in young infants, and chiefly anterior to the time of teething, to be afflicted with a peculiar variety of inflammation of the mouth, which, from its peculiar symptomatic hue, is called WHITE THRUSH. This disorder is by no means so virulent as the former species, nor, perhaps, so painful as the simple ulcerated inflammation. It but very rarely appears in England, but is very commonly prevalent in other parts of Europe.

SYMPTOMS. The formation of a cream-like matter, either in patches on the palate or root of the tongue, or over the entire lining membrane of the mouth. On removing this coating, the subjacent skin is found to be unbroken, but exhibits a red and shining appearance, as from extreme irritation. It is rarely attended with the general characteristics of fever which accompany the ulcerated variety of sore mouth. The mucous lining close to the fundament frequently presents the same exudation of curd-like matter as the mouth, and this manifestation may extend throughout the alimentary canal, and even to the air-ducts, as is the case with the common thrush; but there is rarely much, if any danger.

TREATMENT. The treatment may be said to be identical with that of the milder varieties of APHTHOUS ULCERATION. The exhibition of remedies should only be modified according to the comparative virulence of the disorder.

Diphtheritic Inflammation.

This is an inflammatory affection of the throat, soft palate, and tonsils, accompanied by membranous exudation, but without ulceration. It is common to adults as well as to young children, although far more prevalent amongst the latter. There are two species: the one virulent, gangrenous, and dangerous, if not fatal; the other comparatively of very little import, excepting from its tendency, in very acute cases, to extend into the air-tubes,—a result which constitutes the chief danger to be apprehended in the other form of the complaint. They are distinguished under the denominations of the *malignant* and the *acute or highly inflammatory form.* The latter species betrays little or no general organic derangement, and is rarely, if ever, accompanied by general fever. Whereas the malignant variety is liable to become one of the most serious and fatal of epidemics.

Malignant diphtheritic inflammation is, moreover, often very insidious in its approach, inasmuch as at first it causes but little positive pain, and, until the throat becomes much swollen, the operation of swallowing is comparatively easy.

SYMPTOMS. The symptoms of diphtheritic inflammation vary according to the habit of the child. In sickly, squalid children, who are ill-fed, ill-covered, and packed together in ill-ventilated apartments or hovels, the complaint very soon assumes its malignant or gangrenous appearance. In the acute or inflammatory species of the complaint, the mucous or lining membrane of the throat first appears highly red, and the palate and tonsils considerably swollen, and very shortly becomes chequered with spots or patches of a membranous exudation or coating. This tenacious or concrete lymphy secretion, in severe cases, soon assumes the appearance of an uninterrupted, smooth, white covering. In other cases, the exudation forms in soft, easily-detachable, massive patches, of a dirty yellow or greyish colour, which have an uneven surface.

In malignant diphtheritic inflammation, the innovation of the disease is, as already remarked, frequently very stealthy. The difficulty in swallowing is generally the first symptom which excites attention; and this becomes apparent even when, on examining the throat, the redness and swelling appear insufficient to give rise to this circumstance. On the other hand, as the disease may become fully developed before any complaint is made of the throat, and before any attention is drawn to a peculiarity in the act of swallowing, the throat should be carefully examined whenever a child seems indisposed during the prevalence of diphtheritic inflammation, either in the establishment or in the neighbourhood.

In many cases, the pain on swallowing is very early accompanied by swelling and tenderness of the glands under the lower jaw (sub-maxillary.)

The exudation of lymph, which subsequently takes place, is, in this species of the malady, of a tawny gray colour, of dense structure, and extensive surface, often spreading to the back of the nostrils, and sometimes even to the stomach and intestines, or more frequently, and all the more fatally, to the windpipe and its ramifications.

An excessively offensive fetor generally attends the worst kinds of the inflammation, and blood not unfrequently extils from the gums and lips. The extension of the complaint to the nostrils is indicated by the foul and acrid discharge therefrom;

and the existence of nausea, vomiting, and tenderness of the stomach, or griping and diarrhœa, denote its transmission to the digestive tube; whilst the invasion of croup-like symptoms herald its seizure upon the air-passages. Extreme prostration of strength forms an early feature in the train of symptoms; and a low typhoid fever almost invariably attends, and frequently exhausts the vital energies, even in cases where the lymphy membranous exudation has not extended to the air-passages.

TREATMENT. At the commencement of the very acute or inflammatory form of the affection, especially when it occurs in robust, well-fed children, two globules of *Aconitum* may be given, and repeated after an interval of from six to eight hours. In the majority of cases of this description, however, MERCURIUS will be found the more appropriate remedy, particularly when there is a tendency to swelling of the glands. Six globules may be dissolved in an ordinary-sized wineglassful of water, and a dessert-spoonful of the solution given every four hours. If, notwithstanding the early use of this remedy, the disease threatens to gain ground, professional aid should be sought, as the disease is often very intractable even in this its milder form.

Due attention to cleanliness and ventilation are of the first importance; and generous, nourishing, but easily digestible diet are essential to sustain the patient's strength in the severer forms of the disease. Healthy children ought to be removed from the vicinity.

Mumps.

This is a common and painful complaint amongst children, although not confined to them only. It rages as an epidemy in some seasons, especially amongst the poorer population in low, damp districts. It is usually attributable to cold or to check of perspiration, and the like, and is commonly of more frequent occurrence during the prevalence of keen easterly winds.

The affection commences in the form of a small, hard, and rather painful swelling occupying the locality of the gland below the ear (the parotid). It occasionally affects only the gland of one side, but more frequently those of both. The swelling speedily increases in size, and often extends to the gland beneath the angle of the lower jaw (the maxillary). But in its ordinary character it possesses no alarming features, and will generally pursue a course of about four days, and then harmlessly subside. It is not, however, very unfrequent for the symptoms of the disorder to change their seat from the glands above specified to those of the groin, &c., in males, and to those of the breasts in females. Sometimes, also, the swelling of the parotid gland will, in cases of high inflammation, run on to suppuration, or the formation of matter, (abscess), which may, on ripening, discharge inwardly, and cause suffocation by the entrance of the matter into the windpipe. The glands in other parts of the body sympathetically affected, or affected by a transference of the complaint from the jaws and throat, are also liable to a similar discharge. When the swelling of the glands below the ear and jaw becomes suddenly suppressed, and the brain appears affected, or the respiration impeded, danger is to be apprehended. In common cases there is only a mild degree of fever or other signs of constitutional disturbance.

TREATMENT. MERCURIUS may be reckoned specific in most cases. One dose of two globules will, in general, suffice to confine the disorder to a regular and harmless course; but it will sometimes be necessary to repeat the same dose after an interval of twenty-four to forty-eight hours. When there is a very sudden disappearance of the swelling of the glands in the neck, we may look for more serious phases of derangement; and in these instances we not uncommonly find more heightened fever, accompanied by delirium, and other symptoms indicative of complication of the brain. Such cases are fraught with danger, and ought, therefore, to receive professional aid. *Belladonna*, *Aconitum*, *Hyoscyamus*, &c., are the remedies usually required. When the swelling of the glands assumes an appearance similar to erysipelas, or becomes excessively red and tumefied, *Belladonna* is the preferable remedy; and in case of its failing to subdue the inflammatory symptoms, *Hyoscyamus* may be administered.

It is necessary to protect children who are suffering from mumps against exposure to sudden chills, or changes of temperature, draughts, and the like. The neck and the sides of the face should be bound with flannel or worsted, and the patient should be confined to a well-ventilated, moderately warm apartment.

Vomiting of Milk. Intolerance of Milk.

There are few infants who, in suckling, are not apt to overload the stomach, and, subsequently, to regurgitate a portion of the milk which they have swallowed. This occurrence, in place of being looked upon as a disorder, should be regarded as a healthy effort of nature to prevent that disturbance which would otherwise accrue from the retention of a larger quantity of food than is suitable to the digestive powers. When, however, the regurgitation assumes the form of vomiting, and takes place to such an extent, that the greater part of the contents of the stomach are returned after every meal, it can, of course, no longer be looked upon in the light of a normal circumstance, and will, if unchecked, lead to serious consequences.

This irritability of stomach, under the stimulus of milk, sometimes comes on suddenly, after the infant has previously appeared to be in a thriving state, and is still more prone to manifest itself in children who are reared by the hand on cow's milk, than in those who are nourished from the breast.

TREATMENT. When the derangement does not proceed from any faultiness in the milk, it may frequently be overcome by the medium of appropriate medicine. ÆTHUSA CYNAPIUM is deserving of special notice in such cases. One globule of this remedy may be given morning and evening for the first two days: then daily, or only every other day, according to circumstances; lengthening the intervals as the irritability of stomach diminishes. *Arsenicum*, *Bryonia*, *Cuprum*, &c., may answer better in some rarer instances.

Infantile Dyspepsia, or Indigestion. Weaning-Brash, or Scour.

This important and very frequent derangement is more commonly met with in infants who are reared by the hand than in those at the breast. When it occurs in the last-named instance, it almost invariably arises from some *unwholesome property of the milk.* The infant, in such cases, will take the breast readily enough, and even with avidity; generally, indeed, it never seems satisfied but when sucking, and yet, in lieu of deriving any benefit from these frequent applications to the breast, it becomes more and more fretful, and at length exhibits marked outward signs of ill-health. The face becomes pale and haggard-like, the body emaciated, and the stomach and bowels so irritable, that the milk is either thrown up soon after it is swallowed, or it is passed by the bowels in an undigested, curdled condition. Flatulency, griping, and obstinate, debilitating diarrhœa supervene, and the child, if unrelieved, sinks exhausted in a few weeks.

Indigestion proceeding from *indigestible food*, or from *over-feeding*, is, as already stated, very liable to occur in spoon-fed infants. It is also very frequently excited at the period of weaning, and has accordingly received the appellation of "weaning-brash" and "weaning-scour."

This variety of indigestion is generally ushered in by purging, the stools being commonly of a grass-green or greenish-yellow colour; but, at other times, they are light or clay-coloured, and are frequently alternated with constipation. Sooner or later, frequent vomiting of the contents of the stomach, sometimes intermixed with bile, supervenes. The child is continually restless and fretful, and ever looks as if in a state of suffering. There is thirst, with aversion to food; distension of the belly, coldness of the feet and legs; little or no fever, but a disposition to heat and soreness of the mouth, or formation of small while specks on the inner surface of the lips, cheeks, &c. (*Aphthæ, Aphthous Ulceration*) dryness and harshness of skin, feebleness and emaciation. These symptoms go on increasing in intensity until the vital energy is worn out by their depressing influence, or the child is carried off by the development of inflammatory action and intestinal ulcerations.

TREATMENT. In the *indigestion of suckling*, or that which occurs in infants at the breast, speedy recovery will, in most cases, take place under the substitution of a good nurse of sound constitution, or of appropriate artificial feeding, for the faulty nutriment which has originated the derangement. But when the disturbance produced is already considerable, or if the child does not rally soon after the removal of the exciting cause, the aid of medicine is required, and will materially expedite recovery where such a prospect can be entertained. If the child is much reduced, and there has been much purging, also if symptoms of biliary derangement are superadded, one globule of *Cinchona* should be given morning and evening for the first day, then daily for the next two, and subsequently every other day, until signs of improvement become manifest.

If vomiting, acidity, griping, and flatulency threaten to set in with renewed violence after the substitution of artificial food, one globule of *Pulsatilla* may be given, and repeated after twelve hours, care being taken that the quantity of food given is not excessive, or its quality unfitted to the weakened digestive powers of the infant. *Ipecacuanha* and *Arsenicum* are sometimes required after *Pulsatilla;* the former when vomiting predominates; the latter when both vomiting and purging are excessive, and the child much exhausted and emaciated.

In deranged digestion, induced by improper food—*indigestion of weaning*,—if the progress of decay is not too far advanced, or no organic disease has been developed, a cure will, as in the former case, be accomplished by the withdrawal of the main source of all the mischief. The improper food ought, therefore, at once to be corrected: or the quantity reduced, if that has been too great. At first, asses' milk, or cows' milk, which has been previously boiled, and diluted (one part of water to about three of milk), with chicken-broth, or weak beef-tea or mutton-broth, free from fat, may be substituted for food of a more generous or stimulating or indigestible nature than that with which the infant has been dieted. If there is much thirst, barley-water, rice-water, thin arrow-root, or, still better, pure cold water, may be given in small quantities at a time. The homœopathic remedies that are the best adapted to facilitate recovery, and without the aid of which, indeed, recovery is sometimes hopeless, are principally *Chamomilla*, *Pulsatilla*, *Mercurius*, *Ipecacuanha*, *Arsenicum*, *Nux vomica*, *Cinchona*, *Sulphur*, *Phosphorus*. In the milder forms of the complaint, or when the derangement has only been a few days in existence, *Chamomilla*, *Pulsatilla*, *Ipec.*, and *Nux v.* are, commonly, the most frequently indicated.

CHAMOMILLA is chiefly required where there is hardness and fulness of the belly, severe griping, with drawing up of the legs; constant crying, great restlessness and peevishness; acidity, flatulence, frequent purging, the stools being of a deep grass-green or very yellow colour, or whitish-yellow and frothy, sometimes resembling beat-up eggs, and of an offensive odour, often like that of rotten eggs; occasional sickness, the matter vomited being more or less of a bilious description; thirst, want of appetite.

PULSATILLA is indicated where there is less restlessness and peevishness than in the preceding instance, and little or no thirst, but complete loss of appetite, with acid or otherwise disagreeable risings, disposition to vomiting of the contents of the stomach, frequent stools of a greenish, bilious description, or watery, slimy, and at times of a light or whitish colour.

IPECACUANHA is a most valuable remedy when the affection occurs in the autumnal season, but is at all times an important medicine when copious vomiting forms a more prominent feature in the case than the purging; or when there is both vomiting and purging, the substance ejected from the bowels being chiefly of a greenish-yellow colour, and not unfrequently bearing some similitude to matter in a state of fermentation.

MERCURIUS is required when the alvine discharges are very frequent, but generally scanty, and attended with painful straining; also when small white ulcers (*Aphtha, Thrush*) make their appearance on the inner surface of the lips and cheeks, or on the tongue, &c.; and when, with less flatulency, most of the symptoms mentioned above under *Chamomilla* are present.

NUX V. The interposition of constipation, or alternate states of costiveness and relaxation, with loss of appetite, regurgitations, or vomiting, flatulency, acidity, excessive irritability, great feebleness, and soreness of the mouth, or formation of small white ulcerative specks or spots, give occasion for the employment of this remedy. *Bryonia* is occasionally of service when *Nux v.* is insufficient to remove the constipation; but *Sulphur* is generally still more effective here. (See SULPHUR.)

After the employment of one or more of these medicines, but sometimes even at the commencement of the treatment, when the debility induced by the protracted purging is very considerable, CINCHONA may be used with advantage. The symptoms which, in addition to the consecutive weakness, chiefly point out its applicability, are flatulency and flatulent distention of the belly, thirst, want of appetite; copious and frequent watery evacuations; the bowels are generally moved immediately or soon after a meal, and usually contain particles of undigested food. If *Cinchona* only partially relieves the aforesaid symptoms, FERRUM may then be administered. In cases of a more advanced or serious description than those for which the medicaments hitherto mentioned are the more applicable, ARSENICUM is, generally speaking, the remedy on which the most reliance is to be placed where there is any prospect of effecting a cure. It is, like *Ipecacuanha*, more frequently required when the derangement of stomach and bowels occurs during the autumnal season, but may be resorted to under any circumstances, when the affection presents the following features: Extreme emaciation and weakness, sunken cheeks, pallid face, blue-encircled eyes; fulness of stomach, coldness of the extremities; watery, slimy, greenish, or dark-coloured stools; constant whining; great restlessness and sleeplessness; no appetite, but excessive thirst, with desire for very little liquid of any kind at a time, and increase of the diarrhœa after drinking; great irritability of stomach and bowels, the food being often rejected from the stomach soon after it has been swallowed, or passed by the bowels in an undigested state. *Cinchona* is sometimes required after *Arsenicum*; but all depends upon the nature of the symptoms, and any of the other remedies must be selected in preference, if better indicated. SULPHUR is often serviceable in completing the cure, after the previous employment of other medicaments, but especially such as *Pulsatilla*, *Nux v.*, and *Mercurius*. In other cases, *Calcarea* or *Phosph.* may be required. When there is great tenderness of the belly to the touch, or when the derangement has existed several weeks, organic disease is very liable to be induced. Medical aid should be sought in all cases which do not soon yield to the medicines employed, after the removal of the apparent exciting cause of the disease. Gentle friction with the warm hand, or the application of hot flannel or warm fomentations to the belly, are often soothing when there is much flatulence or griping.

ADMINISTRATION OF THE MEDICINES. In general cases, three globules may be dissolved in six teaspoonsful of water, and a teaspoonful given every four hours; and so on, lengthening the intervals, however, as soon as improvement sets in, —or changing the remedy, if required by the alteration in the symptoms.

Colic. Griping.

By the above appellations are here meant severe griping pains in the abdomen (belly,) not originating in inflammation. In children, they very generally proceed from indigestion, but may also be induced by exposure to cold, and by mental emotion.

Treatment. When the derangement has been induced by indigestible food, such as rich animal food, gravy, pastry, fruit, or crude vegetables, and is attended with flatulence and inclination to vomit, or with relaxation of the bowels, *Pulsatilla* is, commonly, the most effective remedy. (*Ipecacuanha* is sometimes required after, or in alternation with *Pulsatilla*, particularly when indigestible animal food, such as veal or pork, has produced the disorder.) When it has arisen from over-feeding, combined with deficient exercise, and is attended with flatulence, or with inclination to vomit, or vomiting, and obstinate constipation, *Nux v.* is more appropriate. And when exposure to cold, or a fit of passion, has developed the attack, *Chamomilla* is generally of speedy efficacy, particularly if there is looseness of the bowels, with flatulent distension, great restlessness and irritability of temper. When the affection is associated with worms, *Cina*, *Nux v.*, &c., are the most useful. (See *Invermination*.) When it occurs in infants at the breast, or in those who have not long been weaned, or who are being reared by the hand. (See *Indigestion*.) The application of warm flannels or warm fomentations to the stomach often exerts a soothing influence during the attack. The diet should be very light for some days after the disturbance; and the exciting cause avoided, for the future, as carefully as possible.

Weaning.

Some particulars which require to be attended to during the process of weaning, have already been alluded to in another part of this work. Temporary derangement of the digestive functions is the disorder which most children are liable to at the epoch in question, and this derangement may easily be confirmed by want of proper precautions. This peculiar susceptibility to indigestion, at the juncture of weaning, is attributable to change of diet simply; and it is by no means to be conceived that the diet will permanently disagree with the infant, because, upon first trial, some such symptoms are manifested. It is highly necessary, however, to mark the effects of each particular article of food after the repetition of a few days; and in case no improvement be observed with any one species of diet more than another, medicine must be resorted to. Amongst the remedies which will be found the most appropriate we may in this place simply name *Pulsatilla*, *Nux vomica*, *Chamomilla*, and *Ipecacuanha*, and refer the reader to the article on *Indigestion of Infants* for the particular indications which regulate their selection. When restlessness, or great excitement, sleeplessness, and fretfulness set in immediately after weaning, without any signs of deranged digestion, or before these have become established, a globule of *Coffea* may be given. In default of improvement, a globule of *Belladonna* may then be administered, and repeated after a few hours.

Bowel Complaints. Diarrhœa.

Looseness of the bowels may be occasioned, in children, by disagreement of the food, over-feeding, cold, sudden emotions, &c. &c. In infants it is not very rarely occasioned by the mischievous practice of administering aperients, and even powerful purgatives, with the object of clearing the body of the dark-coloured matter, technically known by the name of *meconium*, that collects in the large intestine of the child during the last month or two of its uterine being. And even in children of a more advanced age, bowel complaints are, unquestionably, not unfrequently to be attributed to irritation of the mucous lining by the reiterated employment of aperients. Their active use, or rather abuse, during the existence of the affection, is, moreover, not an uncommon cause of its protraction, not to say its fatal termination.

Diarrhœa is a common attendant upon other diseases, and is, consequently, very frequently a mere symptom, the primary malady consisting in some inflammatory affection. In this place, however, it is purposed to treat of this derangement as a simple functional disorder originating in various sources, and presenting the variety of features detailed under each of the subjoined medicines. It may be, briefly, premised that, in the case of infants at the breast, the motions generally average in number from four to six in the course of twenty-four hours; but they may be more frequent, or, on the other hand, they may be less so in perfectly healthy infants. After the first ten or fourteen days they should present the usual normal colour (not unlike well-mixed mustard, sometimes with a few isolated white specks,) and possessing no other than a slightly sour smell. Excessive frequency, foul odour, and unnatural hues and consistence, such as green and watery, or yellow and watery, white and frothy as if fermented, brown and frothy, or dark, like pitch, sometimes mixed with slime, or consisting wholly of slime (mucus,) accompanied moreover by evident signs of pain and flatulence, must be regarded as unmistakeable indications of derangement. In children of a more advanced age, but also in infants, the tongue is loaded, either white or yellow, and sometimes red at the tip or sides; the appetite is fastidious, fitful, or absent; thirst generally prevails; and the abdomen is often more than naturally warm to the touch, and usually either distended or lumpy at the commencement of the attack.

TREATMENT. CHAMOMILLA is one of the most invaluable remedies in the treatment of the diseases of children, and particularly in bowel-complaints, whether arising from acidity, irritation caused by indigestible food, excited by a chill, or occurring during teething—when the following symptoms are apparent: redness of the face, or of one cheek, hardness and fulness of the belly, attended by severe colic, which is indicated by a state of peevishness, restlessness, constant crying, and drawing up of the legs towards the stomach; sickness, and risings, which are sometimes so acrid as to excoriate the lips; yellow furred or red and parched-like tongue; aphthæ; thirst; frequent evacuations, of a bilious, watery, slimy, or frothy description, of a whitish, yellowish, or greenish* colour, sometimes containing undigested food, or bearing a resemblance to chopped vegetables or to

* Green-coloured stools are, generally, the product of acidity, and they have very commonly a strongly acid smell. Dark, or even black, offensive motions are often connected with deranged liver; and those which are pale, clay-like, or of a very white colour, are frequently to be assigned to deficiency or absence of bile, but sometimes to a more serious cause. Diarrhœa with white evacuations is, indeed, usually very inveterate. if not dangerous.

beat-up eggs, and of an offensive odour, occasionally similar to that of rotten eggs; soreness or rawness around the fundament.

ADMINISTRATION. See page 206.

RHEUM is another remedy of great utility in the treatment of this affection, provided the disorder has not been actually excited by frequent use of this medicine itself in allopathic doses, in which case it will be necessary to have recourse to *Pulsatilla*, *Chamomilla*, or *Mercurius*, as antidotes, according to the nature of the symptoms. *Rheum* is particularly appropriate when acidity or bilious derangement has been generated by indigestion, or has arisen from the prolonged use of antacids, such as magnesia, &c., and when there is flatulent distention of the abdomen, colic, crying, restlessness, straining before and after the evacuations, which are either of the consistence of pap, or watery and somewhat slimy, occasionally of a grayish or of a brown colour,—and when the stools have a very acid odour, and a sour smell is emitted from the body of the infant. It is sometimes necessary to give *Chamomilla* after *Rheum*, to complete the cure; in other cases, and particularly those of an obstinate character, *Magnesia c.* is more efficacious.

PULSATILLA. Diarrhœa arising from indigestion, or from a chill, with watery, slimy, whitish, or bilious, greenish, chopped-looking evacuations, occurring chiefly at night; foul tongue, headache, sickness, acidity, want of appetite, flatulence, and fretfulness; chilliness, with shivering or shuddering, or alternate heats and chills. It is, further, often efficacious, under similar conditions, when fright has been the exciting cause, and *Opium* has not sufficed, or has been administered too late to procure relief.

IPECACUANHA is very useful when, from a sudden change of food, which the stomach is unable to digest, the following symptoms result: bilious derangement, with repeated attacks of vomiting; paleness of the face; frequent crying; diarrhœa, with stools of a bilious, slimy, or greenish yellow, sometimes blackish, or streaked with blood, and of a putrid odour; on other occasions, evacuations resembling matter in a state of fermentation, or containing substances like white flocks or flakes, followed by slight straining. When this remedy is insufficient to effect a complete cure, we should have recourse to *Pulsatilla;* or to *Arsenicum*, should the vomiting increase. (See *Arsenicum.*)

MERCURIUS. This medicine will be found very serviceable in cases where the irritation has arisen from a chill, &c., and the following symptoms present themselves: watery and copious, or slimy and scanty, or bilious stools (sometimes streaked, or mixed with blood,) of a blackish, greenish, or whitish-yellow colour: frothy, or having the appearance of beat-up eggs, and of a very sour or fetid smell, attended with severe colic, nocturnal sweats, and frequently also severe straining and protrusion of the last intestine; diarrhœa, with soreness of the fundament, or redness of the whole body, as from general excoriation; aphthæ,* salivation, eructations, sickness, shivering, and languor.

NUX VOMICA is often useful in cases arising from a chill, or from indigestible food, at the period of weaning, or earlier; it is also, like *Pulsatilla*, useful in some cases in which the disorder has been created by the frequent employment of powerful laxative medicines.

Its indications are: very frequent but scanty evacuations of watery, slimy, whitish or greenish stools, attended with white or yellow furred, or red-tipped tongue, headache, nausea, risings, sickness, acidity, flatulence, colic, and straining, sometimes followed by protrusion of the intestines; extreme fretfulness. This medicine is also of great service, in many cases, when the diarrhœa alternates with constipation, and when portions of

* Small white ulcers.

undigested food are sometimes observable in the stools.

BRYONIA is a useful remedy in cases of diarrhœa, with aggravation after a meal, and passing of the food by stool undigested; or with dark-coloured motions, which recur whenever the weather becomes very warm; also when looseness is alternated with constipation. (*Carbo v.* may be found efficacious, when only temporary benefit results from *Bryonia*, in diarrhœa during the heat of summer.)

ARSENICUM. This medicine becomes indispensable in neglected cases, or in those at an advanced stage of the disorder, when there is reason to fear that it will terminate in wasting.

The following are its characteristic indications: watery or slimy stools, sometimes with portions of undigested food, mostly profuse, of a greenish, whitish, dark-brown or blackish colour, and of a putrid odour, taking place chiefly during the night, or after drinking or partaking of any kind of food, often preceded by crying and restlessness, and followed by exhaustion, or tendency to faint in children of a more advanced age; great thirst; foul or vivid red tongue; sleeplessness; paleness of the face; sunken cheeks; blue circles round the eyes; enlargement of the abdomen, with extreme weakness and excessive emaciation. In diarrhœa with periodical exacerbations, and in that which is attended with vomiting and resembles cholera, *Arsenicum* is one of the most valuable remedies.

LACHESIS is sometimes of much service after *Arsenicum* or *Mercurius*, or indeed in preference to these remedies, when, in addition to most of the symptoms thereunder mentioned, the looseness, &c., is invariably worse after sleeping, and the stools are generally of a pale or whitish colour, or tenacious and like pitch; also when, as with *Bryonia* and *Nux v.*, constipation alternates with diarrhœa.

SULPHUR is an invaluable remedy in some protracted cases, or in those occurring in children who are the offspring of delicate parents,—when there is great weakness, emaciation, distension of the abdomen, redness or soreness of the anus, and excoriations between the thighs and neighbouring parts, or a sort of miliary eruption over the whole body. (*Calcarea* is sometimes required to complete the cure after *Sulphur*. In other cases, *Phosph.*, &c., may be required. See also *Indigestion of Infants.*)

CINCHONA is of considerable service against the debility which remains when the diarrhœa is checked; but it is also useful in the disease itself, particularly when it has been caused by eating fruit or green vegetables, or when the complaint has become inveterate, and is attended with thirst, excessive flatulence, loss of appetite, and great weakness; also when the alvine discharge is apt to take place immediately after a meal, and contains food in an undigested state, or occurs especially during the night,—the stools being copious, slimy, frothy, or watery, or of a blackish or dark-brown, or a very yellow colour.

When febrile symptoms suddenly make their appearance during diarrhœa, *Aconitum* should be resorted to. (See *Inflammation of Stomach and Bowels.*)

Administration of the Medicines. Six globules, of the remedy selected, may be dissolved in an ordinary sized wine-glass of water, and a teaspoonful of the solution given, in severe cases of recent standing, every half hour until three doses have been given: after which the intervals between the doses may be lengthened to every three, and then every six hours, and so on. In less serious cases, as well as in those of long standing (chronic diarrhœa), it will be sufficient to give a teaspoonful thrice a day, or only morning and evening. To very young infants it will be sufficient to introduce a drop or two of the medicine, in solution, into the mouth, for each dose. Whenever a different remedy becomes clearly indicated, it may at once be resorted to. But it is far from commendable to fly from one remedy to another, without sufficient reason, or to change the medicament without allowing a reasonable time for the manifestation of its favorable effects, when no improvement follows the first few doses. (See *Rules for the Administration and Repetition of the Dose.*)

In stupor occurring in children, from the depleting effects of neglected or protracted diarrhœa, *China* and *Arsenicum* in alternation are sometimes of considerable efficacy. Light supplementary nourishment ought at the same time to be given in the case of infants at the breast; and diet of a nutritive quality to children of more advanced age. But such, and all obstinate cases are beyond the sphere of domestic treatment.

Diet and Regimen. As the same dietetic regulations given under the head of *Cholera of Infants* are equally suitable here, the reader is referred thereto. The diet of children who are subject to diarrhœa ought at all times to be of a somewhat restricted nature. With those who are old enough, mutton is the best animal food; young meats, particularly veal and lamb, are less digestible; fish is objectionable, being, perhaps, still more liable to disagree than the last named. Unripe or acid fruits, and most vegetables, but especially potatoes, should be avoided. The clothing ought to be warm, and a flannel roller or bandage may be worn with advantage round the stomach. Wet feet ought to be guarded against; and fine woollen stockings, with thick shoes, should be worn. During the attack, friction, and the application of warm fomentations to the abdomen (belly) sometimes exert a beneficial influence. Change of air, combined with attention to the above-mentioned precautions, materially aids in warding off returns of the disease. When, notwithstanding the employment of these preventive measures, relapses still recur, a course of medical treatment becomes necessary.

Cholera of Infants.

In the autumnal season, infants are very liable to be affected with a sudden invasion of vomiting and purging, unconnected with teething or weaning, and which is sometimes of so violent a character, and so rapid in its course, as to prove speedily fatal if not timely subdued. The majority of cases are not of quite so serious a nature, still it is of importance to give early attention even to those of a milder type.

The disease sometimes sets in with purging alone, the stools being generally green, but occasionally white or yellow. Vomiting, when it does not set in spontaneously with the purging, is early superadded, and frequently exists to such an extent that nothing can be kept on the stomach, the food being constantly rejected from the stomach immediately or soon after it has been swallowed. In some instances, remissions of longer or shorter duration take place; or the purging ceases, but the infant remains, even during these intervals, in a feverish, restless, and otherwise sickly state; the features look sharp, the face pale, and the eyes sunk, half closed, and surrounded by a livid circle; fits of drowsiness supervene, but the child is easily roused, and cries much when disturbed. In protracted cases, the child becomes excessively emaciated, the pulse slow and feeble, the limbs cold, and the child gradually sinks exhausted after three or four weeks of suffering, or is rapidly cut off by a sudden exacerbation of the complaint.

TREATMENT. In general cases, *Ipecacuanha*, *Veratrum*, *Secale cornutum*, and *Arsenicum*, are the remedies which are best adapted to arrest the disease.

IPECACUANHA is, commonly, the most appropriate in the milder variety, or in those cases where the vomiting predominates.

VERATRUM corresponds to the more violent and dangerous form of the complaint, when the vomiting and purging are equally severe, and when there is insatiable thirst and considerable debility. SECALE CORNUTUM if there is predominant diarrhœa, constant crying or whining, with doubling and twisting of the body, great weakness, and aphthous* state of the tongue.

ARSENICUM is more particularly useful in delicate or scrofulous children. It is chiefly called for when the prostration of strength is extreme, the vomiting and purging incessant, the thirst intense, but the sufferings apparently aggravated by drinking even the smallest quantity; further, when the evacuations are putrid, and are preceded by severe griping, with piercing cries, and when there is coldness of the extremities and even of the tongue. *Veratrum* is sometimes required after, or in alternation with *Arsenicum*, when the latter fails to put a speedy check to the vomiting and purging.

CHAMOMILLA may be serviceable in slight attacks, when diarrhœa predominates, and the motions are of a deep green colour, but the weakness not excessive.

ADMINISTRATION OF THESE MEDICAMENTS. Six globules in an ordinary-sized wineglassful of water, a teaspoonful every half-hour, every hour,

* Thrush-like. Ulcerated.

or only every six hours, according to the urgency of the case; lengthening the intervals as soon as improvement sets in.

In protracted cases, inflammation and ulceration are liable to ensue. When the complaint does not promptly yield to the above-named remedies, assistance should be sought. If considerable weakness continues after the subjugation of the vomiting and purging, one globule of *Cinchona* may be given morning and evening for from two to four days. (See also *Diarrhœa.*)

The little patient should be kept as warm as possible when there is any tendency to coldness of the extremities. Friction, performed under the bed-clothes, or before the fire, often assists in restoring the obstructed circulation.

DIET. In the severer forms of the affection, barley or rice-water, to which a little pure sugar has been added, or thin arrow-root made with water, may be given, in teaspoonfuls at a time, to children who have already been weaned, as soon as the stomach is capable of retaining a little nourishment. In the milder varieties,—and in the first named, when a favorable change takes place, and appetite returns,—arrow-root, and then chicken-broth, or well-boiled rice moistened with water or with light gravy, if the digestive powers will allow of this latter addition. For children at the breast, it is sometimes necessary to dilute the milk with a little water, before it can be borne by the highly irritable stomach.

Inflammation of the Stomach and Bowels.

Inflammatory affections of the stomach and bowels, particularly of the latter, are sometimes so insidious in their invasion and progress as to lead to a fatal result without giving rise to any suspicion of their having been in existence. The following are some of the more striking evidences of their presence. Prostration of strength early in the career of the child's indisposition; heat of the skin, but especially of that part which is over the seat of the inflammation, with concurrent excessive fulness, tension and tenderness of the stomach and bowels; sometimes fulness and quickness, but more frequently smallness and quickness of pulse; occasional constipation, but oftener purging,—the stools being generally very green, or thin, yellow and frothy; vomiting, sometimes of feculent matter; dryness and redness of the tongue or of its tip and margins; intense thirst, usually accompanied by an increase of suffering after cold drinks; obstructed or scanty and high-coloured urine; anxious, sunken countenance; rapid and impeded respiration; sometimes dry irritating cough, unattended with any signs of inflammation in the chest; lastly, crying and starting during sleep, heat of head, intolerance of sound and of light, spasms of the extremities, or convulsions. The child generally lies on its back, with its limbs drawn up, is very restless or uneasy, yet averse to movement.

TREATMENT. When the inflammation runs high, or is attended with marked febrile symptoms and obstructed or scanty and high-coloured urine, six globules of *Aconitum* may be dissolved in an ounce of water, (about two tablespoonfuls,) and a teaspoonful of the solution given every three or six hours, according to the urgency of the case. As soon, however, as the temperature of the body becomes lowered, or a greater or less degree of moisture appears on the surface, the medicine must be discontinued, and another remedy selected soon afterwards, if required, in accordance with the remaining symptoms. If, in addition to the symptoms above enumerated, there is heat of the head, with congestion or fulness of its vessels; a wild or fixed look, and intolerance of light; cries and startings during sleep; great acceleration of pulse; thirst; vivid red margins and tip of the tongue; convulsive movements of the limbs; extreme tenderness and distension of the bowels, causing the child to wince and scream under the pressure of the hand; with or without vomiting; and the bowels either confined or relaxed, the motions, in the latter case, being greenish or whitish, *Belladonna* should be administered, in alternation with *Aconitum*, every two to four hours, or given alone, in the same way as described after *Aconite*, when the febrile symptoms are less decided.* In slighter cases, or in those where the head is less involved, but the bowels more irritable,—the stools being frequent, of a deep green, or watery and very yellow or whitish,—the fundament red, or as if excoriated; the bowels excessively inflated; with more or less tenderness on pressure; thirst; dryness of the mouth and tongue; extreme restlessness and peevishness; startings during sleep, or sudden cries, and some tendency to convulsions, *Chamomilla* is of much utility. Again, when there is diarrhœa with painful straining, with green or frothy stools sometimes mixed with blood, hardness and fulness of the belly, and the appearance of aphthæ (small circular white ulcerations) in the mouth, or around the outlet of the last intestine

* When the symptoms are aggravated by cold drinks, or, as is frequently the case, the child will only partake of warm fluids, a drop or two of tepid water may be added to each spoonful of the medicine; or, particularly when the stomach is very irritable, the medicine may be administered undissolved,—one globule being given at each dose.

(fundament), *Mercurius* is of considerable service. Lastly, *Nux v.* may be named as a useful remedy, either after the previous employment of *Aconite*, or independently of that remedy, when there is flatulent distension of the stomach and bowels, obstinate constipation, excessive debility, thirst, foulness of the tongue, with redness of the tip and margins; *Lachesis* when *Belladonna* or *Mercurius* have either failed to relieve, or have effected only partial or temporary improvement; *Opium* when there is vomiting of feculent matter, provided *Belladonna* or *Nux v.* are not better indicated by the other symptoms; and *Arsenicum* when there is extreme irritability of stomach and bowels, dryness and redness of the tongue, intense thirst, vomiting and purging immediately after drinking, coldness or livid colour of the skin, quickness and extreme weakness of the pulse, and entire prostration. But these latter, and indeed most cases of this disease, ought, when possible, to be placed under medical observation, particularly when they do not speedily improve under the action of the medicine administered. Warm fomentations to the abdomen are often soothing. Immersing the child, when not too enfeebled, up to the ribs, in a tepid bath, for half an hour, is also of some service.

DIET. When the inflammation is severe, or

affects the upper part of the alimentary canal, the stomach is so irritable that almost everything introduced into it is speedily rejected; but as soon as these and other acute symptoms have been overcome, the lightest nourishment, such as rice, barley, or gum-water, slightly sweetened, may be given, in the quantity of a teaspoonful at a time, and cold in preference to warm, at the commencement. Light broths, particularly chicken-broth, may then be essayed, and, subsequently, in the case of children who are old enough, well-boiled rice moistened with broth, or a little gràvy, especially that of roast mutton; and so on, gradually increasing the quantity and altering the quality of the food as improvement advances, taking every possible care never to overtax the weakened digestive powers.

Invermination. Worms.

It is often difficult to determine the existence of worms in the alimentary canal. The popular idea as to the symptoms which indicate their presence is founded upon evidence which can but be regarded as demonstrative of irritation of the lining membrane of the stomach and bowels. Nothing, indeed, can be received, with certainty, as confirmatory of their existence but their ejection, and ocular testimony of the fact.

SYMPTOMS. The symptoms which ought, at all events, to excite suspicions as to the existence of worms, are: paleness and emaciation; pungent wringing, and fitful pain about the navel and pit of the stomach; irritation and itching, with heat of the posterior passage, and irregular action of the bowels; fastidious appetite; irritation of the nose; excessive faintness, and a sense of hunger without inclination to eat when food is produced; uneasiness; depression of spirits; languor; restlessness and anxiety. The brain and lungs are often sympathetically affected; and dull or pressive aching pains in the head, convulsions, dilated pupils, fixed, wild look, and a dry, hacking cough, often prevail; or there may be vomiting, hiccup, diarrhœa, straining, suppression of water, difficulty in passing water, grinding of the teeth, and starting during sleep. Frequently there is aggravation after eating sweets, milk diet, salted meats, raw fruit, &c.; and often a sudden disappearance of all the symptoms on the voiding of worms.

There are three species of worms—the *thread-worm*, the *round worm*, and the *tape-worm*. There are two varieties of thread-worms, viz., the long thread-worm and the short thread-worm. The former chiefly inhabits the large intestines, is about two inches long, of a white colour, and resembles a thread. The latter, the ascaris, or ascarides as they are usually denominated, also occupy the large intestines, but are more frequently located in the last intestine, where they generally create an almost insupportable itching; and are frequently to be seen, like minute animated fragments of thread, rapidly moving about in the recently passed evacuations; or they may be observed in congregated numbers around the fundament, and are sometimes even found in the bed in which a child much infested by them has slept. Tape-worm is rarely met with in children. The varieties which give rise to the greatest constitutional disturbance are the round worm and the short thread-worm, particularly the latter. When the symptoms originate from the round worm, they commonly consist in griping about the navel, excessive emaciation, voracious appetite, and a feeling of sickly faintness. Whilst the same indications combined with a nauseating or gnawing pain in the stomach, and more especially, the itching in the nose and in the last intestine, denote the existence of ascarides.

Causes. Anything which tends to bring about a morbid state of the mucous or lining membrane of the stomach and bowels, such as the constant or frequent use of indigestible or innutritious food, a residence in low-lying, damp, ill-ventilated dwellings, &c. &c., favours the generation of worms. Scrofulous or otherwise sickly children are predisposed to be affected with them.

TREATMENT. In cases of thread-worm, when there are considerable febrile symptoms, with nocturnal restlessness, peevishness, and continual itching and smarting in the last intestine, *Aconitum*, for infants one, and for a child more advanced two globules may be given in a dessert-spoonful of water, and repeated about every eight hours, until the febrile symptoms subside.

IPECACUANHA may be administered in the same manner, twenty-four hours after *Aconite*, if the bowels are in a relaxed state, and the child complains of a sense of sinking or faintness in the stomach; also when there is vomiting, oppressed and accelerated breathing, suffocating cough, great listlessness, and aversion to exercise. The employment of *Cina* and *Ipecacuanha* in *alternation* for three or four days, is sometimes very beneficial when the symptoms consist of a combination of those we have mentioned under both remedies. (See *Cina.*)

NUX V. is preferable to *Ipecacuanha*, when constipation predominates; or when there are alternations of diarrhœa and constipation.

ADMINISTRATION. Two globules, at first daily, for three days, and then every other day for a week.

IGNATIA should generally be resorted to when *Nux v.* is ineffectual. Or it may be selected in preference to that remedy when convulsive twitchings of the limbs frequently occur.

ADMINISTRATION. Same as *Nux v.*

SULPHUR is commonly the best subsequent medicine.

ADMINISTRATION. Two globules night and morning, every eight or ten days, for a period of four or five weeks. When only temporary benefit results from the use of *Sulphur*, a similar course of *Silicea*, and then *Calcarea*, may be given.

URTICA URENS (one drop of the tincture in a little water on a lump of loaf sugar) is often a useful palliative against the irritation and itching of the passage, and in default of this remedy, a clyster of one dessert-spoonful of salt dissolved in one pint of water, of which from two to six fluid ounces may be injected.

Against *Round-worm* :—

CINA—(for an infant, one globule, dissolved in four teaspoonsful of water, of which one teaspoonful should be administered in the morning and evening; for a child more advanced, three globules, in four dessert-spoonsful of water, one dessert-spoonful similarly*)—when there is great itching and obstruction of the nose; perverseness; fever chills towards evening; restlessness; cries and startings during sleep; blackness about the eyes; dilated pupils; hard, quick pulse; rapid changes of colour in the face; fits of delirium; clammy tongue; eructations or vomiting; constant craving for food; distension, heat, and hardness of the stomach; costiveness, or purging; sometimes the stools consisting merely of a little mucus, which is passed after much straining; convulsive twitchings of the limbs; lassitude; thick, whitish urine; habitual wetting of the bed at night.

ACONITUM is sometimes required before *Cina;* and indeed, before, or in alternation with, most of the remedies employed in the early stage against both varieties of worms. It may be given in the manner already described. When *Cina* produces only partial improvement, some other medicament must be had recourse to. Generally speaking, *Mercurius* and then *Sulphur* are the most appropriate with which to follow up the treatment; but *Nux v.*, *Ipecacuanha*, or *Belladonna*, &c., are sometimes required; in short, the choice of the remedy must here, as in every other malady, be selected

* See rules for the administration and repetition of doses.

as closely in accordance with the symptoms as possible. Thus MERCURIUS is more especially called for when diarrhœa, with straining and bloody stools, accompanies the presence of worms; or when the motions are scanty, consisting only of a little slime, and there is an increased flow of saliva, with much hardness and distension of the abdomen, particularly about the navel.

NUX VOMICA, when there is considerable derangement of the digestive functions, manifested by foul tongue, inclination to vomit, impaired appetite, thirst, tenderness at the pit of the stomach on pressure; fulness, and sensation of heat in the stomach and bowels; constipation, sometimes in alternation with diarrhœa; depression, peevishness, and exacerbation of the symptoms every morning.

IPECACUANHA, when vomiting predominates, and when a continued sense of uneasiness and faintness is experienced in the stomach. *Pulsatilla*, when the symptoms nearly resemble those that have been enumerated under *Nux vomica*, with the distinction that they are more frequently, though not always, increased towards evening, and when there is a more constant tendency to looseness of the bowels.

ADMINISTRATION. *Nux*, *Ipecac.*, and *Puls.*, same as *Cina*, which see.

BELLADONNA should be resorted to when there are marked symptoms of symptomatic derangement of the brain, or when the sympathetic irritation caused by worms has terminated in inflammatory action. These manifestations are chiefly as follows: starting during sleep, nocturnal delirium, disposition to be frightened or agitated by the most trivial cause; also when there is heat of the head, headache, excessive thirst, quickness of pulse, heat of skin, wild expression of the eye and dilated pupils. *Lachesis* is sometimes required after *Belladonna.* *Sulphur*, as has already been stated, is commonly required after *Mercurius.* It is, moreover, very frequently of service in winding up the cure after the previous use of the other medicines here named.

ADMINISTRATION (i. e. of *Bella.*) For an infant, two globules, in four dessert-spoonfuls of water, a teaspoonful of the solution every six to eight hours; for a child of a more advanced age, four globules, in the same quantity of water, a teaspoonful at the stated intervals.

Great attention should, in all cases of *worms,* be paid to ventilation, exercise, cleanliness, and to the wholesome quality of the diet. Animal food should predominate,—plainly roasted or boiled. Salt may be taken somewhat freely at meals; but salt meats and rich made dishes, as also sweetmeats, pastry, and the greater part of vegetables, especially raw herbs, or roots, or uncooked fruits, are inadmissible.

Mesenteric Disease.

This affection, of which the immediate seat is in the mesenteric glands, may arise from, or be attendant upon, or be followed by affections of the intestinal lining membrane. Nor is it easy, in the first stage of the complaint, to distinguish when there actually exists a disease in the mesenteric glands, or to pronounce that certain given symptoms do not simply arise from irritation in the mucous membrane of the stomach and bowels. Mesenteric disease is most prevalent amongst children of strumous (scrofulous) habit of body, and has been itself classed as a scrofulous complaint. It does not appear in children until the age of seven or eight months, because the glands have not till then become sufficiently developed; but it is of the more frequent occurrence, amongst those of a particular constitutional tendency, from the third to the sixth or seventh year. Its character is clearly tubercular.* It consists in irritation of the mesenteric glands, terminating in their

* Tubercle—a morbid product occurring in various textures of the body, in association with a peculiar and unhealthy state of the system.

enlargement, softening, or suppuration, and is very generally associated with diseased glands in the neck, or with tubercles in the lungs (tubercular consumption).

This disease is most common amongst the ill-fed and ill-conditioned children of the poor, and especially amongst those of a scrofulous habit. Unwholesome food, combined with impure air, forms, in general, the principal exciting cause of the malady; but it may, as already stated, follow in the wake of inflammation or ulceration of the lining or mucous membrane of the bowels, or become developed, in children of bad constitution, after measles, or during protracted or renewed attacks of infantile remittent fever.

SYMPTOMS. A slow, gradual, but regular process of emaciation, combined with tenderness on pressure, and the perception of hard and knotty swellings about the centre of the abdomen, characterise the affection in its established form. There is usually a very fastidious appetite, at times exceedingly craving, at others squeamish, and, sometimes, also a strong desire for food which is of the most pernicious kind, but which when partaken of, does not produce that aggravation of symptoms which accrues therefrom in simple derangements of the digestive organs. Considerable induration and protuberance of the belly ensue as the limbs become more and more attenuated; and however well nourished the child may be, he continues to lose flesh; and marked disorder of the stomach and bowels generally supervenes. Indigestion and derangement of the stomach, with white chalky stools are often observed; and occasionally the presence of worms in the intestinal canal may be distinguished. When the complaint follows its usual slow and protracted course, hectic fever sets in, and the scene closes with debilitating sweats and diarrhœa; but in more acute and rapid cases, decided symptoms of remittent fever appear, and the child is carried off by acute inflammation of the intestines.

During the progress of the ordinary form of mesenteric disease, there is extreme sensibility to cold, and a constant desire to be near the fire; there is also a lethargic indolence and aversion to any movement, with obtuseness of the faculties, and much peevishness. Sleep is rarely much disturbed; the skin is usually cold, dry, harsh, and corrugated, but becomes heated towards evening. Profuse morning sweats now break out, particularly about the head and chest, and the pulse becomes hard and accelerated. Continuous purging then attends, and the child sinks exhausted in a state of excessive emaciation.

TREATMENT. As this disease is of so serious a character, and, when fairly established, so difficult to arrest, we must be excused from attempting to enter deeply into the details of its treatment in a work like the present. Suffice it, therefore, to remark that, in the first stage of the complaint, if there be some fever, with heat of skin, tenderness of the belly to the touch, and other signs of inflammatory action, the remedies which have been enumerated under the head of *Inflammation of the Stomach and Bowels*, may be resorted to.

At a more advanced stage of the malady, when the glands in the abdomen are swollen and tender, and those of the neck or in the armpit are likewise enlarged, *Belladonna*, *Mercurius*, *Sulphur*, *Calcarea*, and *Acidum nitricum*, are the more generally useful remedies. And *Kreosotum*, *Lachesis*, *Cinchona*, *Arsenicum*, and *Phosphorus*, when the diarrhœa, emaciation, and debility are excessive. (See art. *Diarrhœa*, for some of the leading indications for these last-named medicaments.) *Iodium*, *Baryta c.*, *Hepar*, *Cina*, &c., are serviceable in some cases, and *Phosphorus*, *Kali c.*, and *Acidum nitricum*, are sometimes of considerable utility when the lungs are implicated. Fomentations and abdominal frictions occasionally exert a soothing and otherwise beneficial influence.

DIET. The regulation of the diet depends upon

various circumstances, such as the state of the digestive functions, the strength of the patient and so forth. In all cases it should be light, and of easy digestion. Animal broths are required in advanced stages, where there is much debility; but if there is more or less fever, or if symptoms of some degree of inflammatory action are present, —arrow-root, sago, semolina, and the like, will claim a preference.

Derangement of the Stomach.

Under this head I intend treating of a disorder which is of frequent occurrence in improperly fed children.

The ordinary causes of this derangement are: hurried, imperfect mastication: overloading the stomach; fat greasy, indigestible or tainted food; flatulent vegetables; ices; stimulants, &c. The symptoms are so well known, that it is hardly necessary here to enter upon them, particularly as they will be more specially noted under the different medicines.

TREATMENT. We may premise by enumerating the homœopathic remedies which are more especially called for by the exciting causes of the indisposition :—

When derangement of stomach, or a fit of indigestion, has been brought on by imperfect mastication, or by overloading the stomach, *Ipecacuanha* and *Pulsatilla* are, in general, the most useful medicines. In other cases, though less frequently, *Nux v.* or *Cinchona* are more appropriate.

When *rich, indigestible food* has given rise to the disturbance, *Pulsatilla* or *Ipecac.* and *Carbo v.*

When ices, or cold fruits, have been the exciting cause, *Pulsatilla, Arsenicum, Carbo v.*

When tainted food (meat or fish), *Pulsatilla, Cinchona, Carbo v.*

When salt meat, or other salted articles of food, *Carbo v.* or *Arsenicum* chiefly.

And when it has arisen from vinegar or other acids, *Aconitum, Arsenicum,* and *Carbo v.* chiefly.

When the symptoms of approaching stomachic derangement declare themselves immediately, or a few hours after a repast which has been too freely partaken of, a cupful of strong coffee, without milk and unsweetened, is frequently a sufficient restorative.

When sick headache and inclination to vomit, or actual vomiting, and other symptoms of derangement of stomach, as sensation of weight and fulness in the stomach, flatulence, foul tongue, risings of food, or disagreeable and offensive eructations come on immediately, or a few hours after a repast which has been indulged in to excess, we should assist nature by tickling the throat with a feather, and by giving tepid water to drink until the stomach has completely evacuated its contents. If, nevertheless, on the following morning, any symptoms of indigestion remain, we may administer ANTIMONIUM CRUDUM and PULSATILLA alternately, by dissolving six globules of each remedy separately in an ordinary-sized wineglassful of water, and giving a dessert-spoonful first of the one, then the other, every three or four hours, until relief is afforded. These medicaments are also calculated to remove the disturbance above indicated when, in addition to the symptoms of disordered stomach, a degree of *fever* returns every second day.

IPECACUANHA is a very effectual remedy when continuous and most distressing *nausea* forms the most prominent symptom. Its alternate employment with *Pulsatilla* (in the same way as described for *Antim.* and *Puls.*) is preferable in cases which have been brought on by a very hearty and hurried meal, the stomach having consequently been overloaded with imperfectly masticated food; and also when *rash* has been thrown out from the effects of a disordered stomach, attended with anxiety, *oppressed breathing*, and sickness,—but should the difficulty of breathing, and a degree of nausea, or other uneasiness continue, BRYONIA must be resorted to. (*Tartarus emeticus* is sometimes more efficacious than either *Ipecac.* or *Bryonia*, when great drowsiness, with constant nausea and frequent vomiting, relaxed, brownish-yellow motions, accompany the oppression.)

Administration of these Medicines. See the end of the chapter.

Bryonia. In addition to the usefulness of this remedy in the foregoing instance, it is also very serviceable when the following symptoms are present: bitter eructations; *fever*, alternately with coldness and shivering; or redness of the face, heat in the head, and thirst with coldness and shivering, also when diarrhœa or constipation and peevishness, or excessive irritability, are present. (In derangement of the stomach arising from dry, or from succulent vegetables, and attended with excessive flatulency, this remedy is frequently productive of speedy relief.)

Pulsatilla, as has already been stated, is of much service, in alternation with *Antim. c.* or with *Ipecac.*, in recent cases of disordered digestion, when a *rash* has been thrown out in consequence of the derangement, and when there are risings of food, foul tongue, sometimes covered with mucus; chilliness and lowness of spirits. It is, moreover, almost specific when the disturbance has arisen from the effects of rich food, such as *pork* or pastry, or even tainted meat; or from the effects of *ices, cold fruits, or crude vegetables, acid, wine*, &c., particularly when chilliness and depression of spirits accompany the other symptoms. *Arsenicum* is generally preferable to *Pulsatilla* when the derangement has been induced by eating an ice; but their *alternate* employment is often attended with great advantage when *cold fruits* have given rise to the indisposition.

ARSENICUM: When there are acrid and bitter eructations with nausea and vomiting; also, dry tongue, excessive thirst, salt taste in the mouth, and burning or violent pressure in the stomach, with diarrhœa or colic, and griping in the lower part of the belly, particularly when arising from the effects of an *ice* which had been partaken of when warm; or from fruit, stale vegetables, or *acids*. It may, in many cases, be advantageously followed by *Carbo vegetabilis*, which see.

NUX VOMICA is indicated by offensive or acrid eructations, constipation, and confused headache, particularly when arising from *wine* or *other* stimulants which children may have been injudiciously allowed to partake of; when possible, it should be taken the same night, as taken in the morning, although eventually relieving, it frequently causes temporary aggravation in *susceptible* patients. (In derangement of the stomach with heartburn, flatulence, more or less nausea and headache, &c., in consequence of a chill, or of indulging in mental or corporal exertion immediately after a meal, this remedy commonly affords speedy amelioration.)

Aconite: When the affection owes its origin to partaking of sour beer, vinegar, or other acids; and particularly when there is great heat in the head, anxiety, restlessness, full quick pulse, nausea, or vomiting of mucus.

When a fit of passion has produced an attack of indigestion, *Chamomilla* rarely fails to relieve. *Bryonia* is, however, to be preferred when chilliness and shivering accompany the symptoms of derangement of stomach.

Carbo vegetabilis, although last mentioned, is not one of the least useful remedies in this affection, and is often found very serviceable after *Pulsatilla*, *Arsenicum*, or *Nux vomica*, in removing any symptoms that may remain; it is, moreover, particularly useful where great susceptibility to the influence of the atmosphere, especially to cold, exists at the same time: or in sufferings arising from abuse of *wine*, *ices*, or salted meat, &c. Further, in derangement of the stomach arising from having partaken of game or fish which has been too long kept, or meat that has been recooked whilst in a state of fermentation,—as is liable to occur in warm weather. In the latter instances, *Carbo v.*

is to be preferred to any other medicine, and will rarely fail to afford relief;* but if any disagreeable symptoms remain, *Cinchona* may be administered in a little water; and followed if required, by *Pulsatilla.*

ADMINISTRATION OF THE REMEDIES. In slight cases, a single dose, consisting of three or four globules, in a dessert-spoonful of water, will be sufficient; but in those of a severer description, it will commonly be requisite to dissolve six or eight globules in two tablespoonfuls of water, and give a dessert-spoonful of the solution every three to four hours, until the symptoms begin to yield, when the intervals between the doses must be lengthened, or the medicine discontinued. The alternate administration, when called for, has already been alluded to.

DIET. A stomach which has been but slightly overtaxed, will generally recover its tone simply after a few hours' abstinence from food; in cases attended with greater disturbance of the system, it will be necessary, in addition to giving appro-

* A small quantity of finely-powdered charcoal, in a little good French brandy, will be found an equally efficacious mode of administering this remedy as a corrective against derangement of the stomach arising from having partaken of tainted meat or fish.

priate medicine, to enjoin a light diet, even for a few days after the removal of the symptoms.

Vomiting.

This may proceed from a variety of causes, and must therefore be prescribed for in accordance therewith.

When it arises from excess in eating or drinking, *Antimonium*, *Pulsatilla*, *Ipecacuanha*, and *Nux v.* are the most useful remedies. (See *Derangement of Stomach.*) When from foulness of stomach, *Pulsatilla*, *Nux v.*, *Bryonia*, &c. (See *Indigestion of Infants*, and *Derangement of Stomach.*) When from affections of the head, *Arnica*, *Belladonna*, *Lachesis*, etc. (Vid. *Inflammation of the Brain.*) See also *Invermina* and *Colic*, as either of these may prove to be the origin of the affection in particular instances.

In ordinary cases, when there is uncertainty as to the cause of the vomiting, it should be promoted by copious draughts of tepid water when homœopathic medicines are not at hand. But as the medicines are usually of speedy efficacy, and as they form a much more agreeable mode of giving relief, particularly to children, they should invariably be preferred, when there is no reason whatever for concluding that the derangement does not arise from the introduction of poison into the stomach. The medicaments which may generally be resorted to with the most benefit are, *Antimonium c.*, *Ipecacuanha*, and *Arsenicum*. Of these *Antimonium* may be preferred when the tongue is covered with a white or yellow fur, *Ipecacuanha* when it is clean, *Arsenicum* when the vomiting is violent and scanty.

ADMINISTRATION. Six globules of the remedy selected in three dessert-spoonfuls, a dessert-spoonful every hour, or only every three or four hours according to the severity of the symptoms.

When vomiting proceeds from weakness or debility of stomach (*irritable stomach*), *Pulsatilla*, *Nux v.*, *Bryonia*, *Cocculus*, *Arsenicum*, *Hyoscyamus*, *Sulphur*, and *Calcarea*. *Pulsatilla*, is commonly of great service when the stomach is so delicate and irritable that it is only capable of retaining the smallest possible quantity of food at a time; a transgression being invariably followed by vomiting, attended with severe spasms, or vomiting of viscid phlegm, giddiness, diarrhœa, and even fainting. When *Pulsatilla* produces but partial relief, *Cocculus* may be administered. If *Cocculus* fail to relieve, *Bryonia*, and then *Nux v.*, may be given, followed in turn, if required, by *Cinchona* and *Ferrum*. *Sulphur* and *Calcarea* may wind up the cure in all obstinate cases, and *Arsenicum* and *Hyoscyamus* may be given as intercurrent remedies when the vomiting is excessively violent.

Administration of these Remedies. Two globules, morning and evening, in a dessert-spoonful of water, for four consecutive days. An interval of four or eight days to be allowed between the different medicines.

In cases of vomiting which come on either periodically or in consequence of errors in diet, exposure to cold, &c., and in which the matter ejected consists chiefly or entirely of bile (*bilious vomiting, bilious attacks*, accompanied by *headache*, brownish-yellow tongue, bitter or nauseous taste, sometimes pain in the right side and between the shoulders, disgust at the very thought of food,—*Nux v.*, *Pulsatilla*, *Mercurius*, *Cinchona*, *Ipecacuanha*, *Arsenicum*, *Veratrum*, *Sulphur*, *Calcarea*. In a large number of cases, *Nux v.* is the most appropriate remedy, but particularly those which are liable to be brought on by sedentary habits, severe mental application, or by mental annoyance; also when errors in diet (especially as regards vinous liquors) invariably bring on an attack. The *symptoms* which call for *Nux v.* are closely analogous to those above described. A confined state of the bowels is another indication for its employment.

Administration. The globules, at first every two, then every four hours, as the vomiting, &c. subsides.

Pulsatilla is called for by a nearly similar

train of symptoms, but is generally more efficacious when the bowels are more or less relaxed, and is better adapted to persons of mild or sensitive dispositions; whereas *Nux v.* is preferable for those of quick, irascible temper, or who are subject to great depression of spirits, attended with aversion to mental or physical exertion.

ADMINISTRATION. Same as *Nux v.*

When either of these fail to afford much relief, *Mercurius* is often of service. This remedy is moreover called for when the tendency to nausea or vomiting is attended with a distressing feeling of fulness and tension, as if the head were tightly bound.

ADMINISTRATION. Six globules, in three dessert-spoonfuls of water, one every three hours.

IPECACUANHA generally forms a useful remedy when bilious vomiting is apt to be excited by exposure to cold. It is frequently serviceable in other cases, when there is much nausea, with paroxysms of free and copious vomiting, and pain in the entire head as if it had been severely bruised.

ADMINISTRATION. Same as *Nux v.*

ARSENICUM may follow, if the sickness and retching continue to a distressing degree; or it may be selected in preference to *Ipecac.*, when the evacuation of the contents of the stomach is painfully difficult, but the efforts are incessant, or are prone to be renewed on the slightest movement, although the feeling of general uneasiness renders it difficult for the patient to remain quiescent; also when there is excessive thirst, with aversion to drink, or inclination to drink only small quantities at a time, and great debility. Further, when bilious colic and diarrhœa accompany the attack, or when the attacks are invariably preceded or followed by severe nervous headache (megrim), *Arsenicum* is a most valuable remedy.

ADMINISTRATION. Six globules, in two table-spoonfuls of water, a dessert-spoonful at first every hour, then every two to four hours, as the symptoms subside.

VERATRUM may sometimes be administered in alternation every hour or every two hours with *Arsenicum*, when that remedy brings only partial relief. It is an important remedy in the severest forms of bilious vomiting, attended with distressing headache, and preceded or accompanied by copious discharges of pale urine; also when fainting is liable to occur from the violence of the attack.

ADMINISTRATION. Same as *Arsenicum*.

When bilious attacks are attended with febrile symptoms, ACONITUM should be given before any other remedy. In such cases, indeed, it will frequently be sufficient to put a speedy stop to the attack.

Administration. Six globules, in three dessert-spoonfuls of water, one every three hours.

Cinchona, three globules, repeated after twelve hours, may very generally be given with advantage at the termination of every severe bilious attack. It is also of much utility, in some cases, at the commencement—particularly when the affection occurs in debilitated children, and in those who have been dosed with calomel or blue pill for this affection. It requires to be followed by *Hepar sulphuris* in the latter case.

Diet and Regimen. Same as for children who are affected with *Derangement of Stomach* (which see), as also *Jaundice*. During the paroxysm there is usually such disgust for food of all kinds, that it is better not to torment the patient by coaxing him to take something. As soon as the appetite returns, a cup of weak tea, with some cold toast may be allowed.

Constipation.

This is a disorder which is generally sympathetic with some other derangement of the digestive organs, either proceeding from constitutional tendency derived from the parents, or from want of air and exercise combined with too much solid food, especially animal. It is, moreover, often aggravated or confirmed by the frequent use of aperients. The affection is far more common amongst infants brought up by hand, than amongst those that are suckled at the breast.

TREATMENT. In obstinate cases a lavement of tepid milk and water,* or the introduction by gentle rotatory movement, of a twisted strip of paper or linen, moistened with oil, may be resorted to. If, after the lapse of twenty-four to thirty-six hours or so, no relief ensues, recourse may again be had to the lavement with the addition of a little treacle. Repeated friction of the stomach with the hand will sometimes tend to facilitate operation.

Besides this palliative treatment, and in order to overcome any constitutional predisposition to the disorder, one or more of the following medicines may be administered: *Nux v.*, *Bryonia*, *Pulsatilla*, *Opium*, and *Sulphur*, according to symptoms.

* An infant at its birth, or soon after, requires about an ounce or so of fluid; a child between the ages of one and five years, from three to six ounces; and a youth of ten or fifteen, from eight to ten. The tube of the lavement apparatus should be lubricated with oil, and introduced very cautiously.

In ordinary cases, NUX V. and SULPHUR are the most useful, particularly when want of air and exercise have chiefly contributed to bring on the symptoms.

The immediate indications for NUX V. are flatulence, foul tongue, hardness and distension of the stomach and bowels; obstinate constipation, or costiveness, with offensive, hard and knotty, dark-brown coloured stools; also when there is languor and debility, great peevishness, sleeplessness, or drowsiness during the day, with disturbed and restless nights.

ADMINISTRATION. In cases of recent origin, two globules may be given, and repeated after an interval of twenty-four hours. Four days after the second dose of *Nux v.*, if no material improvement has followed, *Sulphur* may be given in the same way, and then again *Nux v.* after five or six days. In cases of long standing, one to three globules may be administered every other day for a week or a fortnight, but as soon as a favourable change ensues the medicine may be discontinued. (See *Rules for the Repetition of the Medicines.*)

When the child seems constantly chilly, or feels cold to the touch, and is almost always dissatisfied and fretful, *Bryonia* is, generally, preferable to *Nux v.* *Bryonia* is, moreover, commonly better adapted to constipation or sluggishness of the bowels occurring during summer, and when the stools are very dark, and of an unusually large size; or when, with infants at the breast, the motions are more formed than is usually the case.

ADMINISTRATION. Same as *Nux v.* The alternate employment of *Bryonia* and *Nux v.* is sometimes productive of the most satisfactory results.

OPIUM is well adapted to robust-looking children, who are, in short, in good health in all other respects, but are subject to costive, hard, knotty, dark-brown motions, often with hardness of the belly, or irregularity at the sides,—communicating the impression of lumps when felt by the hand.

ADMINISTRATION. Same as *Nux v.*

PULSATILLA is indicated when the constipated state of the bowels is accompanied by foulness of tongue, flatulence, and other symptoms of impaired digestion; or when the evacuations are scanty, often very offensive, and either of a dark green or pale colour. *Pulsatilla* is better adapted to children of fair complexion, or who are very sensitive, and easily disposed to shed tears, than *Nux v.* and *Bryonia.*

LACHESIS is frequently a highly serviceable remedy in obstinate constipation occurring in otherwise healthy children; but more particularly in inveterate costiveness with hard and difficult motions, the stools being (as noted under *Opium* and *Nux v.*) knotty (small, hard, and bullet-like, or resembling the excrements of sheep,) or scanty and whitish, like half-baked clay,—generally attended with hardness and distention of the stomach and bowels, flatulency, and other signs of deranged digestion.

ADMINISTRATION. Same as *Nux v.*

SEPIA is sometimes useful after *Lachesis;* in other cases *Sulphur* is more appropriate; indeed there are few cases of constipation, or habitual costiveness, in which *Sulphur* is not more or less necessary to complete the cure.

In some urgent cases, or in protracted obstipation (i. e. where no evacuation whatever takes place from the bowels for about two days in the case of infants, and for several days in the case of children of a more advanced age,) and particularly when the employment of mechanical means (injections, &c.) fails to produce the desired effect, the medicines may be administered at shorter intervals than above stated, and in solution; as, for instance, *Nux v.*, one to two globules, for an infant, and three to four for a child of from two to six years of age and upwards, in six teaspoonsful of water, a teaspoonful every six or eight hours. The lavement, or other mechanical means, may again be resorted to if necessary, after the second or third dose of the medicine. In a large number of cases, of recent origin, the bowels will generally act of their own accord after from two to six days, In children who are able to run about, it is, therefore, only necessary to have recourse to medicine when symptoms of general indisposition supervene, or when constipation threatens to become habitual.

Diet and Regimen. In recent cases, the diet should be very light for some days. In those of longer standing it should be moderate and unstimulating, and the proportion of animal food small. Perfectly ripe, non-acid fruits, such as grapes, strawberries, and gooseberries; and some dried fruits, such as the best qualities of plums and figs, as also stewed apples and pears, together with tender, well-boiled vegetables of a wholesome description, may be allowed with advantage, provided they are found to suit the digestive powers, and do not give rise to acidity, flatulence, &c. But all vegetables which abound in fibrous or ligneous matter, as, for instance, radishes, turnips, cabbages, &c., as likewise green and acid fruits, raisins, currants, &c., should be prohibited. Too dry a diet is also objectionable; a sufficiency of pure water should, therefore, be allowed. Half a tumbler of cold water may be drunk with benefit every morning on first waking, and once or twice more in the course of the day, between meals. Daily exercise, but not beyond the child's strength, particularly if of delicate constitution, is of much utility. Infants should be taken regularly into the open air. If they are spoon-fed, a change should be made in the diet, and such aliments as highly-baked flour, isinglass, and arrow-root discontinued, in consequence of their somewhat astringent property.

Infantile Remittent Fever.

By infantile remittent is here chiefly meant that form of fever which arises from morbid irritability, inflammation, or even ulceration, in the mucous membrane of the stomach and bowels.

The exciting causes of this remittent fever are principally indigestible food, the impression of cold, or the effects of season—the malady appearing occasionally to extend in an epidemic form.

SYMPTOMS. The affection is usually preceded by languor; irritability of temper; drowsiness; with very restless nights; want of appetite; foul tongue; offensive breath; nausea, or vomiting; thirst; slight heat of skin; headache; pain in the stomach; flatulence; constipation, or diarrhœa; and white or turbid urine, which frequently deposits a chalk-like sediment. Ere long these symptoms present themselves in a more aggravated form, together with a further development of morbid phenomena, such as hurried and oppressed breathing; quickness of pulse; occasional flushes in the face; vomiting of food or bile; distention and tenderness of the belly; obstinate constipation; sometimes diarrhœa, or frequent desire to go to stool with but little effect; motions discoloured, fetid, frequently mixed with mucus, and occasionally with blood. The hands and feet are often cold, while the rest of the body is parched; the head hot and heavy, or attended with other symptoms resembling water in the head, such as lethargy, &c. The tongue, at first moist, loaded, and occasionally very red along the margins, often becomes dry over a triangular spot at the point; and the lips are sometimes covered with a brown fur. As soon as the fever is regularly established, remarkable aggravations, with consecutive remissions, take place during the twenty-four hours. When the febrile exacerbation takes place at night, it is accompanied by vigilance and tossing; when during the day, there is, on the other hand, drowsiness and stupor. An annoying cough with bronchitic indications,* succeeded by wheezing

* Indications of affection of the tubes of the lungs (the air-passages.)

and expectoration, sometimes appears. Although, as is characteristic of remittent fever, the febrile symptoms never entirely subside, still the patient will frequently appear to be steadily recovering for a time; and the unwary or inexperienced may consequently be led to pronounce an unduly favorable opinion, which will too often be contradicted by the occurrence of a relapse, followed perhaps again by another encouraging but deceptive remission, and so on,—unless the progress of the disease be checked,—until either the mesenteric* glands become affected, or dropsical effusion into the cavity of the belly, or unequivocal signs of disease of the brain supervene; or the little sufferer becomes so emaciated and reduced by protracted disease, that the vital powers give way, and he sinks exhausted.

TREATMENT. As already observed, infantile remittent fever is so liable, particularly in scrofulous or otherwise inherently delicate children, to terminate in water in the head, inflammation in the chest, mesenteric disease, or in general dropsy, that professional aid should be sought without delay as soon as the febrile exacerbations

* The mesentery is the membrane in the centre of the small intestines, and by means of which they are attached to the spinal column.

threaten to increase in severity or become more frequent or almost incessant. Excessive distension of the belly, startings and sudden cries during sleep, flushed face, heated head, dilated pupils, twitchings and jerkings of the limbs, drowsiness and stupor, accelerated and laborious breathing, with increase of cough, indicate that great danger is to be apprehended.

In mild attacks, occurring in tolerably healthy children, the disease may, generally, be readily subdued in a few days, by means of one or more of the following remedies: *Ipecacuanha*, *Pulsatilla*, *China*, *Nux v.*, *Aconitum*, *Belladonna*, *Mercurius*, *Bryonia*, *Lachesis*, *Chamomilla*, and *Sulphur* combined with light farinaceous diet. Solid food, particularly meat and fish, must, in general, be strictly prohibited, even though the appetite should be good, which it occasionally is, and even ravenous at times. (See also the remarks on DIET at the conclusion of the chapter.)

With regard to the indications for the remedies quoted, IPECACUANHA may be given if, as is commonly the case, the attack has been excited by over-feeding, or by indigestible food, and particularly when the patient has contracted a habit of *bolting* the food without having previously masticated it properly, and the symptoms encountered are as follows: general dry heat, or harsh and parched skin, especially towards evening; thirst; extreme restlessness; burning heat in the palms of the hands; perspiration at night; quick, oppressed breathing; foul tongue; nausea, and vomiting; or fastidious appetite, with sickness after eating; great languor, apathy, and indifference. Should these symptoms remain unaltered after several doses of *Ipecac.*, or should the bowels become very relaxed, the motions fetid, whitish, bilious, or of variable colour at different times, and accompanied with griping and distension of the belly, turbid, reddish, orange-coloured urine, fever towards evening or during the night,—PULSATILLA must be prescribed, followed, if required, by CINCHONA, especially if the nausea or vomiting has subsided, but the bowels remain relaxed, and are considerably distended, or tense and drum-like.

NUX VOMICA is also a most efficient remedy in mild cases, or in the early stage of any variety of the disorder, when the bowels are confined, or very costive, with frequent inclination to go to stool; or when there is straining, followed by scanty watery motions, generally mixed with mucus, or occasionally with a little blood; belly tumid and rather painful; further,—when the child is excessively peevish and ungovernable; the tongue foul, or vivid red at the tip and margins; the appetite impaired; or there is nausea, with disgust at food; restlessness; fever towards morning, but also in some degree during the night.

When the patient is of a plethoric habit; or in all cases in which the febrile action is excessive, the thirst great, the pulse full and greatly accelerated, the skin dry and much above the natural temperature, the water scanty and high coloured, ACONITUM is, very generally, of considerable value, either alone or in alternation with some other remedy which is more appropriate to the remaining symptoms.

CHAMOMILLA is sometimes useful after *Nux v.* when bilious diarrhœa or vomiting supervenes. It is further indicated if the tongue is red and cracked, or coated yellow; sleep lethargic, or restless and agitated, attended with frequent starts and jerkings of the limbs; flushes of heat in various parts of the body. Also when the head is hot and heavy, the skin hot or parched, the face flushed, the pulse quick; and when there is thirst, foul tongue, nausea, or bilious vomiting; no motions; or frequent and scanty, greenish evacuations with straining; turbid, bright yellow or orange-coloured urine.

BELLADONNA may succeed *Chamomilla* if the head continues hot, the pulse excessively quick and full, the tongue loaded, or coated white or yellow in the centre, and very red at the edges; also thirst, nausea or vomiting; great heat of the belly, with tenderness on the slightest pressure; oppressed breathing. If the more active inflammatory symptoms yield to the action of *Belladonna*, —MERCURIUS will sometimes suffice to complete the cure; but more particularly when the following symptoms remain; loaded tongue, nausea or vomiting, with continued tenderness of the belly; thirst, sometimes with aversion to drinks when offered; cloudy or milk-like urine; no motions, or diarrhœa with excessive straining, the stools generally consisting merely of a little slime, sometimes mixed with blood. If, on the other hand, the head continue hot and heavy; the pulse quick; the tongue foul, or very dry, particularly at the tip; and other symptoms of stomachic derangement are prominent; together with a tumid and painful state of the belly, constipation, or alternate diarrhœa and costiveness;* excessive restlessness, and quick, laborious respiration, particularly at night, with drowsiness during the day, BRYONIA is to be preferred.

LACHESIS may follow *Belladonna*, or *Mercurius*, when the signs of intestinal irritation or inflammation continue with but little abatement. Or it

* *Nux v.* and *Lachesis* also correspond to this symptom.

may precede these remedies, when the tenderness and distension are more marked at one particular spot (the most trivial pressure there being intolerable) than over the entire belly, when the stools are of a very pale colour, and when the fever is highest at night.

SULPHUR may be given with advantage to complete the cure, in many cases, after the previous employment of any of the foregoing medicines. It is, however, when the attack is characterised by the following features, that this remedy is more directly called for; heat, especially towards evening, but also in the morning, or during the day; flushes, alternately with paleness of the face; dryness of the skin; hurried and laborious breathing; palpitation of the heart; nocturnal perspiration; languor and great weakness, particularly in the inferior extremities; tense, tumid, and painful belly; whitish urine; dry, hard, or loose and slimy motions.

These, then, are the more generally useful remedies in cases of the above description; and will materially tend to facilitate recovery, or prevent the disease from assuming a hopeless character. When, however, the malady occurs in children of relaxed and feeble habits, or of a decided scrofulous constitution, it becomes, especially if neglected, and not checked at the commencement of its course, a most intractable and frequently fatal disease, from the proneness which it then has to terminate in one or other of the serious complications alluded to at the commencement.

The remedies from which the most benefit is to be anticipated under such unfavorable circumstances, are, in addition to those previously mentioned, *Silicea*, *Sulphur*, *Calcarea*, *Baryta c.*, *Arsenicum*, *Cocculus*, *Cina*, *Sabadilla*, &c.

SILICEA, when there is great emaciation, languor and debility, paleness of the face, want of appetite, or craving for dainties; shortness of breath or movement; feverish heat in the morning or towards evening. This remedy is also a most important one when the patient is afflicted with worms, and when the disease is in a great measure attributable to that cause. *Cina* and *Sabadilla* may likewise be found useful along with *Silicea*, in the latter instance, the former particularly when the urine is milky or deposits a white crust. (See *Invermination.*) The indications for *Sulphur* have already been given.

CALCAREA. Great debility, with flabbiness of the muscles, dryness of the skin, and excessive emaciation; frequent flushes, or general heat, followed by shivering towards evening; exhaustion, or dejection after speaking; impaired, fastidious, appetite, with weak and slow digestion, or, on the contrary, extreme voracity; perspiration towards morning; hard, tense, and tumid belly. (*Baryta c.* is sometimes useful after *Calcarea.*

ARSENICUM. Extreme prostration of strength and emaciation, with desire to remain constantly in the recumbent posture; dry, burning heat of the skin, with great thirst, but desire to drink little at a time, or merely to moisten the lips, which are frequently parched; impaired appetite, and sometimes excessive irritability of the stomach, so that very little food can be retained; hard and tense belly; restless, unrefreshing sleep, with frequent starts, or twitching of the tendons; fretful and capricious disposition.

COCCULUS. Great weakness, with excessive fatigue, depression, and tremor after the slightest exertion; heavy expressionless eyes; flushes of heat in the face; nausea, or aversion to food, distension of the belly; constipation; oppressed respiration; perspiration on attempting any trivial exertion; lowness of spirits.

Belladonna, *Lachesis*, or *Baryta c.* will be required when the head becomes much affected. BELLADONNA, especially when there is heat, heaviness, violent throbbing of the vessels of the head and neck, flushing, and delirium; or deep and protracted sleep, with twitching of the tendons, coldness of the hands; pale, cold face; small quick pulse; hot, tumid, and tense abdomen. LACHESIS, either before or after *Belladonna*, when the patient lies as if in a deep, prolonged sleep; with grinding of the teeth; or somnolency alternately with sleeplessness; tremulous, intermittent, or scarcely perceptible pulse. (See WATER IN THE BRAIN.)

BARYTA. Lethargy, tossing, or agitation, moaning and muttering, feeble and accelerated pulse.

Other remedies, such as *Antimonium*, *Acid. phosphoricum*, *Phosphorus*,* *Hepar s.*, *Rhus*, *Kali*, *Acidum nitr.*, *Lycopodium*, &c., may be required according as the symptoms happen to vary: we have merely given some of the medicines which have been found of valuable service, when the indications of the disease have corresponded with those above given. It may be added, that when the skin is hot and parched, the sleeplessness and restlessness are often temporarily removed by sponging the body with tepid water; this expedient is, however, only to be had recourse to, when the remedies fail to afford this relief, and that in a more permanent degree.†

* *Phosphorus* and *Acidum phosphoricum* are more especially useful in protracted cases, with debilitating diarrhœa and very white or milky-looking or turbid urine, which deposits a white coating.

† Homœopathic Practice of Physic.

ADMINISTRATION OF THE REMEDIES. In general cases, with well-marked exacerbations, it will be found advantageous to administer the medicine during the period at which the symptoms exist in a more or less subdued form. Six globules of the remedy selected may be dissolved in an ordinary-sized wineglassful of water, and a dessert-spoonful of the solution given about an hour after each exacerbation. To very young children, of from one to two years of age, a teaspoonful of the solution may be given at the stated intervals. At the commencement of the attack, before the fever sets in, the above dose may be given every three to six or eight hours, according to the urgency of the symptoms, in the course of the first day. And in milder cases, with less distinctly marked remittent fever, a dose may be given morning and evening.*

DIET AND REGIMEN. The utmost possible attention should be paid to diet in the treatment of infantile remittent fever. There is, generally, much aversion to food during the height of the disease, and we should on no account entice the patient to take more than the weakened digestive powers can sustain, even when the appetite is returning. When there is diarrhœa, or symptoms

* See rules for the administration and repetition of the dose.

of intestinal inflammatory action,* the dietetic regulations should be the same as we have given under the head of Bowel Complaints, and Inflammation of the Stomach and Bowels. In which chapters, moreover, some additional indications will be found for some of the remedies enumerated above. In protracted cases, change of air is often of great service.

DISEASES OF THE RESPIRATORY ORGANS.

Cold in the Head, or Common Catarrh.

This common complaint is perhaps more distressing to the infant at the breast than to children more advanced in age; because, by rendering the nostrils impervious to the air, the operation of suckling is rendered difficult, and is repeatedly interrupted, the child being frequently compelled to relinquish the nipple in order to breathe. These constant and uneasy attempts of the infant at feeding, sometimes, moreover, give rise to irritation and excoriation of the nipple.

Symptoms. The characteristic symptoms of the affection are sneezing, watering at the eyes, and flow of mucus from the nose. With these are

* Chiefly characterised by heat of skin, and great tenderness of the belly on pressure with the hand.

sometimes associated.—Cough, hoarseness, rattling of phlegm, flushing of the face, and heat of skin. The child sleeps with its mouth open, and snuffles during the act of respiration.

When the second or secretive stage of cold in the head sets in, the discharge from the nose is at first clear and watery, but soon becomes thick, yellow, or greenish-yellow, and ultimately of the nature of, or resembling the matter of an abscess.

Treatment. In the first stage of the affection, and when the lining membrane of the nostrils is dry and swollen, a little oil of almonds or cream may be applied to it with a feather, as a palliative to the local irritation. Benefit will also result from placing the infant in a warm bath and subsequently keeping it warm and unexposed to great variations of temperature. The homœopathic remedies which are most frequently serviceable in arresting or curtailing simple catarrh are: *Aconitum*, *Nux v.*, *Arsenicum*, *Mercurius*, *Chamomilla*, *Tartarus emeticus*, *Euphrasia*, *Pulsatilla*, *Sepia*, *Calcarea*, *Sulphur*, *Dulcamara*, *Sambucus*, *Carbo v.*, and *Graphites*.

At the commencement of the attack, but especially when there is burning heat of skin, also when a short, dry cough attends, *Aconitum* is the most useful medicament. One to two globules may be dissolved in three teaspoonsful of water, and a teaspoonful given every four hours. Twelve hours after the last dose of *Aconitum*, NUX V. (one to two globules in three teaspoonsful of water, a teaspoonful every twelve hours,) may be resorted to; if the nose continues obstructed and there is no discharge, or if any it is slight and watery, and takes place only during the day.* ARSENICUM is required when there is a copious discharge of acrid, watery mucus, which produces soreness and swelling of the nostrils, and when there is excessive restlessness and agitation. If it fail to relieve these symptoms within twenty-four to thirty-six hours, *Lachesis* may be employed.

MERCURIUS. Where *Arsenicum* has been used with some advantage, but there remains a rather scanty, yellowish, or greenish, or a somewhat thick, whitish yellow discharge. Or it may be preferred to *Arsenicum* if the discharge is of the same description as mentioned under that remedy, but not so acrid, and when it is accompanied by some degree of fever, or by copious nocturnal perspiration. *Mercurius* is, moreover, better adapted

* When, in the case of infants at the breast, the nose remains so much obstructed as to interfere with the act of sucking (notwithstanding the previous use of *Nux v.*), a globule of *Sambucus* may be given every five or six hours until some amendment becomes apparent.

to plethoric, lymphatic children than *Arsenicum.* The administration of *Arsenicum* and *Mercurius* may be conducted in the same way as described for *Nux v.*

CHAMOMILLA, which is a remedy of peculiar value in many infantile disorders, is frequently serviceable when the discharge is watery, and is attended with a distressing loose cough, particularly at night; also when there is some heat of skin, and much mucus rattling in the chest. BELLADONNA is sometimes of service in alternation with *Chamomilla;* and *Tartarus emeticus*, or *Tart. emet.* and *Ipecacuanha* alternately, when the cough and rattling of phlegm do not diminish, or, on the contrary, threaten to increase notwithstanding the administration of *Chamomilla.* See also PULSATILLA. The dose of *Chamomilla* or of *Tartarus em.*, may consist of three globules in six teaspoonsful of water, and a teaspoonful of the solution every six hours. In the alternate administration the same number of globules of each remedy, with the same quantity of water, may be employed, and a teaspoonful first of the one solution then the other, given at intervals of about twelve hours, or only six in severe cases. If it is found difficult, or almost impossible to administer the medicine in solution, we may give one globule for each dose.

EUPHRASIA is generally preferable to *Bella-*

donna, *Chamomilla*, *Arsenicum*, or *Pulsatilla*, when there is considerable redness of the white of the eye, excessive watering of the eyes, with copious discharge of mucus from the nose.

Administration same as *Nux v.*

Pulsatilla is best adapted to that stage of nasal catarrh at which the discharge has become thick, green, or yellow, or greenish yellow. It is also well indicated when these symptoms occur in conjunction with a loose cough and mucous rattling in the chest.

Administration same as *Chamomilla.*

Sepia is often serviceable after the previous employment of *Pulsatilla;* when the complaint is much mitigated, but threatens to become protracted.

Calcarea is sometimes very effective when the noise continues much stuffed, and the discharge puriform, (resembling the fluid formed by the process of suppuration.)

When cold in the head assumes the chronic form, the remedies which, in addition to *Sepia* and *Calcarea*, are commonly most useful in arresting it are—*Sulphur*, in general cases,—*Carbo v.* when exacerbations always take place towards evening, —*Dulcamara* when the complaint becomes aggravated on exposure to cold air, or increases or diminishes as the temperature of the atmos phere varies,—and *Graphites* where there is great languor and prostration. In such cases, one globule may be given morning and evening, every third day, until improvement ensues.

Cold in the Chest. Pulmonary Catarrh. Bronchial Catarrh.

This complaint consists in an inflammation of the membrane which lines the various air-tubes and cells of the lungs.

SYMPTOMS. Chilliness succeeded by fever, with quick pulse and hot skin; cough, more or less intense, at first dry or with scanty expectoration of transparent and viscid, or frothy, mucus (phlegm), which subsequently becomes copious, and sometimes streaked with blood. Young children invariably swallow the phlegm which is detached, except when it is ejected during the attack of vomiting which not unfrequently occurs after a violent and suffocative fit of coughing. The breathing is ever exceedingly quick and laboured, the nostrils are dilated during inspiration, and a rattling or wheezing noise is heard on applying the ear to the chest; the face is generally pale and puffy, and the countenance anxious; the tongue is usually foul, the appetite gone, and the strength much reduced; the bowels may be either costive or relaxed, and the secretions vitiated. The symptoms are always exacerbated at night, and the affection is often complicated with inflammation of the substance of the lungs.

When a favorable termination is approaching, the fever abates, the respirations become less frequent, and the cough looser and less choking, in four or five days; but when it takes an unfavorable turn, the difficulty of breathing increases, the face becomes livid, and the body covered with a clammy sweat; stupor or convulsions supervene, and the patient is carried off in a state of suffocation, commonly within eight or ten days from the commencement of the attack. The chances of recovery depend on the extent of the inflammation and the constitution of the patient. Healthy children succumb comparatively rarely when appropriate treatment is resorted to sufficiently early.

TREATMENT. In the first or inflammatory stage of the affection, particularly if the patient is of a plethoric habit, *Aconitum* is an indispensable remedy when the skin is hot and dry, and the pulse full and much accelerated. It is further indicated by the presence of a short, dry, and frequent cough; rapid and laborious respiration, thirst, anxiety, and extreme restlessness.

ADMINISTRATION. Three globules, in three

dessert-spoonsful of water, a teaspoonful of the solution every four hours. As soon as improvement results—the skin becoming moist, and the respiration easier—the intervals between the doses may be lengthened, or some other remedy substituted, if indicated by the remaining symptoms. It will sometimes be found necessary to have recourse to *Aconitum* again, if the heat of skin, the fulness and quickness of pulse, &c., return. When, notwithstanding the employment of *Aconitum*, the breathing continues to be very rapid and much oppressed, and the temperature of the skin considerably above the natural standard, which is liable to be the case if the complaint is complicated with inflammation of the lungs, BELLADONNA should be resorted to, particularly if the patient is of a full habit, or of lymphatic or sanguine-lymphatic temperament. A dry, fatiguing cough, aggravated at night, and frequently followed by fits of sneezing, or accompanied by a rattling noise in the chest, is an additional indication for *Belladonna*. It may be administered in the same way as *Aconitum*, or given in alternation with it when the nocturnal fever and restlessness are excessive. BRYONIA and CHAMOMILLA are often required to complete the cure after *Aconitum* and *Belladonna*. In many instances, however, either the one or the other will claim a preference to *Belladonna*. The symp toms which more particularly point out the appropriateness of *Bryonia* are, quick and difficult breathing; dry or loose cough, (in the latter case the matter which is expectorated consists of viscid phlegm,) aggravated after taking food or drink; rattling of mucus in the chest; foul tongue; parched mouth and lips; thirst; and a constipated state of the bowels. CHAMOMILLA is called for after *Aconitum*, when the cough is severe, and accompanied by wheezing, thirst, and diarrhœa. ADMINISTRATION of *Bella.*, *Bry.*, and *Chamomilla*, same as *Aconitum*. In the second or secretive stage, *Pulsatilla* is often of service when the acute inflammatory symptoms have been subdued, and the cough has become looser, the mucus thicker, more copious and more easily detached; the bowels costive or relaxed.

ADMINISTRATION. Four globules, in four teaspoonsful of water, a teaspoonful morning and evening. When the disease has attained an advanced stage, and the secretion of mucus in the tubes and cells of the lungs has accumulated in excessive quantity, impeding respiration and threatening suffocation, the cough being at the same time very violent, and the paroxysms frequently followed by vomiting, or by rigidity of the limbs, the face livid, and the forehead covered with perspiration. IPECACUANHA is, generally, of considerable service.

ADMINISTRATION. Six globules, in an ordinary-sized wineglassful of water, a teaspoonful of the solution every two hours, until a favorable result is effected, or a change of remedy called for. The alternation of *Tartarus emeticus* with *Ipecacuanha* is, occasionally, very beneficial. Should these medicines fail to relieve the symptoms above named, and the pulse become very feeble and irregular, the surface cold, and the strength nearly exhausted, *Arsenicum* will sometimes succeed in averting a fatal issue.

ADMINISTRATION. Same as *Ipecacuanha*, or with shorter intervals between the doses, if it seem advisable. *Puls.*, *Tart.*, &c., may be required after *Ars.*

These, then, are a few of the more important medicaments in some of the ordinary forms of inflammation of the bronchial tubes; but there are several other remedies which may be indicated in particular cases, such as *Spongia*, *Hepar sulphuris* (see CROUP) *Lachesis*, *Nux v.*, and *Kali bich.*, &c. *Sulphur* is often of service in preventing the affection from assuming the chronic form, when the fever and difficulty of breathing have been overcome by *Aconitum*, etc. All cases which are attended with much fever and greatly accelerated breathing, ought to be held as more or less dangerous, and provided for accordingly.

DIET. The thirst being generally excessive in the early stage of the complaint, it is perhaps commendable to withhold the breast from infants, and to give water, or two parts of water to one of the breast-milk—or very thin gruel, slightly sweetened—in its place, until the active febrile and inflammatory symptoms have yielded. To older children, gum-water, whey, barley-water, and such like, may be given at the commencement. But when recovery is steadily setting in, a gradual return may be made to a more nutritious diet.

Inflammation of the Lungs.

Inflammation of the substance of the lungs rarely, if ever, occurs as a primary affection in young children; being very generally associated with and occurring as secondary to inflammation of the bronchial tubes. It consequently, in children below six years of age, almost invariably appears in connexion with quick pulse, hot skin, great restlessness, fever, cough, mucous rattling in the chest, accelerated breathing, and considerable prostration of strength. Percussion* yields a dull

* The act of striking upon the chest with the object of pro-

sound. With children who are more advanced in life, the true signs and symptoms of inflammation in the lungs, such as crepitating respiration, dullness on percussion, viscid, rust-coloured expectoration, &c., &c., are usually as well marked as in adults.

TREATMENT. *Aconitum*, *Belladonna*, and *Bryonia* are the principal remedies in the early stage. Their leading indications have been given in the preceding chapter, which see. *Phosphorus* and *Tartarus emeticus* are the next in most frequent use; but it requires professional knowledge and experience to regulate their selection.*

Croup.

The disease of which I now purpose to treat, has so repeatedly and so strikingly illustrated the sufficiency of the homœopathic system to cope successfully with the most formidable of acute diseases, as to refute most signally the allegations to the contrary which have been so falsely and industriously fostered and propagated.

ducing sounds, from the nature of which the state of the subjacent parts may be established.

* Some particulars connected with the treatment of inflammation of the lungs in adults, will be found in the "Homœopathic Domestic Medicine," by the Author.

Croup consists of a peculiar inflammation of the mucous membrane that lines the windpipe and its ramifications, generally terminating in the formation of a thick viscid substance, denominated false membrane, which adheres to and takes the form of the parts it covers. The principal exciting causes of the affection are exposure to cold or damp, particularly during the prevalence of north or north-easterly winds; residence in a low, badly-drained locality; combined with deficient or improper food, and consequent derangement of the digestive organs. It frequently appears as an hereditary malady; and when once a child has been attacked by it, he is very liable to a recurrence. This predisposition is, however, very generally overcome after the patient has been treated homœopathically during one or more seizures, or has been placed under a constitutional course of treatment on recovering from an attack. From the period of weaning to the eighth or tenth year is the time during which children are most subject to this distressing malady.

On the continent, and especially in Germany, France, and Switzerland, it is more dreaded and more common, as well as more violent, than in England. The duration of the complaint varies; sometimes it runs a fatal course in twenty-four hours; but in the major number of cases it is prolonged to the fourth or fifth day before the patient sinks. In some cases again, it assumes a chronic form, and may be protracted over a period of two or three weeks.

SYMPTOMS. If croup has precursory symptoms, they will occur for two or three days before the identity of the disease be described and confirmed, and they generally consist in the manifestation of the symptoms of a common catarrh, usually accompanied by a dry, rough cough, and hoarseness. In certain localities, where the complaint is known to be endemic,* and in families predisposed by constitution to suffer from it, no attention should be spared in watching and treating any such symptom. When the disease is not foreshadowed by a premonitory stage, the first intimation of its presence may be in the characteristic sudden, abrupt, shrill, brazen, trumpet-like, single cough which the child will emit during the night, and even whilst asleep: the peculiar sharp and stridulous intonation of the voice, the loud and very laboured breathing, and the crowing sound which may often be heard during the act of inspiration. The pulse is accelerated and hard; the skin is highly hot and feverish; a sensation of strangulation prevails, and the patient seems to long to

* Peculiar to a place or country.

swallow something which would remove an apparent obstrnction about the gullet. Some children will grasp the throat convulsively, as if to squeeze out some foreign body. There are, frequently, sudden pauses in the malady, when all the symptoms appear to subside; but these are, commonly, but indications of a worse period of return; and after them the sense of suffocation is, in general, redoubled; the head is tossed back convulsively, as if to stretch the throat; the features assume a ghastly pale or livid tint; the extremities of the body are clammy and cold; the prostration excessive; the voice nearly inaudible; the eye becomes glazed and dull; and unconsciousness or convulsions supervene.

Treatment of the Premonitory and First or Inflammatory Stage. The homœopathic medicines being of such easy access, and so convenient to administer, the treatment of this serious malady is thereby, in uncomplicated cases, commonly rendered at once safe, prompt, and effective even in the hands of the most unpractised and unprofessional persons, provided the disease is not allowed to attain an advanced stage before the remedies are resorted to. When the attack is preceded by catarrhal symptoms, in the form of a rough, dry, hard cough, accompanied by hoarseness or by wheezing, HEPAR S. will, in the majority of cases be the means of preventing the development of the affection, by arresting it in this early stage. But when fever and difficulty of breathing become superadded, or when they, together with the characteristic ringing cough, the peculiar faint, sharp voice, and the crowing sound during inspiration, suddenly affect a child, it will be necessary to administer ACONITUM in alternation with *Hepar*. The immediate employment of these two will, very generally, be speedily followed by an improvement in the breathing, an abatement of the fever, and a loosening of the cough. If, however, some degree of oppressed respiration, attended with a loud, grating, and wheezing noise, still remain, SPONGIA must then be had recourse to, or given in alternation with *Hepar s.*,—as also with *Aconitum*, if a considerable degree of fever, with quick, full pulse, and, sometimes, hot and flushed face, continues or reappears.

ADMINISTRATION OF THESE MEDICINES. When *Hepar s.* is given in the premonitory catarrhal stage of the complaint, four or five globules may be dissolved in two tablespoonsful of water, and a teaspoonful of the solution given every three or four hours. When it is given, in alternation with *Aconitum*, during the inflammatory stage of developed croup, six or eight globules of each remedy may be separately dissolved in two table spoonsful of water, and a teaspoonful, first of the one, then of the other, administered every hour, or only every four hours or so if the symptoms are not very urgent. In giving *Hepar s.* or *Spongia* alone—in the absence of inflammatory fever, with dry, hot skin, and full, hard, and much accelerated pulse—the medicine may be prepared in the proportions above stated (or *one grain of the second trituration*, of either remedy, may be mixed in the two tablespoonsful of water,) and a teaspoonful administered every four hours, until signs of amendment set in, or a change of remedy be required by an alteration in the symptoms. Again, when it seems necessary to employ *Aconitum* along with *Hepar s.* and *Spongia*, in consequence of the continuance of active fever, six globules of each medicine may be separately dissolved in two tablespoonsful of water, and a teaspoonful, first of the one, then of the next, in rotation, given every hour or two.* As soon as improvement becomes apparent, the intervals between the doses may be lengthened. To children under two years of age, if some difficulty is experienced in exhibiting the medicine in the form of solution, one globule of the remedy may be placed on the tongue at each

* i. e. A dose of one medicine at a time, every hour or two.

repetition of the dose. In the worst forms of croup, it is sometimes necessary to administer the medicine every half or even every quarter of an hour.

When the disease has reached the second stage —or that in which the *false membrane* is formed, and the difficulty in breathing and the wheezing become greatly aggravated—sometimes a flapping or valve-like sound accompanies the act of ex- or inspiration, in consequence of a partial detachment of a portion of the membrane; the voice sinks to a whisper, the cough grows hoarser and more suffocative, and the countenance looks blanched or livid. A congested state of the lungs, and, subsequently, of the brain, with the concomitant symptoms already detailed, then ensues.

Treatment of the Second Stage. The chances of recovery in this stage of the affection are, naturally, materially diminished. Medical aid should, therefore, be sought without further delay, if it has not already been obtained. If the disease has advanced thus far, before remedial measures have been adopted, *Hepar s.* and *Spongia*, exhibited alternately in the manner described above, frequently succeed in averting a fatal termination. In some cases, viz. where there is much increased vascular action, with fulness and quickness of pulse, *Aconitum* must be included in the alternate or rotatory administration. If, on the other hand, as will occasionally happen—either from some neglect on the part of the attendants—or from the impossibility of preventing the patient from exposing himself to a chill during the outbreak of perspiration—or from some undetected peculiarity in the case, to which the medicaments do not correspond—the early employment of *Aconitum*, *Hepar sulphuris* or *Spongia*, fail to subdue the complaint, *Lachesis*, *Phosphorus*, *Belladonna*, *Arsenicum*, and *Sambucus*, or *Tartarus emeticus*, are the remedies which, in general cases, may chiefly be relied on. *Lachesis* and *Phosphorus*, or, sometimes, *Spongia* and *Phosphorus*, commonly in alternation, when there are signs of congestion in the chest, or even of extension of the inflammation to the substance of the lung, or to its enveloping membrane (the pleura,) with consequent dullness on percussion;* *Belladonna*, or *Belladonna* and *Spongia*, in alternation, when symptoms of congestion in the brain, with tendency to stupor or to convulsions, supervene; *Arsenicum* when the patient has become cold, excessively debilitated, and seems to be sinking; and *Tartarus emeticus* or *Sambucus* and *Tartarus emeticus*, in alternation, when there is much

* See note, p. 268.

rattling of phlegm in the chest, and slow and much impeded respiration. These medicines should be given in rapidly repeated doses, and in about the same proportions as *Acon.*, *Hep. s.*, and *Spong.*, as long as any gleam of hope remains. When reaction follows the administration of any of the remedies we have recommended for the latter periods of the second stage (viz. *Lach.*, *Phosp.*, *Bella.*, *Ars.*, &c.,) or whenever any signs of a relapse threaten, after all the dangerous symptoms have been overcome, it is advisable to fall back upon *Hepar s.* and *Spongia.* There are other remedies, such as *Kali bich.*, *Bromium*, *Iodium*, *Bry.*, *Cham.*, *Sulph.*, &c. &c., which may be useful in complicated attacks; but, in the majority of cases, the seasonable employment of *Aconitum*, *Hepar s.*, and *Spongia* will be found adequate to conquer the disease in a few hours. When, on the removal of the inflammatory symptoms, the disease becomes subject to remissions, succeeded by sudden exacerbations of a dangerous suffocative, *spasmodic* character, a rare occurrence in true croup when treated homœopathically, *Arsenicum* and *Lachesis*, in rapid alternation, and, failing these, *Sambucus* and *Moschus* may be resorted to. (See also *Spasm of the Opening of the Windpipe.*) But as croup is subject to intervals of *comparative* ease, followed by exacerbations, the use of *Aconitum*, *Hepar s.*, and *Spongia* should not be discontinued without due reason. In the second stage of the complaint, a suddenly fatal issue sometimes results from suffocation, caused by a detached portion of the false membrane obstructing the passage of the windpipe.

DIET AND REGIMEN. During the existence of croup, a little milk and water may, at the utmost, be given from time to time. Even when every symptom of danger has been surmounted, the greatest possible caution must be observed in the exhibition of food. In the advanced period of the second stage, when *Arsenicum*, &c., are insufficient to prop the sinking energies, a little burnt brandy may be administered now and then, in the quantity of a few drops. Wine may be preferred in the case of children below three years of age. The child should be kept warm, confined to one apartment; and every possible precaution taken to guard against a chill throughout, and for some time after the croup seizure. The disease is, as previously remarked, much less liable to return after it has been treated, once or twice, homœopathically; but when the home of the child is in a cold, bleak, and much exposed, or a low, damp situation, approximate to large surfaces of water, a change of quarters should, if practicable, be repaired to. In chronic croup, or hoarseness remaining after an attack of croup, *Hepar s.*, *Phosphorus*, and *Carbo v.* are commonly the most serviceable medicines: they form, moreover, useful preventatives against recurrences, when administered after a seizure.

Accidental Obstructions in the Windpipe, etc.

Young children are generally in the habit of carrying everything in the mouth, as also of eating quickly and unequally, of talking or laughing whilst feeding, &c. During the course of teething, in particular, every thing which a child can catch hold of is put into its mouth. Any one of these circumstances may lead to the accidental lodgment of some improper material in some part of the windpipe (or throat). As the symptoms which arise from the presence of some foreign substance in the windpipe present a great analogy to those of hooping-cough, spasm of the glottis (opening of the windpipe), and even croup, we should ever at once inquire into the history of the case before resorting to remedial measures. The circumstance of the child having previously been observed to play with some small substance; or the disappearance of a needle, pin, button, &c., which had been in the vicinity of the child: the suddenness of the invasion of the symptoms; and the absence of constitutional disturbance, such as fever, &c., immediately after the seizure, contribute to confirm our suspicion as to the cause of the morbid phenomena.

SYMPTOMS. The characteristics of accidents of this kind are usually very similar to those attendant upon the diseases above alluded to. A sudden convulsive and suffocating cough, returning at intervals, but sometimes continued for many minutes without intermission (if the obstruction remains); hoarse or almost inaudible voice; impeded breathing, particularly during expiration; and sometimes a flapping or other noise from the movement of the body up or down the windpipe, if it happen to be a pea, bead, button, or the like; the face red, or even purple, and the eyes starting and discharging copiously during the fit of coughing.

TREATMENT. In cases of a very urgent nature no time should be lost in seeking the assistance of a surgeon; as an operation, having for its object the admission of air through an artificial opening, made by an incision in a part of the windpipe, frequently offers the only chance of success in such instances. Meanwhile, however, the follow-lowing remedies may be resorted to:

IPECACUANHA and TARTARUS EMETICUS. Of

each six globules, separately, in a tablespoonful or about half an ounce of water; a teaspoonful of the solution, first of *Ipecac.*, then of *Tart. emet.*, alternately, after every paroxysm of aggravation; using two teaspoons, one for each medicine. If no relief follows after two or three doses, *Belladonna* may be substituted for these remedies, and given in the same way. But if the patient becomes livid in the face, *Opium* should be preferred. When the foreign substance is not fixed or firmly impacted in some part of the windpipe, and is known to consist of a bead, pea, or even a small coin, its expulsion may sometimes be accomplished if we encourage the act of coughing or vomiting, by tickling the throat with a feather, or by introducing the handle of a spoon, or the fore-finger into the throat as far as the root of the tongue. Inverting the body suddenly, has also succeeded in some cases. When the extraneous body has been removed, *Aconitum* and *Hepar s.* will generally be found the most appropriate remedies against any inflammatory consequences which have been excited by the local irritation.

Nearly the same description of symptoms may arise from the stoppage of a large piece of meat in the throat, as those which are occasioned by the entrance of some foreign substance into the windpipe.

TREATMENT. If the obstructed substance can be reached with the finger, it should be removed thereby as soon as possible; but when it is too deeply seated to admit of its extraction in this manner, it should be pushed down the gullet by means of a piece of whalebone, scraped smooth, and having a small piece of sponge firmly secured to the end which is introduced into the mouth and throat. A sudden and violent effort to vomit, induced by tickling the throat, by placing snuff on the tongue, or by striking the patient a sharp blow with the flat of the hand between the shoulders, will frequently effect the ejection of a piece of meat or other food which has stuck in the throat. The only chance of saving the patient, in cases of urgency, generally consists in the performance of an operation. Fish bones, pieces of glass, pins, &c., may often be removed by means of a piece of sponge fastened to a strip of whalebone, as above noticed. In this case, however, the sponge should be gently passed downwards by a sort of spiral or rotatory movement, until it is below the object, the exact locality of which the child can frequently indicate by pointing with his finger. A little water should then be given, in order to cause the sponge to swell, whereupon it should be slowly drawn upwards. Swallowing imperfectly masticated bread, &c., will occasionally succeed in removing fish bones. There are various other contrivances for procuring the removal of foreign substances from the throat, but most of them require the skill of the practised surgeon for their successful accomplishment. When a spasmodic contraction of the gullet interferes with the manipulations, *Ignatia* will sometimes speedily reduce it; if not, *Lachesis* or *Chamomilla* may be resorted to.

Spasm of the Opening of the Windpipe.

This affection is by some denominated the spasmodic croup, or acute asthma of infants. It bears a considerable resemblance to croup, yet differs from it in many respects, as, for instance, by the extreme suddenness of the attack—while that of croup is generally preceded, for one or two days, by hoarseness and a slight cough—and by the cessation of suffering the patient enjoys between the attacks, whereas when croup has once set in, the excitement is more or less permanent; moreover, this disease generally attacks in the evening or at night, whereas croup, in most cases, makes its first appearance during the day.

Croup, as we mentioned in the article upon that subject, is an inflammation of the membrane of the windpipe, exciting the formation of a peculiar secretion, which, if not checked, concretes into an abnormal membranous tissue, constituting what is technically called the *false membrane* of croup; whereas, in the asthma of Millar, the suffering appears to arise from a *spasmodic contraction of the top of the windpipe*, impeding the progress of respiration.

The attack commences during sleep, from which the child suddenly awakes as if frightened, and appears as if making ineffectual attempts to fetch breath; after much effort it succeeds by means of a sudden spasmodic inspiration, attended with a prolonged crowing noise; if the fit continues, the face becomes purple, and the extremities partake of the same hue, frequently associated with a clenching of the thumbs inside the palm, and spasmodic contraction or extension of the toes. As the complaint advances, the bowels become deranged, or the general health impaired; and if proper means are not promptly taken, the spasmodic attacks recur frequently, and at short intervals, and occasionally the little patient perishes during one of the paroxysms, or is carried off by a general convulsive fit.

The disease rarely occurs except in infants of delicate constitution, when due means should be taken to endeavour to eradicate it by a proper course of treatment; it is frequently associated with dentition, or a deranged state of the digestive organs, engendered by improper food, vitiated air, fever, &c. Although the affection may early prove fatal by suffocation during a paroxysm, it may, on the other hand, be protracted for several months, occurring at intervals from various exciting causes, such as fits of passion, vexation, or indigestion.

TREATMENT. The medicines which, in general cases, are the best adapted to the treatment of this disease are: *Arsenicum*, *Ipecacuanha*, *Lachesis*, *Sambucus*, *Chamomilla*, *Belladonna;* and also *Aconitum*, *Pulsatilla*, and *Nux. v.* Of these, IPECACUANHA is commonly to be preferred, when the attack has been excited by indigestible food, and when the child has been affected with sickness, or with purging, or both, before it was put to rest.

ADMINISTRATION. Three globules in six teaspoonsful of water—a teaspoonful of the solution every quarter of an hour until three doses have been given, after which the intervals may be lengthened if improvement has set in; but if no material alteration for the better has ensued, PULSATILLA may be substituted for *Ipecacuanha.* When no cause can be assigned for the attack, and the patient is of delicate or exhausted constitution, ARSENICUM will usually prove the more suitable remedy; excessive agitation and perspiration, and extreme prostration of strength during and after the paroxysms, with small, irregular, or intermittent pulse, are characteristic indications for *Arsenic*. It may be administered the same way as the preceding, and if no melioration results after three or four doses, LACHESIS may be resorted to. The last-named remedy may be preferred to *Arsenic*., or indeed to any other remedy, when the complaint suddenly attacks an otherwise healthy child, and no exciting cause of the seizure can be determined.

ADMINISTRATION. Same as *Ipecacuanha*.

When the affection is associated with deranged bowels, and acidity of stomach, CHAMOMILLA will be found a useful remedy. It is further indicated when the attacks are prone to come on even during the day, particularly after a fit of passion or vexation; or when they are connected with the process of teething, and when general convulsions supervene. (See *Teething*.) BELLADONNA must, however, be had recourse to immediately, if the latter symptoms do not yield to the use of *Chamomilla*, but on the contrary, the succeeding paroxysm of convulsions increase in duration or intensity. In all cases that are complicated with symptoms of affection of the brain or its membranes, arising from difficult dentition or other causes, and accompanied by a tendency to, or the actual development of, severe general convulsions, *Belladonna* is an important remedy.

ADMINISTRATION. Three globules in six teaspoonsful of water, one teaspoonful to be given when the fit is subsiding, or when it has terminated. If an aggravation ensues the result must be awaited. If no change occurs the dose may be repeated, but not until another convulsive fit commences. When an alteration for the better becomes manifest, the medicine may be discontinued, and only resorted to again should threatening signs of a relapse appear.

ACONITUM is required when the irritation of teething is evidently the exciting cause of the disease, and there is quickness and fulness of pulse. (See *Teething*.) *Pulsatilla* and *Nux v.*, are chiefly indicated in cases dependent upon derangement of the digestive organs. *Ignatia* and *Cocculus* may also be found serviceable in these cases. When the complaint occurs in highly scrofulous children, with enlargement or fulness in the region of the thymus gland,* *Belladonna*, *Spongia*, *Baryta*, *Carbo v.*, &c., are required. It may sometimes be necessary to have an operation performed, in the hope of preventing suffocation when the malady proceeds from the pressure of the enlarged gland.

* A gland which is of considerable size in the fœtus, but which diminishes during youth, and usually disappears entirely in old age. It is situated in the chest, under the upper part of the breast-bone.

Diet and Regimen. During the spasmodic seizures, even when somewhat protracted, little or no food beyond a little warm milk and water, will, in general, be necessary in the first instance. In order to aid in the prevention of recurrences, the state of the digestive organs must be carefully attended to, and all nourishment which is of an indigestible nature should be strictly inhibited. If the child be at the breast, supplementary diet should be withheld, and a healthy nurse, possessing a full supply of milk, procured. A change of air is advisable, and every source of annoyance and excitement ought, where practicable, to be removed or avoided.

Hooping-Cough.

This is a malady peculiar to children, in the great majority of cases, although instances are not wanting of its seizing adults. It is very rarely caught more than once. It derives its name from the peculiar *whooping*, crowing sound, which accompanies the inspiration after every cough, and which generally becomes lengthened towards the end of the paroxysm. Right or wrong, the affection is commonly looked upon as contagious; and it most undoubtedly occurs very frequently in an epidemic form. Like *Croup, Hooping-cough* is most prevalent between the months of January and

June, but more especially at the turn of the spring. There is one remarkable feature about hooping-cough, in which it differs from the generality of the acute complaints of the respiratory organs, which is the length of its continuance; for from the first manifestation of morbid symptoms to the disappearance of the malady, there is usually a lapse of from two to three, and sometimes even five or six months. By some this malady is divided into two stages, the incipient or febrile, and the congestive and nervous. By others, again, it has been divided into three stages, viz., the first or *febrile*, the second or *convulsive*, and the third or *nervous*.

SYMPTOMS. During the first period, which varies in duration from one to five or six days, we remark the common feverish cold, (catarrhal fever), manifested by discharge from the nose, sensibility of the eyes, thirst, heat of skin, quickness of pulse, and a hacking, dry, and irritable cough. After the lapse of a few days, in the generality of cases, but in some without any notable premonitory symptoms, the cough assumes the characteristic convulsive form, attended with prolonged inspirations possessing the peculiar noise already alluded to. Occasionally this crowing or whooping noise is absent, or not well marked. During the fits of coughing, which occur in paroxysms at intervals of from half an hour to three or four hours, the face and neck become red, swollen, and livid; the eyes appear as if protruding from their sockets, and stream with tears; the pulse is accelerated; the vessels of the head are much distended; the patient is excessively agitated, and lays hold of any person or fixed object within his reach for support during the fit. After the seizure has lasted for a longer or shorter period, it is terminated by the act of vomiting, and the expectoration of a quantity of phlegm; whereupon the child is usually empowered to return to his play or previous occupation; but it is often some little time before complete tranquillity is restored. In severe cases, blood is discharged from the nose, eyes, chest, and stomach; and sometimes the patient falls down insensible from the intensity of the paroxysm. The attacks generally return with some degree of regularity, although they are often more frequent or more violent at night, and are liable to be brought on at any time by excitement, too full a meal, or exposure to cold. The straining, during the fits of coughing, occasionally gives rise to involuntary discharges from the bladder and bowels. In mild cases, respiration is free during the intervals, and the child, with exception of some little debility, is in every respect apparently healthy. But in more severe cases, or when there has previously been some derangement of the digestive organs, the appetite is bad, the bowels disordered, the tongue very foul, and the temperature of the skin considerably increased at night. In the worst forms of complaint, again, fever is never absent, and the respiration is, continuously, more or less laboured and impeded, indicating the existence of some serious internal complication. Such cases sometimes terminate fatally in a very sudden manner; they are, however, only met with in children of unsound constitutions. Other dangerous complications, as for instance, with affections of the brain or its membranes, are liable to occur, particularly in recently weaned infants, or those who are undergoing the process of dentition.

In favorable cases, occurring in healthy subjects, the disease begins naturally to decline in about three or four weeks, and then continues, generally speaking, for about two months longer in a modified form. The expectoration, which was at first tenacious and scanty, becomes more profuse and less viscid; the cough loses its harshness; the paroxysms are not so violent and protracted, and the intervals between them are of longer duration. Young children commonly swallow the phlegm as soon as it is discharged from the air-tubes, except when it is ejected during the act of vomiting. Relapses of the paroxysmal convulsive character of the cough are of frequent occurrence on any exposure to cold; and the duration of the affection in its second (and third) stage is sometimes considerably prolonged hy an ungenial state of the atmosphere.

TREATMENT. In the incipient, febrile, irritative, or catarrhal state of the cough, it is not unfrequently possible to check the further progress of the disorder by means of such medicines as *Aconitum*, *Belladonna*, *Mercurius*, *Chamomilla*, *Pulsatilla*, *Nux v.*, *Ipecacuanha*, *Carbo vegetabilis*.

ACONITUM is required when there is considerable fever, with thirst, heat of skin, and quick full pulse; also when the cough is dry and very frequent, and when there is slight redness and tenderness, or sensibility of the eyes; or when a feeling of soreness and burning are complained of the throat and chest.

ADMINISTRATION. Six globules in two tablespoonsful of water: to children of from four to six years of age and upwards, a dessert-spoonful; and to those under four years, a teaspoonful of the solution every four hours. As soon as the fever lessens, the intervals between the doses must be lengthened, or another remedy resorted to if the remaining catarrhal symptoms indicate the necessity for such change. In the second stage of the cough, the alternate use of *Aconitum* with the other remedy employed is, occasionally, of service when some degree of fever prevails. The great value of *Aconitum* consists in the circumstance that whilst it most effectually answers the purpose of arresting general fever and keeping down incipient tendencies to local congestions and inflammations, it accomplishes this desirable end without inducing any consecutive weakness,—which so frequently results from the employment of aperients and other depleting measures, such as leeches, bleeding, &c., resorted to in the old mode of practice. The importance of this point, not only in this but in many other severe acute diseases, need scarcely be commented upon.

BELLADONNA is one of the most important remedies in the catarrhal stage of hooping-cough, particularly when it occurs in plethoric children, when there is heat of skin, dry, hollow, or harsh and barking nocturnal cough, or which becomes materially aggravated at night, and is followed by violent and great sneezing; incessant crying, and nocturnal restlessness. This medicine is also particularly well adapted to the angina or sore throat, which is not an unfrequent concomitant at the commencement of the affection.

ADMINISTRATION. Same as *Aconite*, only at longer intervals (every six or twelve hours.)

MERCURIUS. Hoarseness, watery coryza, with soreness of the nostrils; dry fatiguing cough, generally occurring in two successive fits; profuse night sweats.

HEPAR SULPHURIS. Hoarse, dry cough, worse at night, and commonly succeeded by a fit of crying. This medicine is also useful in forwarding the secretory process.

CHAMOMILLA. Dry, hoarse cough, or cough with difficult expectoration of tenacious phlegm, followed by a feeling of soreness at the part from which the mucus seems to have been detached; also when there is thirst, with fever towards evening, exacerbation of cough at night, even during sleep; great peevishness; excessive acidity and diarrhœa. The paroxysms of coughing are excited by an almost incessant irritation in the upper part of the windpipe and chest.

ADMINISTRATION of *Merc.*, *Cham.*, &c., same as *Bella.*

PULSATILLA. Cough loose, and accompanied with flow of tears, weakness of the eyes, sneezing, thick discolored discharge from the nostrils, slight hoarseness, and inclination to vomit after coughing; deranged digestion; occasional diarrhœa, especially at night.

DULCAMARA. When the attack has come on after exposure to a cold, damp atmosphere; and the cough is loose, with *copious and easy expectoration.*

NUX VOMICA is of great service when the cough approaches the second stage. It is indicated by the following symptoms: dry, fatiguing cough, attended with vomiting, and occurring particularly from about midnight until morning, the paroxysms sometimes so protracted and violent as to produce apparent danger of suffocation, with lividness of the face, and, occasionally, bleeding from the mouth and nose. (ARNICA is better adapted to this latter symptom, when the discharge of blood is copious.) Foul tongue, loss of appetite, constipation, also indicate the appropriateness of *Nux v.*

IPECACUANHA is, like the former, of great use when the cough is attended with danger of suffocation, and each inspiration appears to excite a fresh fit of coughing. It is further indicated when the fits are accompanied by spasmodic stiffness of the body, and blueness of the face, great anxiety, and accumulation of phlegm in the chest.

CARBO VEGETABILIS is often of considerable utility when the cough, notwithstanding the employment of one or more of the previously named remedies, assumes more and more of the characteristics of established hooping-cough; or when it sets in from the first in a convulsive form, and becomes exacerbated towards evening, or in the early part of the night, attended with pains in the chest, redness of the throat, and painful deglutition. The existence of excessive flatulence, and of eruptions about the face, head, and other parts of the body combine to determine the selection of this medicament.

ADMINISTRATION of *Nux v.*, *Ipecac.*, and *Carbo v.* same as described for the remedies required in the *second or convulsive* stage of hooping-cough. (See below.)

SECOND OR CONVULSIVE STAGE. TREATMENT.

Drosera, *Veratrum album*, *Cuprum aceticum*, *Arnica*, *Ferrum metallicum*, and *Conium maculatum*.

DROSERA is one of the principal remedies in the treatment of the disease when it has reached this stage; and in cases where it is clearly indicated, and the constitution has not been enfeebled by the transmission of hereditary weakness or other causes, it will, very generally, speedily declare its beneficial effects, and materially modify or shorten this trying and painful period of the disorder. The particular indications for the use of this medicine are, violent paroxysms of cough, occurring in such rapid succession as to threaten suffocation, and attended with the characteristic shrill sound during inspiration; after each fit of coughing, vomiting of food, or of stringy mucus;* relief on moving about; no fever, or fever consisting in regular attacks of chills and heat, followed by slight, warm, nocturnal perspiration; or outbursts of *warm* perspiration during the paroxysms of coughing.

VERATRUM ALBUM is very useful either at the very commencement of the convulsive stage, or at a more advanced period, when the child has become *reduced* in strength and *emaciated;* or when it suffers from *cold sweats*, particularly on the forehead, with *involuntary emission of urine, vomiting, spasms*, and other symptoms common to this stage; also pain in the chest and inguinal region; low fever, with small, weak, and accelerated pulse; thirst; aversion to conversation.†

When the vomiting, as also the cough, become more distressing at night than at any other time,

* Phlegm.

† *Carbo vegetabilis* is frequently useful in bringing this stage of the affection to an early and successful termination, after the previous use of *Veratrum* or *Drosera*, or both of these important remedies; particularly when, notwithstanding the decrease of cough, the tendency to vomit still remains. (See also FERRUM.)

Conium may follow *Veratrum*, if the latter fails to relieve this peculiarity.

CUPRUM ACETICUM.- This remedy is often found strikingly useful in the convulsive or nervous stage, *particularly when convulsions, mith loss of consciousness, ensue after each paroxysm.* Also when we find vomiting after the attacks, together with continuous rattling of mucus in the chest, and wheezing. In almost all such cases, a marked benefit has followed the employment of this remedy; sometimes it has been found sufficient of itself to cut short the disease, or has so far modified it that other remedies, which had before seemed to fail, have after its exhibition, acted with the most marked effect, and completed the cure.*

ARNICA is useful as an intermedial medicine, when the bleeding from the nose or mouth is considerable; and also in the affection itself, when each paroxysm is succeeded by crying. (*Hepar s.* is also useful, when the latter symptom follows a hoarse dry cough.)

* *Cina* is also a useful remedy when there are convulsions, or *tetanic rigidity* of the whole body during or immediately after the fits of coughing, particularly in children affected with *worms.* In cases which are complicated with the presence of worms in the intestines, *Mercurius* may be preferred to *Cina* when there is copious sweating at night.

Ferrum metallicum. This medicament will be found very useful as an intermediate remedy, when there is invariably vomiting of food on coughing soon after a meal. When the vomiting occurs only during the night, and when there is much rattling of phlegm in the chest, with diarrhœa and great prostration of strength, *Tartarus emet.* is often very useful.

Kali carbonicum has been found of much efficacy in hooping-cough, when a swelling and puffiness in the form of a little bag appeared between the eyelid and the eyebrows.

Administration of the Remedies in the Convulsive or Nervous Stage. In mild cases, two globules may be given every second day; but in those of a more severe description, six globules may be dissolved in two tablespoonsful of water, and a teaspoonful given every four hours during the first day—every six hours the second—every twelve the third; and so on, *lengthening* the intervals or entirely suspending the medicine, according to the greater or lesser degree of improvement effected. In cases requiring *Veratrum* or *Drosera*, it has been found useful to give the first dose immediately after a fit of coughing, and only to repeat after the next paroxysm if it proves as severe as that which preceded; an interval of twenty-four to forty-eight hours should then be permitted to elapse, or *longer*, if improvement becomes manifest, before another dose is given. If the complaint becomes worse in place of improving, after two or three doses of *Drosera* or *Veratrum* have been administered, or if new symptoms supervene, not covered by the remedy last employed, another must be selected.*

When the cough has lost its convulsive character, recourse may be had to the medicines which have been mentioned as the more appropriate in the catarrhal stage, particularly *Pulsatilla*, *Dulcamara*, *Chamomilla*, *Carbo v.*, but also *Nux v.*, and *Ipecacuanha*, &c., when called for. *Bryonia* is also serviceable, especially when the cough is always excited or aggravated after eating or drinking.

During the progress of the disease, symptoms of local inflammation must be narrowly looked for, and treated accordingly. (See *Cold in the Chest*, or *Inflammation of the Air-passages;* and also *Inflammation of the Brain; Water in the Brain; Remittent Fever*, and *Bowel Complaints*, when any of these complications attend.) When hooping-cough occurs during the process of dentition, *Aconitum*, *Chamomilla*, *Belladonna*, and *Mercurius* are more or less useful. (See above, and likewise the chapter on *Dentition*, for indications.)

* See rules for the repetition of the dose.

DIET. The diet must be light and of easy digestion; bread-pudding, semolina, and other light puddings of this description, provided the fever be not high,—in which case, weak gruel, barley-water, and the like, must alone be allowed; when the more serious symptoms have been subdued, or in all mild cases, we may give a little chicken-broth or beef-tea, and so on, gradually increasing the amount of nutriment as the disease declines. The drinks should consist of water, toast-water or barley-water.*

During the first stage the patient should be confined to one, well-ventilated, apartment. When the second stage is unattended with fever, and signs of affection of the chest, change of air is often beneficial.

Convulsions.

Early childhood is, from various causes, peculiarly predisposed to this distressing malady. Convulsions generally arise from the physical peculiarities of infancy, in the preponderance of the brain, and nervous system in general, over the other parts of the frame—hereditary predisposition called into activity by dentition—repelled eruptions—irritating substances in the stomach—

* Unmedicated jujubes, or gum-arabic and sugar-candy may be allowed, occasionally, for moistening the throat or mouth, when the cough is dry and irritating.

intestinal worms—mechanical injuries—fright, and lastly, from some occult cause, frequently a derangement of the organic structure, in many instances bidding defiance to the powers of medicine. In average cases, they are not quite so dangerous as is popularly supposed, or as might be presumed from appearances. The presence of real danger cannot be correctly drawn from the violence of the manifestations—slight convulsive movements frequently proceeding from or denoting, in conjunction with other signs, the presence of more serious mischief than severe convulsions. They generally, as may be concluded from what has been remarked above, take place in children who have their nervous system in a state of exalted sensibility or irritability, in consequence of an impaired state of health; but they may occur suddenly in apparently healthy children, without premonitory warning, or without any assignable exciting cause. When harbingers of a convulsive attack are present, they usually display themselves in the form of occasional twitchings of the fingers or toes, clenching of the thumb, downward torsion of the hand or foot, and retraction of the toes. The pupils are observed to be suddenly dilating or contracting; or one is being contracted whilst the other is dilating; the eyes are either fixed or in constant and rapid motion.

An irregularity in the breathing, a livid appearance about the mouth, and frequent changes of colour, are also deserving of notice.

SYMPTOMS. During an attack of convulsions of a mild character, the face is sometimes alone affected with slight twitchings, combined with distortion of one or both eyes; or only one limb, or one half of the body may be convulsed, sometimes alternately or successively with the other half. In the severer varieties, all the limbs are more or less affected, and likewise the muscles of the face and those of respiration. The eyes seem about to start from their sockets, and are much distorted, or roll about in various directions; or the eyelids open and shut in incessant motion; the tongue is protruded, or alternately elongated and contracted; the mouth foams; the breathing is impeded; the hands are firmly clenched; the limbs violently jerked or tossed about; and the face and head, which are often red at the beginning of the seizure, assume a dark or purple hue towards the conclusion, as also, at times, the entire surface of the body. As the attack declines, the convulsive movements become less violent and of less frequency, the contractions of the muscles relax, and the child, after a fit of crying, recovers his natural appearance. A quiet sleep often ensues; accompanied by a copious perspiration, from which the child awakes calm and refreshed. At other times, the paroxysm is succeeded by a secondary state of great languor, attended with complaints of headache, &c.

Convulsions vary in duration as well as intensity; sometimes the paroxysm will last only a few minutes, but occasionally it is protracted for hours, and after a short interval of cessation it may recur with undiminished violence. When very severe or frequently repeated, a fatal issue, or an irrecoverable state of paralysis may be the consequence. Neither fever nor loss of consciousness necessarily accompany an attack; but when they do, or when the pulse is much accelerated, and the skin exceeds the natural temperature, which is more liable to be the case in robust, plethoric children, an inflammatory disease (of the brain or its membranes, for instance) is commonly to be dreaded.

TREATMENT. During the attack itself it is rarely necessary, in general cases, to interfere much. It will be sufficient to loosen the child's garments, raise the head, sprinkle the face with cold water, and to give admittance to fresh air. It is only when the paroxysm is of great severity or lasts long, or when the attacks return in rapid succession, with unmitigated or even increased violence, that it is necessary to administer medicine before the attack has exhausted itself. The application of cold to the head, by pouring a stream of water upon it from a little distance, is a simple and frequently effectual mode of curtailing a paroxysm. The effect is heightened when the feet and legs are, at the same time, immersed in warm water. If the bowels are much loaded, three to six ounces of tepid water may be injected.* The medicines which are most commonly resorted to in Homœopathic practice, either during or after the paroxysms, are *Camphora*, *Chamomilla*, *Ignatia*, *Coffea*.—Or *Aconitum*, *Belladonna*, *Mercurius*, *Cina*, *Arsenicum*, *Ipecacuanha*, *Sulphur*, *Opium*, etc.

CAMPHORA. The application of *Camphor* to the nostrils of the child, for a few seconds each time, will sometimes succeed in abridging a paroxysm of great severity.

CHAMOMILLA is frequently of great service in convulsions, occurring in very young children from the irritation of teething; but it is also useful at a more advanced age, particularly in children of a nervo-sanguine temperament, who are extremely sensitive, and peevish; or when the attacks have been excited by fever, colic, a chill, or a fit of

* See art. *Constipation*.

passion or vexation. The characteristic indications for its administration are: restlessness, fretfulness, and disposition to drowsiness when awake; one cheek red, the other pale; diarrhœa; (if this remedy be exhibited at this stage of the disorder, it will frequently prevent the fit from becoming fully developed;) eyes half-closed; great thirst; quick and loud breathing; rattling in the throat; moaning; twitches of the eyelids and muscles of the face; contortion of the eyeballs; jerks and convulsions of the limbs, with clenched thumbs; lastly, constant rolling of the head from side to side; loss of consciousness. (*Belladonna* may be exhibited after *Chamomilla*, should the latter fail to do much good.)

ADMINISTRATION. We may, for very young children, dissolve one globule in four teaspoonsful of water, and administer one teaspoonful at the commencement of the attack; if fresh paroxysms come on some hours after, but decreased in intensity, we ought not to repeat the remedy, but allow it to exhaust its action; if the convulsions increase, on a second or third attack, we may give another spoonful—unless other symptoms declaring themselves, intimate that we ought to have recourse to any of the under-mentioned medicaments. (See also the directions given under CINA.)

IGNATIA is often very effective in convulsions

arising from the irritation of worms; and is sometimes successful during dentition, in cases which withstand the employment of *Chamomilla*, and *Belladonna*. It is more peculiarly adapted to listless, inanimate children; or to pale, delicate infants, of peevish dispositions, with alternations of vivacity and sadness,—laughing and crying almost in the same breath.

The characteristic symptoms are: the infant, while reposing in a light or moaning slumber, becomes suddenly flushed with burning heat, awakes, and springs with a convulsive start, and the utmost soothing scarcely quiets the excitement; there is a tremor of the entire body, attended by violent crying or agonizing shrieks; and the muscles of single limbs seem convulsed. *Ignatia* is further indicated when the fit returns every day at a regular hour, followed by fever and perspiration, or every other day at variable hours. (In some instances *Belladonna* will be found requisite after *Ignatia*.)

ADMINISTRATION. Same as *Chamomilla*.

COFFEA is useful when convulsions are liable to be excited in delicate and sickly children by the most trivial cause, but particularly by any mental excitement of a pleasing or joyful description.

ADMINISTRATION. Same as *Chamomilla*.

ACONITUM. In robust, plethoric children, this

remedy is frequently of much service as an auxiliary when the pulse is full and accelerated. It may, under such circumstances, be given either previously to, or in alternation with, the medicament otherwise indicated, until the unnatural rapidity of the circulation has been subdued.

ADMINISTRATION. As soon as the paroxysm is over, two globules may be dissolved in four teaspoonsful of water; a teaspoonful every four to eight hours when given before any other remedy; or every four to six hours, in alternation with the other medicine employed.

BELLADONNA is one of the most important remedies in all cases which proceed from, or are connected with, a more or less serious disturbance in the brain. It is more particularly indicated when the child starts suddenly from sleep, and stares about wildly; the pupils being much dilated; the body or individual members rigid; the head and hands dry and burning; the blood-vessels much distended. Further, when there is insensibility, with involuntary passing of water after returning to consciousness, and when the slightest touch will sometimes provoke a renewal of the attack. This medicine is also indicated when the paroxysms are preceded by smiles or laughter.

ADMINISTRATION. In the same manner as *Chamomilla.*

It is frequently found that *Chamomilla* and *Belladonna* answer in alternation; or, as already remarked, that when one has alleviated the evil, the other will dissipate the remaining symptoms.

CINA is useful, particularly during the second teething, for children of a melancholy temperament, and scrofulous constitution, who are troubled with worms, or habitually wet the bed. The characteristic symptoms are,—spasms, commencing with constriction of the chest and impeded respiration, and followed by stiffness of the limbs, paleness of the face, with sunken, blue underlined eyes, and rigidity of the whole frame.

ADMINISTRATION. Same as *Chamomilla.* But in some cases it will be found useful to prescribe one globule every four days, for a week or fortnight, in order to remove the susceptibility to the attack.

MERCURIUS is useful in spasms which are caused by the presence of worms; the stomach being swollen and hard before, during, and after the fit; the child is, at the same time, attacked with painful eructation, and a species of salivation; and the limbs are tossed about and convulsed. After the paroxysms, the patient lies, for a considerable time, exhausted and apparently dying.

ADMINISTRATION. Same as *Chamomilla.*

The foregoing are the more generally useful

remedies in ordinary cases; but the subjoined are sometimes called for in the particular instances specified.

CICUTA VIROSA is more or less serviceable when there is a clear indication of the presence of worms; or when the child is first attacked with severe griping and colic, terminating in convulsions. The characteristic features of the fit are: tremor of the limbs; jerks like electric shocks, terminated by insensibility. (*Nux v.*, *Ignatia*, and *Mercurius* are also useful when convulsions occur in children who are troubled with worms. See *Invermination.*)

ADMINISTRATION. Same as *Cina.*

ARSENICUM has proved very valuable in severe cases of convulsions, during dentition, with the following symptoms: a burning heat diffuses itself over the whole body of the child; the feet are stretched out, and the hands drawn convulsively backwards; the child then throws its hands about, and rolls over with violent shrieks, changes its position, and bends forward with clenched fingers and extended thumbs; it is irritable, restless, and perverse; evinces insatiable thirst, but drinks little at a time; is affected with diarrhœa, sometimes of undigested food; frequently vomits immediately after taking food; the paroxysms recur frequently, and all attempts at soothing seem only to irritate the child.

ADMINISTRATION. Same as *Cina.*

IPECACUANHA is chiefly useful when the attack has been excited by indigestible food; and when the paroxysms are either preceded, accompanied, or followed by great difficulty of breathing, nausea, or vomiting; also when the child has a constant inclination to remain in the recumbent posture. *Nux v.* or *Pulsatilla* may likewise be serviceable when improper food has originated the attack. (See *Derangement of Stomach.*)

SULPHUR is particularly indicated in spasms arising from repelled chronic eruptions.

In cases of convulsions from FRIGHT, *Opium*, two globules, may be resorted to, when the following appearances are present: general trembling; jactitation* of the limbs; vacant stare; cries; snoring respiration; insensibility. Change of air is sometimes necessary to aid in overcoming the liability to returns of convulsions in delicate children. Attention should be paid to the general health; and every known exciting cause, such as mental emotions, indigestible food, &c., avoided as strictly as possible. (See also the articles on *Teething, Invermination*, and *Derangement of Stomach.*

* Tossing.

Convulsions being frequently merely symptomatic of these disorders.)

Teething.

With some children the first teeth appear as early as the third or fourth month, but the average period of their first appearance is about the sixth or seventh month. Their protrusion through the gum is often, however, delayed to a later period, owing either to the constitutional condition of the infant, or to some other and unascertainable accidental cause.

The first set of teeth amounts to twenty in number, and this set is rarely completed in less than a year and a half, and sometimes remains imperfect until the third year.

The front or middle incisors, four in number, two in each jaw, are the first to appear; next come four more of the same description of teeth, one on each side of the former, then the four anterior molars or grinders, then the four canine or eye-teeth, and, lastly, the four back grinders.

They usually appear in pairs, the lower jaw commonly taking the precedence of the upper in the order of cutting them. Sometimes, though rarely, the canine appear before the front or anterior molars.

The SECOND SET of teeth, which succeeds the

first in the order in which that is shed, date from about the seventh or eighth year on the average, and the process of changing teeth may be said to extend over a period of from five to six years. And this set, which remains permanent, saving accidents or decay, is not completed until the appearance of the *wisdom teeth* (the last grinders,) between the 17th and 20th year on the average.

The second set of teeth comprises thirty-two in number, i. e. those before described, with the addition of eight additional grinders and four wisdom teeth.

Indispositions during Teething.

During the progress of TEETHING there are many little inconveniences to which children are apt to be subject, but which indicate no serious consequences, and which, with care as to diet, air, exercise, ventilation, and the like, will usually run their course without prejudice, and subside of themselves. The diet of the mother, or nurse, ought also to be carefully selected; no precaution should be omitted in providing against any of the inflammatory complications, especially about the mouth and throat, to which children are, during dentition, peculiarly liable, and with this object in view, in order that no extraneous morbid complications should escape early observation, the mouth and gums should be constantly and carefully examined; pulmonary and cerebral derangements,* particularly the latter, are more especially the disorders to which children are subject during teething. But when the process is being favorably carried on, the symptoms will usually be as follows:—in which case the precautions as to diet, before indicated with that of keeping the head cool, will suffice to ward off any more serious affections.

SYMPTOMS. Peculiar restlessness, especially at night, sudden paroxysms of crying, alternate flushing and pallor—gums swollen, red and hot, especially along the upper edge—disposition to gnaw anything—difficulty in sucking, arising from the tender state of the gums—considerable and constant flow of saliva, and slight diarrhœa, which two last symptoms are to be looked upon as favorable indications, and not as derangements to be counteracted. In these we may detect the salutary effort of nature to afford relief to the system susceptible as it is of inflammatory and congestive tendencies during dentition. The sudden or irregular suspension of these symptoms, with the continuance of the others, in an aggra-

* Affections of the lungs and brain.

vated form, or the manifestation of new ones, such as excessive fretfulness, incessant thirst, with trembling of the lips, convulsions, etc., especially with indications of great heat of head and of the body generally, and suppressed urine, may be looked upon as a sufficient ground for the exhibition of medicine, for although they may subside of their own accord, and may occur and remit from time to time, until a tooth cuts through, still, a fatal result or some permanent injury may be the sequel of neglect.

TREATMENT. When there is merely considerable excitement, restlessness, want of sleep, starting, &c.

COFFEA (one globule) should be administered. In the event of no amelioration after a few hours, ACONITE (similar dose) may be resorted to.

If either medicine be attended with good effects, no repetition should take place until a return of the symptoms is threatened.

If only partial relief be obtained, they may be followed up with *Chamomilla.*

This remedy should have the priority and preference when indicated by excessive excitability, great thirst, starting at any noise, convulsive and spasmodic twitchings during sleep, dry, hacking, irritative cough; short, quick, and sonorous breathing; acidity, vomiting, excessive looseness with green, whitish, and watery motions, (particularly when the nurse is in the habit of drinking coffee.) MERCURIUS is sometimes required after *Chamomilla*, when the excessive looseness continues, and is occasionally followed by protrusion of the last intestine, or is accompanied by glandular swellings and a tendency to the formation of aphthæ in the mouth or around the fundament; or when there is hardness of the belly, and convulsions, followed by great weakness. In the event of only partial or temporary improvement from the employment of *Merc.*, *Sulphur* may be resorted to.

Each of these remedies may be administered as follows:—one globule, in a teaspoonful of water, at intervals of twelve, twenty-four or forty-eight hours, or oftener if the symptoms are very urgent, until improvement sets in.

NUX V. should generally be administered in the same way when constipation prevails, followed or alternated by *Aconite*, if there be considerable febrile action.

ACONITE is at all times indicated by great inflammation, swelling, and painful tenderness of the gums; heat of skin; flushed face; suppressed or scanty, high-coloured urine. Dissolve one globule in three teaspoonsful of water, and administer one teaspoonful of the solution every six or eight hours.

BELLADONNA is indicated by symptoms of determination of blood to the head and cerebral* derangements, manifested by the following: great heat and pulsation about the head; redness and puffiness of the cheeks; violent throbbing of the vessels of the neck; restlessness and alternate heaviness; tossing back of the head; startings and sudden cries during sleep, the child awaking with a fixed and terrified look; dry, nocturnal cough; increased temperature of the skin and accelerated pulse; watery and suffused, or red and sparkling eyes, with sensibility to light; dilated pupils; convulsive movements, either confined to the eyes, face, and arms, and consisting of mere twitchings, or of a more violent and general description.

ADMINISTRATION OF BELLADONNA. Six globules in a wineglassful of water, a teaspoonful of the solution every three, or six, or twelve hours, being guided by the intensity of the symptoms, and the effect produced. As soon as signs of improvement set in, the medicine must be discontinued. (See *Rules for the administration and repetition of the Dose*) When the fever is high, *Aconitum* may be given alternately every three or four hours with *Belladonna;* or, in not very urgent cases, a tea-

* Appertaining to the brain.

spoonful of the above-mentioned solution of the last-named medicine may be given in the morning, and one of *Aconitum* of the same strength at bed-time; and so on until relief is afforded.

With respect to the extraneous complications to which allusion has slightly been made, and to which, during *teething*, children are more especially subject, they must necessarily be submitted to the course of treatment recommended under the head of each particular malady. (See *Inflammation and Dropsy of the Brain, Inflammation of the Lungs, Constipation*, &c. &c.)

Various kinds of eruptions, often appear and disappear with the progress of the teeth, but neither these nor a moderate degree of looseness of the bowels ought to be interfered with unnecessarily.

Diet and Regimen. Strict attention should be paid to diet, and great care taken not to overload the stomach of the infant; and the same precaution, as already observed, is equally necessary in reference to the nurse. Exposure to a chill should be guarded against; nevertheless, it is essential that the head should be kept cool, and that the infant should be regularly taken into the open air. Whilst the gums are hot, tender, and intolerant of the slightest pressure, the use of ivory rings, a crust of bread, &c., tend but to aggravate matters. The employment of *Aconite* is, as previously remarked, the most appropriate remedy in such a state of matters, when a remedy seems called for. Its alternation with *Arnica* is often still more soothing—giving one globule of the one and then the other medicament at intervals of twelve hours. As dentition advances, pressure appears to relieve the child, and may then be encouraged. Lancing the gums is rarely necessary under homœopathic treatment; it ought only to be resorted to when the medicines fail to palliate, and there is excessive local irritation, combined with attendant symptoms of extreme nervous disturbance. The incision may, in most cases, be slight, and generally on or towards the outer side of the gum.

DISEASES OF THE BRAIN, ETC.

Irritation of the Brain.

This complaint is perhaps more peculiar to children who have a constitutional predisposition to *water on the brain.* It is not necessarily indicative of organic disease, although it is certainly a species of warning that there is a susceptibility to the suscitation of such derangement; and, moreover, if neglected, it may lead to organic and chronic disease.

SYMPTOMS. At the onset of this malady a peculiar susceptibility of the senses prevails. The eye cannot bear to be exposed to too strong a light, and there is great dislike to the slightest noise. The child is, at the same time, peevish; restless, or distressed with wakefulness. A spasmodic closure of the eyelids is not an unusual concomitant symptom; and there are frequent twitchings or convulsive movements of the limbs —the foot or hand being suddenly jerked upwards —or the hands are firmly clenched—or the thumb is fixed across the palm. The skin is, sometimes, hot, and the pulse accelerated; but more commonly the temperature of the body and the condition of the pulse are normal. The more frequent exciting causes of irritation of the brain, are the injudicious and culpable use of stimulants; debility from loss of humors, mental emotions, such as passion, fear, &c.; or the hurtful effects of low, damp localities, and badly-ventilated dwellings.

TREATMENT. *Coffea*, *Aconitum*, *Lachesis*, *Belladonna*, *Chamomilla*, *Nux v.*, *Ignatia*, *Cinchona*, and *Arsenicum* are amongst the more important remedies in ordinary cases of morbid irritation of the brain.

COFFEA. In simple cases, chiefly characterised

by wakefulness, restlessness, sensibility to noise, and great nervous excitement; two globules of this medicine may be dissolved in three teaspoonsful of water, and a teaspoonful of the solution given every four hours. If some improvement has followed the use of this remedy, it may be resorted to again as soon as symptoms of a relapse threaten; but if no melioration succeed, ARSENICUM may be given in the same way; and if the latter fails to relieve, LACHESIS may be resorted to, particularly if considerable excitement continues. Due attention must, however, be paid in all cases to the entirety of the symptoms, and the selection of the remedy made in the strictest possible accordance therewith.

ACONITUM is required when there is heat of skin, and acceleration of pulse, combined with sleeplessness and more or less agitation or excitement.

BELLADONNA. When the case verges closely on acute inflammation of the brain or its membranes, the head and face being hot, the face rather flushed and the vessels distended; the sensibility to light and noise excessive, and the eye preternaturally brilliant. The state of wakefulness is apparently accompanied by ineffectual efforts to sleep, and when sleep ensues, it is liable to be broken by the slightest touch or sound—the child starting up as if alarmed. Further, an unusual sensitiveness of the skin, spasmodic closure of the eyelids, occasional twitchings of the limbs, a throwing back of the head, and constant crying, are additional indications for *Belladonna.* (See *Inflammation of the Brain* and also *Teething.*)

ADMINISTRATION of *Aconitum* and *Belladonna* same as *Coffea.*

CHAMOMILLA is of service in this affection, when the irritation proceeds from acidity, attended with diarrhœa, colic, and great fretfulness. It is also particularly useful when a fit of passion has given rise to the morbid symptoms.

ADMINISTRATION. Two globules in four teaspoonsful of water, one teaspoonful every twelve hours, or oftener if necessary. (See *Diarrhœa.*)

NUX VOMICA is sometimes required in irritation of the brain, but more especially in cases which have been induced by the injudicious employment of stimulants (such as wine, &c.) Some degree of sensibility to light, occasional twitchings of the limbs, sensitiveness of the whole surface of the body, foul tongue, and constipation, are the principal symptoms which denote the appropriateness of *Nux v.*

ADMINISTRATION. Same as *Chamomilla.*

IGNATIA is chiefly indicated when twitchings of the limbs or other convulsive movements, sometimes of a severe kind, accompany the other symptoms of this derangement.

ADMINISTRATION. Same as *Chamomilla.*

CINCHONA is more especially requisite when debility, arising from protracted diarrhœa, has given rise to the state of morbid, nervous irritation; or when it has been developed by the injurious consequences of exposure in a low damp situation. Wakefulness, restlessness, emaciation, and extreme sensibility of the entire surface of the body, are the leading indications for the selection of this medicament.

ARSENICUM is useful under nearly similar circumstances as *Cinchona,* but with less striking sensitiveness of the surface. It is well adapted to children of a scrofulous or otherwise delicate constitution.

ADMINISTRATION of *Cinchona* and *Arsenicum* same as *Chamomilla.* (See also rules for the repetition of the dose.)

In cases arising from fright, a globule or two of *Opium* may be administered with advantage.

DIET AND REGIMEN. The diet ought to be of easy digestion and unstimulating, but, when not contraindicated by inflammatory signs, sufficiently nourishing. Exposure to light and noise should be avoided. The apartments ought to be well ventilated; and when the locality of the dwelling in which the child is kept is unfavourable, a removal will be necessary. The application of warmth to the feet, combined with frequent sponging of the head with cold water, will be found beneficial.

Determination of Blood to the Head. Congestion.

This affection is not of uncommon occurrence during infancy.

SYMPTOMS. The prominent convex state of the open part of the head,* combined with heaviness and want of animation, approximating stupor. Occasionally there is some degree of heat of the head, but the pulse sluggish, or perhaps irregular. The bowels are variable, more especially costive; the face flabby, full, and of a deep or livid colour; the veins about the forehead and neck prominent and distended; the eyes present a vacant expression, or they seem difficult to fix on any object, and the pupils are commonly dilated. The sleep is heavy but disturbed, and the breathing is frequently thick and oppressed.

Congestion is more liable to terminate in effusion (water in the brain), than in inflammation of

* The mould.

the brain, although the latter result does occasionally ensue. In rapid cases of effusion its occurrence is generally indicated by insensibility, with relaxation of the limbs or paralytic weakness; but in those in which the fluid is sereted more slowly, the head gradually enlarges, and the belly becomes retracted, the extremities relaxed and debilitated, and complete stupor or general convulsions supervene.

TREATMENT. In the majority of cases OPIUM is one of the most useful medicines in recent congestion, whether arising from a fright, from repulsed scarlatina or measles, or some undiscoverable cause; and whether occurring in infants immediately after birth, or in children of a more advanced age.

Its principal indications are: somnolency, or heaviness and stupor; dark-colored or livid countenance; dilated pupils; convulsed or half-closed eyes; considerable drowsiness; very disturbed sleep; and the child when roused looks vacant or seems incapable of fixing the sight; prominent state of the mould; full, slow, and rather irregular pulse: oppressed breathing; constipation. A dose of one or two globules will, when early administered, often cause the above-described symptoms to disappear in a few hours; but if no perceptible amendment becomes soon apparent, the medicine must be repeated, provided some other remedy is not required by a change in the symptoms.

NUX V. and BRYONIA are often serviceable after the previous employment of *Opium*. In slight cases, chiefly marked by extreme drowsiness, and associated with constipation, they may be preferred to that remedy. *Nux v.* particularly when the stomach has been overloaded with indigestible food, or when wine has been thoughtlessly and culpably given in excess. *Pulsatilla* is often useful in cases arising from an overloaded or disordered stomach, especially when the patient is of a lymphatic temperament. *Bryonia* is sometimes useful in completing the cure when *Nux v.* is insufficient to accomplish it. The administration of these may be conducted in the same way as *Opium*. (See also art. Derangement of stomach, and administer as there stated if requisite.)

BELLADONNA, preceded if needful by *Aconitum*, is to be preferred in congestion with symptoms of approaching inflammation of the brain (see that article, and also the indications given for the selection of this remedy in the preceding chapter)—or when drowsiness, heat of the head, puffed, bluish red countenance, dilated pupils, sudden starts on closing the eyes, muscular twitchings or general convulsions, with a projecting condition and violent throbbing of the moulds form the most striking features of the case.

ADMINISTRATION. Three globules in six teaspoonsful of water, a teaspoonful of the solution every twelve hours. When convulsions are present the repetitions of the dose may be regulated in accordance with what is stated in the article on that subject. In more advanced cases of congestion with symptoms of threatening effusion, or of established effusion, *Belladonna*, *Helleborus*, *Lachesis*, *Digitalis*, *Arsenicum*, and *Zincum* are the medicines on which the chief reliance is to be placed as long as hope remains. As auxiliaries in the treatment of congestion, the use of the warm bath, and the application of cold to the head and warmth to the feet may be mentioned. Medical aid should be sought in all cases which do not speedily give way to the medicines administered.

Inflammation of the Brain. Brain Fever.

Acute* inflammation of the brain or its membranes, analogous to that which occurs in adults, is only encountered in children of a robust and plethoric habit of body. It is chiefly characterised by redness and heat of the face, with violent throbbing of the vessels, and intolerance of light

* *Acute* is a term applied to diseases which run a short course, but are accompanied by violent symptoms.

and sound. The sleep is restless and much distubed by frequent starting, or by delirium. The pulse is quick and full; the eye unusually brilliant, and sometimes inflamed looking; the expression of countenance peculiar; and the breathing rapid and oppressed. There is commonly, also, great irritability of stomach, constipation, and suppressed or scanty urine. If these symptoms be not speedily arrested, they are very liable to be followed by stupor, with partial or general convulsions, ending in death.

TREATMENT. *Aconitum* and *Belladonna* are the principal medicines. When timely resorted to they will rarely, if ever, fail to overcome the affection.

ADMINISTRATION. Six globules of each medicine may be separately dissolved in two tablespoonsful of water, and a teaspoonful first of *Aconitum*, and then of *Belladonna* given, in alternation, every six hours. As soon as the skin becomes moist, and the pulse diminished in force and frequency, the *Aconitum* must be discontinued, and *Belladonna* given alone as long as it appears to do good.

If improvement does not set in soon after the employment of these remedies, assistance should be sought. (See also WATER IN THE BRAIN.)

Water in the Brain. Dropsy of the Brain.

This frequent and dangerous affection most commonly occurs in children of scrofulous constitution. Its symptoms proceed from a diseased state of the brain or its membranes, which is liable to give rise to a watery effusion,—hence the denomination water or dropsy of the brain. The less the disease assumes an inflammatory aspect, and the more slow its progress, so much the more surely, generally speaking, will water be thrown out.

SYMPTOMS. The malady in its more common form, generally comes on very insidiously, and often creates no alarm for several days—the signs of indisposition being attributed to the effects of teething or to peevishness. The first of these indications of deranged health consists in great languor and tendency to fatigue from the slightest exertion. The child consequently shuns movement; totters in its walk; or drags one leg after the other. There is excessive fretfulness, particularly when the head is raised, and pain is frequently complained of in the back of the neck, in the eyes, limbs, and stomach. The stomach is exceedingly irritable, vomiting being generally induced whenever the child sits upright or is placed in the erect posture: the head is hot; the eye looks inflamed, or the pupil is contracted, and the countenance wears a peculiar bold expression. There is some fever, especially at night, with grinding of the teeth during sleep, and starting, or fits of screaming on being awakened. The evacuations are unhealthy, or the bowels are obstinately confined; the urine scanty or suppressed. The child answers correctly when spoken to, but often stutters or hesitates in using a particular word. As the disease progresses, pain is commonly less frequently complained of; the child becomes quiet when allowed to remain in the horizontal posture, but utters a shrill, peevish cry when lifted up. Drowsiness or stupor now prevails; the head sinks upon the pillow; the eyes are half closed; the pupils dilated or immoveable, or alternately dilated and contracted, and attended with impaired or double vision or with squinting. A diminution or a complete cessation of sickness, sometimes combined with a slight return of appetite, occurs at this stage; but emaciation proceeds rapidly; the child moans and frequently lifts its hands to its head with a tremulous motion, and often sighs deeply. This, the second stage, may continue for eight, twelve, or fourteen days; after which the affection enters upon the third stage, with its convulsions of greater or less intensity. There is constant moaning or raving, but complete loss of consciousness; the eyes are dim, glazed, and turned upwards; the pulse may be invariably fast throughout the whole course of the disease; or after having grown slow and weak at the termination of the first stage, it may now become much accelerated for a short period, and then gradually decline. The limbs become relaxed, the belly retracted. and the breathing very unequal. Extreme prostration, with increased stupor, supervene: and the child is carried off in a state of collapse,* or the scene is terminated by a severe convulsive fit.

In the acute and less frequent variety of the complaint, the symptoms are much more strongly marked. In robust children it occasionally sets in very suddenly with fever or violent convulsions, the child dying on the third or fourth day. In other cases the child is seized with severe headache; the face is red, the head hot, and the vessels full and throbbing; the child starts at the slightest noise; the eye is preternaturally brilliant, and is very sensitive to the light. The pulse is, at first, full and very quick; and the respiration hurried and labored. The stomach is excessively irritable; the tongue white and furred, and per-

* Utter prostration of the vital powers.

haps enlarged; the bowels usually very costive; or the motions unnatural, generally presenting a singular green color; the urine scanty, or sometimes altogether suppressed. The countenance is strikingly peculiar, presenting a mixed expression of terror and pain; the hands are frequently raised to the head; and the child is extremely fretful, particularly when taken up from the bed; whilst the screams which occasionally escape from it are piercing and frantic. As the disease advances, the pulse becomes slow, feeble, and unequal or irregular—any movement has, however, a tendency to accelerate it. The complaint then passes through the stages already described, and terminates in a like manner.

Water of the brain occurs very frequently during the progress of other diseases, such as fevers, (infantile remittent,) scarlatina, measles, smallpox, hooping-cough, affections of the chest, bowel complaints, difficult dentition, &c., becoming suddenly apparent on any rapid subsidence of the symptoms, or creeping on insidiously in the course of the primary malady. It is, therefore, incumbent to pay attention to any unaccountable invasion of sickness of stomach, associated with an unusual degree of peevishness, intolerance of light and sound, heat of head, &c. The premonitory symptoms are, however often absent in these cases; and stupor, convulsions, or paralysis give the first indications of a secondary disease of the brain or its membranes.

Chronic Water or Dropsy of the Brain.* This form of the disease is sometimes a sequel of the preceding variety. But, more commonly, it sets in slowly and insidiously without any antecedent acute stage. The head gradually enlarges, whilst the face retains its natural size; and if the child affected be of tender age, the bones of the head separate to a considerable extent, the moulds become transparent and prominent, and a sense of fluctuation is detectible on pressure. In some cases the head is unusually large originally, and does not increase in magnitude during the course of the disease. The first general symptoms usually observed are languor, lassitude, and loss of flesh. The physical power is much enfeebled; and one or the whole of the senses are impaired, or become entirely suppressed as the malady advances. In some cases, the intellectual faculties are preserved much longer than could be imagined from the extent of the disease. Occasionally the head attains an enormous size, and is incapable of

* A term applied to diseases of long standing; it is used in opposition to *acute*.

being kept erect by the debilitated and attenuated frame which supports it. Violent general convulsions sometimes occur, and certain limbs remain constantly in a rigid state. At other times the convulsions are only partial, affecting merely the face, the muscles connected with the act of breathing, or those of one or more extremities. Some degree of giddiness in the erect posture is occasionally complained of; or there may be heat and pain in the head; vomiting; nocturnal fever, with great restlessness and movements of the head from side to side, or sinking of the head deep into the pillow; repeated working of the tongue and lips, or continuous action of the lower jaws as in the process of chewing. Squinting is not an unfrequent attendant. Dissolution is generally preceded by drowsiness, and followed by stupor, convulsions, and relaxation of the limbs; but the immediate cause of death is often to be found in some other disease, such as ulceration of the bowels, pulmonary consumption, or an inflammatory affection of the chest.

TREATMENT. In a malady of this serious and dangerous character, professional aid should be sought without delay. The following remedies may, nevertheless, be named as the most appropriate to resort to in the majority of cases:—

Aconitum, Belladonna, Hyoscyamus, Bryonia, Rhus, Helleborus, Mercurius, Sulphur, &c. In the most acute, but rarer forms of the complaint, occurring in robust, plethoric children, *Aconitum* is required when the pulse is full and rapid, the head hot, the respiration hurried or oppressed, the stomach more or less irritable, and the urine very scanty or suppressed.

ADMINISTRATION. Six globules in two table-spoonsful of water,—to children under two years a teaspoonful, and to those above that age a dessert spoonful of the solution every six hours. As soon as the violence of the fever has been subdued, and the skin has become moist, which will commonly be the case after two or, at most, three doses have been administered—

BELLADONNA should be had recourse to, particularly when there is great heat in the head, redness of the face, with fulness and violent throbbing of the vessels of the head and neck; loud complaints of pain in the head; or frequent clasping of the hands round the head; increase of suffering from the slightest noise, and extreme sensibility to light; frequent flushings; unusual brilliancy of the eye, and bold or wild expression of countenance; sickness of stomach; delirium; frantic screams. This remedy is further indicated when the child buries or sinks its head deep into the pillow, or moves its head from side to side; also when there is drowsiness or stupor; contraction or dilatation of the pupils; moaning; partial or general convulsions; grinding of the teeth.

ADMINISTRATION. Same as *Aconitum*. Cold applications to the head are often of considerable assistance, in conjunction with the use of *Bella.*

In the more common, less acute form of the disease, *Belladonna* is still a very important and most efficient remedy; and even in the chronic variety it is of considerable service when early resorted to. In both cases, however, it will generally be found advantageous to administer it in alternation with *Hyoscyamus*, or with *Helleborus* if the mould is full and prominent, at intervals of from six to twelve, or twenty-four hours, according to the urgency of the symptoms. When no improvement follows the employment of *Belladonna* either in the acute form of the complaint, or in the first stage, or the commencement of the second stage of the low and protracted type, BRYONIA may be substituted for it, especially if the bowels are obstinately confined, the urine suppressed, or the act of passing it painful and difficult; the respiration oppressed; and the lower jaw in frequent movement.

ADMINISTRATION. Same as *Aconitum*. (*Helleborus* is often required after *Bryonia*.)

In the second and third stages, the remedies by means of which we may yet entertain some hope of warding off a fatal issue, are chiefly *Lachesis*, *Digitalis*, *Rhus*, *Opium*, *Stramonium*, *Arsenicum*, *Sulphur*, and *Zincum*. Without entering minutely into the numerous indications which lead to the selection of these, it may be briefly observed that LACHESIS is better adapted than *Belladonna* to the low form of the malady, when it occurs in sickly or debilitated children, or when the case under treatment has previously been complicated by the abuse of mercurial preparations; also when there is constipation, with extreme prostration of strength, moaning, drowsiness or stupor, and tremulous, intermittent, or scarcely perceptible pulse. DIGITALIS is sometimes indicated in the second stage of water in the brain, particularly when the pulse is slow, weak, and irregular.

RHUS is an important remedy in the low protracted variety of this disease, especially when it has attained the second stage. The following are some of its leading indications; intense headache, giddiness, heaviness, and drooping of the head on the chest or shoulder; distressing, pressive, aching pains in the back of the head, combined with a sensation of creeping, or as if something were loose and moving about; drowsiness; slow, or quick and weak pulse; convulsive movements of the limbs, attended with complaints of severe pain in the head, and followed by remissions during which the patient lies in a torpid state. In water in the brain occurring in conjunction with general dropsy after scarlet fever, this medicament is often of signal service. *Belladonna* and *Hyoscyamus* may, however, be required, here, previous to the employment of *Rhus*, especially, if, as is frequently the case, the disease sets in in a very acute form.

OPIUM is sometimes serviceable in the second or even the third stage, when there is complete apathy and absence of complaint; half-closed eyes, contracted, or dilated and immoveable; drowsiness or stupor, and constipation. STRAMONIUM when the convulsions are frequent and severe, and do not yield to the employment of *Belladonna* and *Hyoscyamus*, &c. ARSENICUM, when the face is pale, the emaciation and debility excessive, the pulse quick, weak, and unequal or irregular, and when marked intermissions are observed in the course of the affection. SULPHUR is occasionally useful in winding up the cure after the employment of *Bryonia* or *Arsenicum*. And ZINCUM in desperate cases, after the previous use of *Belladonna* or any of the other remedies, when there is ice-like coldness of the extremities, or of the whole surface of the body; blueness of the hands or feet; impeded breathing; small, weak, and scarcely perceptible pulse. Should any improvement ensue after a few doses of *Zincum*, *Belladonna*, or any of the other remedies which may then appear better indicated, should be resorted to.

In chronic water or dropsy of the brain, *Helleborus*, *Arsenicum*, *Sulphur*; and *Pulsatilla*, *Rhus*, *Conium*, *Arnica*, together with *Belladonna* and *Hyoscyamus*, are amongst the more serviceable remedies. Compression of the head is also of some utility.

The more acute the inflammation, the greater are the prospects of cure in general cases of water in the brain. It is in these that the employment of *Belladonna* and *Hyoscyamus*, preceded, if necessary, by *Aconitum*, act with striking success—a copious outbreak of perspiration, with diminished rapidity and oppression of breathing, and increased flow of urine taking place soon after their timely administration. On the other hand, when the disease comes on gradually and insidiously in the wake of some other malady, and especially if it occurs in a child of scrofulous habit, the chances of recovery are much less; still, even in these varieties, a cure may often be accomplished when the case seems almost hopeless. Protracted slowness and feebleness of pulse, or a sudden fall in the pulse occurring in concomitance with dilated or immoveable pupils, and laborious and irregular breathing, are unfavorable signs.

When the chronic form of the complaint follows an acute attack; or when, during its progress, delirium, convulsions, and stupor supervene, a fatal result can with difficulty be warded off. But when this variety is manifested in its more common form, and is regularly confirmed, the child affected with it may live for many years,—death being ultimately occasioned, as we have elsewhere observed, by some other disease.

DIET. In the first stage of the acute variety, toast-water, or, at the utmost, barley-water, or thin water-gruel, are alone required. In the low form of the complaint, and in the second stage of the acute, the patient's strength may be supported by a sufficiency of nutritious but light, easily-digestible food. In the chronic form of the malady the diet must be nourishing, at the same time care should be taken not to overload the stomach. The practitioner is much more frequently called upon to diminish than to increase the amount of food given to the children of parents who are in comfortable circumstances. Habitually overloaded stomachs, and the want of a sufficient supply of pure air, form fruitful sources of the derangements of childhood in general.

FEVER. ERUPTIVE FEVERS.

Diet in Fevers.

THE great essentials in the treatment of fever are:

Perfect rest, mental and bodily.

Pure air and a cool apartment; the temperature of the patient's room should never, when practicable, exceed 55 degrees.

Feather-beds should be discarded and mattresses substituted; and the bed-clothes ought to be light, but sufficient.

Nature herself generally prescribes the regimen to be observed, by taking away appetite; while the thirst present, as an eminent medical writer has well observed, may be considered as her voice calling for fluid. Water is the best diluent; no solid food, broth, or even gruel and the like, should be permitted in cases where the fever runs excessively high; and the utmost caution is to be observed, in allowing gruel or weak broths during the decrease. An error in this respect often causes irreparable mischief, and it is always safer to err a little on the side of abstinence, than on that of indulgence.

Toast-water, or weak barley, or rice-water, sweetened with a little sugar or raspberry or strawberry syrup, orangeade, whey, and thin gruel may be allowed, when the fever is somewhat abated. On the approach of convalescence, indicated by the subsidence of thirst and the desire for food, Hecker's farina,* semolina, sago, arrow-root, and such like, as also cocoa and beef-tea, may be given, though then we must still carefully avoid incurring the risk of a relapse, by giving any aliment, or any undue amount of nutriment, likely to tax, in however slight a degree, the digestive powers. This is best accomplished by the administration of very small quantities at a time, and at short intervals, gradually augmenting or diminishing the allowance, according to the effects produced. In all kinds of severe acute diseases, the above rules should be strictly attended to; but in those of a subacute character, which retain a mild type throughout their course, the diet may, from the first, be of the same description as that we have mentioned as the best adapted to the convalescent stages of the severer forms. Fruits, such as grapes, gooseberries, and juice of a sweet orange, are often allowable, as the inflammatory symptoms decline, in most forms of fever unattended with diarrhœa.

* This wholesome preparation may be had pure at the Homœopathic Pharmacy, 239 Arch street.

Simple Fever.

This disease seldom presents any distinct character, and generally runs its course in twenty-four hours; as, however, it frequently forms the initiative of other more serious disorders, it deserves attention. Before attacks of scarlatina, measles, smallpox, &c., it is usually present, although occasionally showing itself as a distinct affection.

SYMPTOMS. Shivering, followed by general heat, restlessness, thirst, accelerated pulse, great uneasiness and lassitude terminated by profuse perspiration.

TREATMENT. Throughout the work, this disease will be found treated of, both when arising from indigestion or cold, and when appearing as the precursor of other affections; but when it is manifested by the symptoms above detailed, and cannot be traced to any particular exciting cause, and particularly when *hot dry skin* is present, ACONITE, three globules, may be administered* in a teaspoonful of water, and repeated every six to eight hours, until the febrile symptoms subside, which they will speedily do under the employ-

* In all cases where directions for the *administration* of a medicine are given, the attention of the reader is directed to the "*Rules for the Administration and Repetition of the Dose.*"

ment of this remedy, sometimes shortly after the first dose, if the attack be simple fever properly so called; if, on the other hand, it be the forerunner of any more severe disorder, *Aconite* will, very commonly, either at once check its further progress, or materially modify its malignancy. The former is more peculiarly the case with purely inflammatory attacks: the latter holds good as far as relates to eruptive diseases, and some other affections, which run a regular course.

Scarlet Fever.

This appellation is employed to denote an affection, characterised by a bright red eruption, which appears in patches upon the skin and lining membrane of the mouth and throat, and which is accompanied by fever, with pain and more or less difficulty in performing the act of deglutition.

Scarlet fever generally occurs in an epidemic form towards the end of summer and autumn, particularly in cold, wet seasons, and prevails as such until the opening of spring. It is also capable of being spread by contagion. Different degrees of malignancy may spring from the same fount of infection. The habit of body materially influences the type of the malady; but when the existing epidemy is of a peculiarly severe or malignant character, it assumes a more or less serious form in all whom it attacks.

When it manifests itself in its simple form, uncomplicated with any internal inflammation,—the rash coming out freely, remaining its usual time, and presenting its characteristic, boiled-lobster-like, hue,—the prospects of recovery are favorable.

SYMPTOMS. General uneasiness and feeling of weakness, nausea, sometimes vomiting, with transient chilliness, or fits of shivering, commonly form the antecedents of the eruption. To these are soon afterwards superadded,—headache, thirst, heat of skin, occasionally drowsiness, bleeding at the nose, fever, extreme quickness of pulse, and a feeling of soreness or pain in the throat. In one or more days the face becomes tumefied. and numerous small reddish spots appear on the face, neck, and chest—the skin, in the intermediate spaces, retaining its usual colour. In a few hours, this eruption spreads over the whole body, and even extends to the lips, tongue, and throat. About the third day, the small red spots and the majority of the interstices are supplanted by large, indefinitely-marked patches, presenting the vivid hue before described, gradually growing paler towards their margins, and often overspreading entire limbs, but especially the groins, hips, and joints, with a uniform scarlet color. The fever nsually diminishes after the evolution of the eruption. In five or six days, the efflorescence disappears, when the skin scales, and comes off in large pieces.

We sometimes find scarlet fever with scarcely any or even no external redness, but, at the same time, marked sore-throat and bright redness of the tongue; in such cases the disease, instead of showing itself on the skin, has fixed upon the mucous membrane; and even the sore-throat and redness of the tongue, present in most cases of this disease, may be considered indicative of an internal scarlatina.

Scarlatina was formerly confounded with measles, from the resemblance which the two eruptions bear to each other at their commencement; but they are easily distinguishable, even without taking into consideration the peculiar appearance of the skin above mentioned—characteristic of the disease,—by the eruption, in scarlet fever, generally developing itself in from twenty-four to forty-eight hours after the commencement of the fever; whereas that of measles rarely sets in before the third or fourth day; the absence of symptoms of cold, such as cough, sneezing, flow of tears—the usual precursors of measles—constitutes another mark of difference. The greatly accelerated pulse, which denotes the approach of scarlatina, is also never met with, to the same extent, in any other disease.

TREATMENT. In those cases in which this disease appears in its simple form, BELLADONNA is a specific remedy. Even in cases with symptoms of more or less disturbance of the brain, and in those attended with vomiting and excessive tenderness of the bowels, or with rapid and laborious breathing and other signs of affection of the chest, it is of the highest importance.

It should be administered as soon as the throat becomes sore, or when dryness and burning are complained of in the mouth and throat, accompanied by much thirst, but almost complete inability to swallow even drinks or saliva; further, when the throat is of a *bright-red* color, having its surface excoriated, or covered with white specks, or stringy mucus, or presenting the appearance of thrush; the tonsils swollen, and the tongue of a *bright fiery red* hue, or, as is sometimes the case at a more advanced stage of the disease, interspersed with dark red patches.

ADMINISTRATION. Six globules in two tablespoonsful of water. a dessert-spoonful every six hours, until the disease begins to subside, or a change takes place in the symptoms, calling for the employment of some other remedy. To children of from one to six years of age, a tea-spoonful of the solution may be given at the stated intervals.

If the disease have taken a favorable turn, we may allow the *Belladonna to continue its action;* but if after the second or third repetition of *Belladonna*, the inflammation and swelling increase instead of diminishing, as is frequently the case in scrofulous constitutions; or if we perceive increased secretion of mucus or of saliva, with swelling of the glands and muscles of the neck; or also soreness of the gums, offensive breath, exacerbation of suffering at night, chills or shivering, sometimes alternated with heat, and nocturnal sweating, we must have immediate recourse to MERCURIUS.

ADMINISTRATION. Same as *Belladonna.* If *Mercurius* produces only partial improvement, or if the throat symptoms are always more complained of after awaking from sleep, and the pain is much increased by the slightest external pressure, *Lachesis* should be resorted to. When there is little or no glandular enlargement, but a large quantity of viscid mucus is secreted from the inflamed and tumefied lining of the throat, which adheres so tenaciously that it is with difficulty to be expelled, and sometimes even threatens suffocation, *Nux v.* is of considerable service. (*Pulsatilla* is also useful in such cases, particularly when the patient is of phlegmatic temperament.)

ADMINISTRATION. Same as *Belladonna*, and *Mercurius*.

When, at the commencement of the attack, there is violent fever, with dry heat of skin, headache, and hardness of pulse, a dose of *Aconite* (three globules) should be given six or eight hours before *Belladonna* is resorted to. In some cases the alternate use of these two is beneficial at intervals of four hours, until the fever yields.

OPIUM may follow the administration of *Belladonna*, when there is burning heat of the skin, drowsiness, stupor, stertorous breathing, open mouth, eyes half closed, restlessness, with vomiting or convulsions. Again, when violent delirium, accompanied by extreme restlessness, and incessant movement of the hands, &c., appears at the commencement of scarlet fever (or, indeed, any of the eruptive fevers,) *Opium* is more serviceable than any other remedy, and will generally prevent a fatal issue from paralysis of the brain, which is so prone to appear under the said circumstances. *Zincum* may sometimes be required when *Opium* is insufficient to avert the threatening danger; or the aid of *Belladonna* may be needed to complete the recovery, after the favorable change produced by *Opium*. Such cases, as also those which are complicated with putrid ulcerous sore-throat, and a faint or a deep red eruption, interspersed with livid spots, in place of the true vivid red, scarlet rash, should, when possible, be treated by a homœopathic practitioner.

The dose of *Opium* may consist of six globules, or a drop of the tincture, added to an ounce of water, a dessert-spoonful every four hours; as soon, however, as a marked improvement sets in, we may discontinue the medicine.

When the eruption is very intense, and extends over the entire frame, and particularly when the patient affected is of the scrofulous constitution, *Sulphur* is often of much service.

ADMINISTRATION. Same as *Belladonna.*

Aconitum may be given, in alternation with *Sulphur*, when there is great restlessness, with dry heat of skin, and fulness and quickness of pulse.

If, notwithstanding the employment of these the throat becomes exceedingly painful and inflamed, *Belladonna* must be resorted to.

The symptoms of derangement of stomach and bowels, which sometimes come on during scarlet fever, generally give way to the remedies employed against the disease itself. But when they become exceedingly distressing, it is necessary to arrest them by means of *Ipecacuanha*, *Pulsatilla*, or *Chamomilla*. When nausea and vomiting are the most prominent gastric symptoms, *Ipecacuanha* is to be preferred; when there are both vomiting and diarrhœa, but less nausea, together with occasional pains in the bowels and chilliness, *Pulsatilla;* and when there is diarrhœa alone, *Chamomilla.* In some instances all three may successively be called for.

ADMINISTRATION. Three globules, in three dessert-spoonsful of water, a dessert-spoonful every three to six hours, according to the severity of the symptoms. In other cases *Mercurius* or *Arsenicum* may be required for diarrhœa occurring during or after scarlet fever. (See DIARRHŒA.)

If the bowels are confined, a lavement of tepid water may be employed; but if they have been properly acted upon at the invasion of the disease, there is no necessity for artificial interference, even though they should remain inactive for several days.

When the rash disappears suddenly or prematurely, *Bryonia* is commonly the remedy which is most capable of bringing it out again. In other cases, *Phosphorus* and *Sulphur* are required. But if the consecutive symptoms resemble those before alluded to under *Opium*, that remedy must be selected in preference.

These are the principal remedies employed by Homœopathists in the treatment of Scarlatina, as it is ordinarily met with. There are, of course, other and more virulent forms in which the disease occasionally appears, but the treatment of such cases ought to be conducted by an experienced practitioner, and not by an unprofessional person.

We frequently find this affection, in a complicated form, distinguishable from pure scarlet fever by the absence of the peculiar hue of the skin, to which allusion was made at the commencement, and by the pressure of the finger leaving no white imprint. Against this, so widely different type of the disorder, *Aconitum* is often a specific.

ADMINISTRATION. Same as *Belladonna.*

Sometimes it is found necessary to administer a dose of *Coffea*, a few hours after the first or second dose of *Aconite*, when the patient complains of severe pain in the head, trunk, or extremities, and is extremely restless, fretful, agitated, and disposed to shed tears, and then again to return to *Aconite* after an interval of the same length; and so on, alternately, until the cure is completed; which, under favorable circumstances, is speedily accomplished by means of these remedies.

The accession of any special complication, such as water in the brain, inflammation of the windpipe, &c., in the course of scarlet fever, or at its termination, must at once be attended to, and treated in accordance with its peculiar features.

In strumous habits, many troublesome consequences are frequently left. And it may here be remarked, that even after the desquamatory process is completed, the whole of the danger is not altogether passed; any exposure to cold, or infringement of dietetic rules, being likely to entail unpleasant and even dangerous consequences.

CHAMOMILLA may be employed with advantage, either alone or alternately with *Belladonna*, against rawness of the face, &c., occurring after scarlet fever.

AURUM. Against an offensive and purulent discharge from the nose, with soreness and swelling of the interior.

MERCURIUS VIVUS is a good remedy against soreness of the nose and face, with swelling of the submaxillary glands; followed by *Hepar sulphuris*, *Silicea*, *Sulphur*, and *Calcarea*, if necessary.

BELLADONNA. If there is puffiness of the face, with swelling of the hands and feet, lingering fever in the evening, glandular enlargements, chaps about the mouth, severe headaches, stammering, &c.; it may sometimes be advantageously alternated with the medicines just mentioned.

Dropsical swelling of the whole body is a very serious and not unfrequent sequel, sometimes requiring a most careful and discriminating treatment. The extent of the swelling does not always indicate the degree of danger, as children, in whom the external tumefaction is inconsiderable, are often carried off by water in the chest or head. The following remedies will generally be found the best adapted to the successful treatment of the same: *Helleborus*, *Arsenicum*, and *Rhus*. Of these, *Helleb.* is generally the most appropriate when the body has become suddenly swollen (or dropsical); *Rhus*, when the legs or feet are more especially affected; and *Arsenicum* when *Helleb.* does not soon produce a favorable impression. There are other remedies which may be required under particular circumstances; but a professional man can alone determine their choice, and the special indications which call for their selection. Against inflammation of, or discharge from, the ears, *Belladonna*, *Hepar sulphuris*, or *Pulsatilla* are the best remedies,—in the case of boils, *Arnica*,—which may be followed by *Bryonia* and *Sulphur*, where necessary; and for deafness, *Belladonna*, *Pulsatilla*, *Dulcamara*, and *Sulphur*, are to be chiefly recommended.

Belladonna, as Hahnemann discovered upwards of forty years ago, is undoubtedly a most valuable preservative against *pure* scarlatina when epidemic, whatever may be said to the contrary by those who have either not employed it properly, or who have tried it in an impure or complicated form of the complaint. In those rare instances in which it fails, even when had recourse to at a sufficiently early period, it, at all events, has the power of materially modifying the character of the disease. With very young children, one globule, with those from six to ten years of age two globules (in a teaspoonful of water every second day, or every day when the fever rages extensively), and with adults, or robust children above ten years of age, three globules daily, or night and morning, for from two to three weeks at farthest, will generally be found sufficient to obviate any risk.* Should

* We have, in common with others, repeatedly proved the truth of Hahnemann's discovery of the prophylactic, or preservative powers of *Belladonna.* Dr. Schneider, of Magdeburg, has recently employed it on a most extensive scale, against the pure, smooth scarlet fever; he found that when he gave it to a large proportion of the children of the town or village in which the fever raged, not one of those to whom it was administered sufficiently early, and continued long enough, was seized: whereas nearly the whole of those to whom *Belladonna* was not given were more or less severely, and often fatally, affected. The prescription he employed was as follows: Five drops of the pure tinct. to one drachm of spirits of wine. Of this, eight drops to a teacupful of water. *Dose.* To children up to three years of age, one teaspoonful every morning; to those between three and five years, one teaspoonful morning and evening; and to those of a more advanced age, two teaspoonsful in the morning

the disease continue to rage, this treatment may, in some instances, be renewed. If, however, the ruling epidemy be scarlatina in an unusual or complicated form, the remedies employed as preservatives must be such as possess properties which correspond to the peculiar features of the disease. Thus, *Aconitum* and *Belladonna* in alternation (allowing twenty-four hours to elapse after the administration of *Aconitum* before *Belladonna* is given, and from forty-eight to seventy-two hours after *Belladonna*, before *Aconitum* is repeated, and so on) have been employed successfully in epidemies not possessing the clear scarlatina hue, with a smooth and glossy surface, In other epidemies, again, *Coffea*, *Calcarea*, &c., might be required. But there are few in which *Belladonna* will not be more or less useful. The food must be plain and wholesome, and wine and acids avoided whilst *Aconitum* or *Belladonna* are being taken. *We must, in administering preservatives, carefully watch their effects; and if a medicinal action set in, discontinue immediately.*

Diet and Regimen. During the course of this malady, the greatest possible attention must be

and one in the evening.—*Allg. Hom. Zeitung*, 10, 33. In warm weather the mixture ought not to be kept more than from two to four days.—*Epitome of Hom. Domes. Med.* p. 9.

paid to this point. Whilst the fever runs high, no other nourishment must be given than toast-water, or weak barley-water; and even after the fever has abated, every care must be taken, and a return gradually made to a more nourishing diet, as negligence in this respect may be productive of the most serious consequences. Cocoa, milk and water, Hecker's farina,* arrowroot, beef-tea, with thin slices of stale or toasted bread, should commonly form the prelude to the usual mode of living. In mild attacks, the patient may be allowed gruel or weak broths. (See also *Diet in fever.*)

Stimulants, such as wine, &c., ought never to be given for the purpose of removing debility during convalescence, as they are very liable to give rise to serious and dangerous local inflammations. The employment of such medicines as *Arsenicum*, *Veratrum*, *Pulsatilla*, *Nux v.*, and *Lachesis*, &c., are sometimes, though rarely, required to give tone to this debilitated state of the system, when it threatens to prove tedious. During the course of the disease, the patient should be confined to his bed; and whilst he is protected from draughts, he should not be oppressed with an excess of clothing, or almost stifled by the close and vitiated air of an ill-ventilated, over-heated apartment.

* This preparation may be had *pure* at the Homœopathic Pharmacy, 239 Mulberry Street.

Measles.

This eruptive fever is distinguished by its connexion with catarrhal symptoms affecting the mucous or lining membrane of the eyes, nose, windpipe and its ramifications.

SYMPTOMS. The form of measles which is most generally met with, is ushered in by the usual signs of fever,—viz., lassitude or languor; shivering; heat of skin; or alternations of heat and chills; and thirst. Giddiness, headache, and pain in the back are also complained of. As the affection proceeds on its course, the patient is seized with sneezing; discharge from the nose; suffused and watery eyes; hoarse, dry cough; puffed and feverish face; vomiting and purging; or constipation; or sluggishness of bowels with very offensive evacuations; scanty secretion of urine; full, frequent and strong, or quick, small irregular and oppressed pulse; sometimes delirium; and commonly an exacerbation of fever towards evening. These symptoms occur in various degrees of intensity. They are often so slight as to attract very little notice, and cannot be determined from common cold or other febrile disease. Exposure to infection, or the prevalence of epidemic measles, being the only means of influencing a decision as to the true character of the premonitory symptoms. In the course of three to four, but sometimes not before the lapse of seven or eight days, the eruption begins to appear on the face and neck, and subsequently on the body and limbs, in the form of small, round, red dots or pimples. These are very slightly elevated, but sufficiently so as to give a sensation of hardness to the hand when passed over the surface of the affected skin. They soon run together into extensive patches of irregular shape, their margins presenting somewhat of a crescentic or semicircular curve. In the average number of well-developed cases, the entire surface is usually bedecked with the eruption about the fifth day. On the sixth day it begins to fade on the face, and generally altogether vanishes with a bran-like exfoliation of the cuticle, about the ninth or tenth day from the invasion of the fever, or the sixth from its own appearance. Deviations from this course are, however, not of unfrequent occurrence. The eruption is sometimes very slight; but the patches which are well marked, and which in healthy measles are of a lightish red color, exhibit a striking contrast with the natural color of the sound skin in the interstices. The throat, when examined, will be observed, about the fourth or fifth days, to be covered with small red points or patches, which are formed by the extension of the eruption to the mucous membrane, and are occasionally productive of difficulty in swallowing. A greater or less degree of difficulty of breathing, with some pain and tightness of chest, precede the evolution of the eruption; and, occasionally, violent sickness and vomiting, or even convulsions, supervene. In such cases the rash, when it appears, is frequently combined with an eruption of miliary vesicles.

In favorable cases, although the fever does not wholly cease, it nevertheless abates considerably in violence as soon as the eruption is developed.

Measles is not so much to be dreaded for itself, as for the deleterious consequences which, in bad constitutions, it frequently entails in the form of consumption, scrofula, diarrhœa, inflammation of the eyes, &c. A complication with other diseases, as inflammation of the lungs or brain; and an unhealthy, livid-looking, or imperfectly-developed eruption, with concentration of the disease on the windpipe and its ramifications, likewise tend to render the malady of serious import.

TREATMENT. In *mild* epidemic measles, occurring in a simple and uncomplicated form, a few doses of *Pulsatilla*, combined with free ventilation, without exposure to currents of air, darkening of the apartment, if the eyes be rather sensitive to light—and the use of light, unstimulating food, when the appetite continues unimpaired, are the only remedial means required. *Pulsatilla*, it may be added, is useful in all the stages of the complaint, viz. the catarrhal, the eruptive, and the convalescent, —in the latter, where there are consecutive symptoms, in the form of inflammation of the eye and eyelids, discharge from the ear or earache, and diarrhœa. Even in the severer varieties of measles, *Pulsatilla* is more or less useful, but the aid of other medicaments is usually required in such cases. *Pulsatilla* ought to be given as soon as the slightest catarrhal signs make their appearance during the prevalence of measles; for, independently of its general appropriateness to that stage of the complaint,—particularly when discharge from the nose, frequent sneezing, inflamed, watery, and sensitive eyes, headache, hoarseness, and some cough which is aggravated by lying down, and is occasionally accompanied by an inclination to vomit, constitute the more prominent symptoms,—it appears to assist in bringing out the eruption, and thereby curtails as well as alleviates the catarrhal stage.

Administration. Two globules every twelve hours for from two to three days. As soon thereafter as the rash makes its appearance, the medicine may be resumed in the same way, unless some other remedy becomes indicated. When the accompanying fever is severe, the pulse being quick and full, the skin hot and dry, the thirst great, and the secretion of urine scanty, it will be necessary to give *Aconitum*, two globules every six or eight hours, in alternation with *Pulsatilla.* And if the intensity of fever persists, notwithstanding *Sulphur* may be substituted for *Pulsatilla*, and exhibited in alternation with *Aconitum*, until the febrile symptoms yield. The troublesome itching which usually attends the scaling off of the cuticle or scarf-skin, may be relieved by sponging the body with warm water. When the prevailing epidemy is of a more severe type, although the treatment just mentioned will often suffice to ward off serious complications, and conduct the patient safely throughout the entire course of the affection, there is, nevertheless, frequently a necessity for resorting to other medicaments, both in the premonitory or catarrhal stage, and during the disease. An inherent delicacy of constitution contributes to extend the range of required medical treatment, and to entail a variety of consecutive symptoms,—some of the more important of which have already been alluded to. As the treatment of the complicated and malignant grades of measles ought only to be confided to professional hands, it is not intended, in the following brief observations, to enter into the subject in detail, but merely to point out a few of the medicines which are more frequently indicated in the said cases. It may be remarked, beforehand, that the catarrhal stage even of the mild and simple form of measles may, in particular habits, be attended with symptoms of equal severity as that which precedes the development of the more serious and dangerous species. The medicines which are sometimes called for, soon after or in preference to *Pulsatilla,* in the catarrhal or premonitory stage of measles, when the symptoms occur with great severity are, *Aconitum, Belladonna, Hepar sulphuris, Chamomilla, Ipecacuanha, Opium,* and *Calcarea.*

ACONITUM is required when the febrile symptoms are the most prominent, the pulse being quick and full, the skin hot and dry, the thirst great, and the urine very scanty and high-colored. (See *Common Cold.*)

ADMINISTRATION. Six globules in two tablespoonsful of water; a dessert-spoonful of the solution every eight hours until the skin becomes moist and the pulse reduced. To children under three years of age, the dose may consist of a teaspoonful of the above at the intervals stated.

BELLADONNA is more especially adapted to full,

plethoric, and scrofulous habits. It is indicated when the patient complains of severe pain in the forehead and back; and when the eyes are watery, very sensitive to the light, and much inflamed; the head hot; the pulse quick; and the skin above the natural temperature. Further, when there is a dry, harsh, or hollow, barking cough, aggravated at night, and sometimes accompanied by accelerated and oppressed respiration, with rattling of phlegm in the chest; hoarseness; frequent fits of sneezing, with discharge from the nose; thirst; vomiting; great restlessness, sleeplessness, and occasionally delirium, or convulsive twitching of the limbs.

ADMINISTRATION. Same as *Aconitum* with which remedy *Belladonna* may be alternated if the symptoms mentioned under the former are superadded to those just described.

IPECACUANHA is chiefly called for when, as is frequently the case about the third or fourth day of the fever, there is *distressing tightness of chest*, with laborious breathing; extreme restlessness and agitation; deep sighing or moaning; excessive nausea; vomiting, or both vomiting and purging; obstruction of the nostrils; dry cough.

ADMINISTRATION. Same as *Aconite.*

BRYONIA is indicated by nearly the same train of symptoms as *Ipecacuanha*, but is to be preferred to that remedy when the bowels are in a constipated state.

ADMINISTRATION. Same as *Aconite.* The latter may be given alternately with *Bryonia* when the febrile symptoms run high.

HEPAR SULPHURIS is often very useful when a dry hoarse cough, closely resembling that of croup, forms the most prominent feature in the catarrhal stage of measles.

ADMINISTRATION. Same as *Aconite*, with which it may be taken alternately when the pulse is full and rapid, the skin hot, and the thirst considerable.

CHAMOMILLA is occasionally of service with very young and delicate children, when the cough is very severe at night, and continues even during sleep; also when there is difficulty of breathing, colic, diarrhœa, and sometimes vomiting.

ADMINISTRATION. Two globules in four teaspoonsful of water, a teaspoonful of the solution every six or twelve hours, according to the severity of these symptoms.

OPIUM is called for when, antecedent to the appearance of the eruption, the patient is seized with violent delirium, with incessant movement of the hands, &c.

ADMINISTRATION. Six globules in two tablespoonsful of water, a dessert-spoonful every four hours. When a marked improvement follows the first dose, the interval must be lengthened before the medicine is repeated, if its repetition seem necessary.

CALCAREA is sometimes required when convulsions occur immediately before the eruption comes out; and when there is extreme restlessness and anxiety; obstruction of the nose; hoarseness; dry cough.

ADMINISTRATION. Same as *Opium*.

When the eruption has made its appearance, the following are the more important remedies in measles of a bad or complicated character; *Bryonia*, *Pulsatilla*, *Sulphur*, *Phosphorus*, *Arsenicum*, etc.

BRYONIA. This remedy is appropriate when the eruption does not come fully out, and the disease concentrates itself upon the chest, with incessant cough, pricking pains, quick and oppressed respiration, and acceleration of pulse; or when there is foulness of tongue, considerable thirst, and severe aching in the limbs, with aggravation of pain from movement: lastly, when the rash presents a deeper hue than usual—or is combined with an eruption of miliary vesicles, or livid spots.

ADMINISTRATION. Six globules in two tablespoonsful of water, a dessert-spoonful every four hours. If improvement follows, the medicine may be continued with longer intervals between the doses; but if no amendment takes place, and fresh symptoms, incidental to the prevailing epidemy, supervene, another remedy which corresponds thereto must be selected.

(*Aconitum* is sometimes useful in alternation with *Bryonia*, when the affection retains the inflammatory form, and the shooting or pricking pains in the chest are associated with heat of skin, and rapidity and fullness of pulse.)

PHOSPHORUS is indicated in cases somewhat analogous to the preceding medicament; the chest being chiefly affected, and the eruption imperfectly developed. It is also indicated when there is hoarseness with pain in the windpipe; great debility; shrunken features; low fever; stupor; and diarrhœa. (*Arsenicum* is sometimes required after *Phosphorus*, when the chest has been relieved, but the fever, prostration of strength, and diarrhœa remain.)

ADMINISTRATION. Same as *Bryonia*.

PULSATILLA, as already observed, is often useful in measles of a bad type, as well as in the milder form of the disease. A combination of signs of marked disturbance in the digestive organs,—as foul tongue, nausea, vomiting or purging,—with those detailed under its indications in the catarrhal stage of simple measles,—and, sometimes, a total absence of thirst, are the principal symptoms which denote its appropriateness. The presence of external or internal inflammation of the ear is, moreover, a marked indication for *Pulsatilla.*

ADMINISTRATION. Same as *Bryonia.*

SULPHUR is often serviceable after the previous employment of *Pulsatilla,* or indeed any other remedy, when the eyes are much inflamed, and there is earache, with thick discharge and dullness of hearing; and loose cough, with thick, whitish yellow expectoration. It is also useful when the eruption is faint, or never comes freely out, and there is low fever, with headache, aching in the limbs, and much debility.

ADMINISTRATION. Same as *Bryonia.*

Measles sometimes terminates fatally in consequence of a retropulsion of the eruption from exposure to cold or change of temperature, or when the sudden and premature recession takes place from unknown causes. In such cases BRYONIA, administered as above, is generally found efficacious in re-evolving the eruption, and preventing this disaster; but if diarrhœa with mucous discharge follow the suppression, PULSATILLA is indicated; if *vomiting,* with great oppression at the chest, be the more prominent symptom, IPECACUANHA should be substituted, and followed in turn by ARSENICUM, if symptoms of improvement do not speedily show themselves:—In the case of children, CHAMOMILLA is to be preferred to *Ipecacuanha*, where there is labored respiration and diarrhœa with colic, vomiting, and tenderness of the abdomen (belly:) BELLADONNA. may follow or supersede *Chamomilla* if the diarrhœa subsides, but the tenderness of the abdomen, the impeded breathing, &c., continue unabated. (See *Inflammation of the Stomach and Bowels:* as also the other indications already given in this chapter, for the whole of the above remedies.)

For the treatment of coughs which sometimes remain after measles, a variety of medicines may be indicated.

For the diarrhœa which the disease occasionally leaves behind it *Cinchona*, *Pulsatilla*, *Mercurius*, and *Sulphur* are, in general, the most appropriate remedies;—for their several indications see *Diarrhœa*. For running from the ear *Pulsatilla* and *Sulphur* are very serviceable, but other remedies are sometimes required. For inflammation of the glands below, and in front of the ear, *Arnica* and *Dulcamara;* for tenderness of the skin *Rhus;* and for a burning, itching, rash, which bleeds after scratching, *Arsenicum* and *Sulphur* are severally indicated.

When measles rages epidemically, PULSATILLA and ACONITE, administered alternately, for a fortnight, allowing an interval of twenty-four hours after each dose (three or four globules) of *Aconitum*, and one forty-eight hours after that of *Pulsatilla*, will sometimes ward off an attack or give a milder character to the affection if it breaks out. This precautionary treatment may be once more renewed after the lapse of a week if the disease continues to spread.

DIET. In this respect the same rules may be followed as given under SCARLET FEVER. The patient ought not to be kept too warm; but, whilst we ensure free ventilation, care should be taken not to expose him to a current air; or to a very low temperature, lest the eruption should thereby be driven in, or its full development prevented.

Roseola. False Measles.

This eruption bears a close resemblance to, and, as is the case with *Red gum*, is often mistaken for measles. It is frequently dependent upon the irritation of teething, or derangement of the digestive organs, and is chiefly discriminated from measles by the absence of catarrhal symptoms. This rash calls for no particular treatment beyond pure air with the avoidance of exposure to cold, unless there is great restlessness and febrile excitement,—in which case *Aconitum* or *Coffea,* &c., may be resorted to (see *Dentition,*) or when there is disturbance of stomach and bowels, for which the employment of such remedies as *Ipecacuanha, Chamomilla,* &c., may be necessary. (See *Indigestion of Infants* and also *Diarrhœa.*)

Smallpox. (*Variola.*)

It is proposed here, to divide this disease into two varieties—the *distinct,* when the pustules on the face are clearly defined, and do not run into one another—and the *confluent,* when they coalesce and form one continuous whole.

When the symptoms are less severe than those properly characteristic of the disease, and the eruption on the face slight, it is called the modified smallpox. We generally find this description in such persons as have been properly vaccinated in infancy, a precaution which, although not always a preservative from the attacks of smallpox, greatly lessens its virulence, and gives a milder character to the complaint, when taken.

SYMPTOMS. The disease is frequently very sudden in its attacks, commencing with chilliness and shivering, followed by febrile symptoms, headache, severe pains in the small of the back and loins, languor, weariness, and faintness; the patient also complains of oppression of the chest, and acute pain in the pit of the stomach, increased by pressure. The eruption generally makes its appearance at the close of the third day, first on the face and hairy scalp, then on the neck, and afterwards spreads over the whole body. Its establishment is followed by an abatement of fever, in distinct smallpox. Catarrhal symptoms, as sneezing, coughing, wheezing, and sometimes difficulty of breathing, are frequent concomitant symptoms. A convulsive fit is, occasionally, the first decided indication of illness, and has been held to be a favorable sign. The space of time which elapses between the reception of the infection and the invasion of the febrile symptoms is, generally, computed to be about a fortnight.

The eruption first displays itself in the shape of small, hard, red pimples, which, in about three days, present a vesicular appearance, surrounded by an inflamed circular margin, and become depressed in the centre as they enlarge. About the sixth or eighth day, the lymph in the pustule becomes converted into pus,* and the depression in the centre disappears. This has been denominated the process of *maturation*.

When the pustules are very numerous on the

* Matter.

face, the features generally become much swollen, and the eyelids are frequently closed up. On the first day, a small lump, like a millet-seed, may be felt in each of the elevations above noticed, distinguishing this eruptive fever from almost all others. The pocks continue coming on during the first three eruptive days, and each pock runs its regular course; thus, those which first appeared are forming into scabs or dying off, while the others are suppurating. The general desiccation commonly takes place on or about the eighth or fourteenth day, according as the pustules may happen to be distinct or confluent. An extension of the eruption to the mucous membrane of the mouth and throat is a common occurrence.

When the pustules have attained their full development, they generally burst, in mild cases emitting an opaque lymph, which dries into a crust and falls off; whilst, in severe ones, a discharge of puriform matter, forming scabs and sores, which leave, on their healing, permanent marks or pits. Red stains, caused by increased vascular action, always remain for a while after the eruption; but if no ulceration has taken place, they disappear in process of time.

In CONFLUENT SMALLPOX, all the precursory symptoms are more severe, the fever runs high, and frequently continues so throughout the course of the disease; the pain in the pit of the stomach and difficulty of breathing are more complained of, and in children the eruption is more frequently preceded by convulsions and delirium; the latter symptom, indeed, is often present with adults during the suppurative or secondary fever, which frequently assumes a typhoid character, and sometimes carries off the patient on the eleventh day. All cases in which we have a deeply-rooted morbid constitutional taint to contend against, generally require the utmost skill to ward off a fatal result. An extensive inflammatory blush on the face or trunk almost invariably precedes the confluent variety of small pox.

Salivation* (which is more peculiar to adults), and soreness of the throat, with aphthæ, or pustules on the tongue and pharynx,† frequently occur in both forms of this disease, and particularly in the confluent. In children, diarrhœa is a more common occurrence during the course of the confluent variety.

When smallpox terminates fatally, the immediate cause of death is, for the most part, to be found in some inflammatory affection of the brain or organs of respiration. Complications of the

* Increased secretion of saliva.

† The back part of the throat; the opening into the gullet.

said character, therefore, and a bad type of the disease, must always lessen the prospects of recovery. A species of eruption which never matures properly, but remains flat and looks pale, being unsurrounded by a red areola—a large number of confluent eruptions on the face—hoarseness, with cough of a croup-like sound—the appearance of livid spots on various parts of the surface—and lastly, profuse discharges of blood, and symptoms of gangrene* are all to be considered as unfavorable signs.

Before proceeding to the medicines to be administered in the different stages of the disease, a few words may be said upon the general treatment of the patient.

Cool and fresh air are our best auxiliaries, the variolous virus† being of a nature to react upon the organism, and warmth being calculated to increase its activity. So beneficial is cool air found in this malady, that taking a child to an open window when attacked with convulsions, will generally afford immediate relief. Great cleanliness must also be observed, and the linen frequently changed.

TREATMENT. Now that the homœopathic principle of *vaccination*, the discovery of the celebrated

* The first stage of mortification.

† The matter, product, or poison of smallpox.

Dr. Jenner, is so universally acted upon, this formerly so loathsome and fatal disease has in a great measure been deprived of all its virulence. For although it cannot be denied that the process of vaccination is not an effectual preservative against the disease, nevertheless it is comparatively seldom that those who have once or oftener been properly vaccinated, are ever very seriously or dangerously affected, if they do not wholly escape.

In ordinary forms of simple, distinct smallpox, *Aconitum* or *Coffea* are the most useful in the febrile stage;—*Ipecacuanha* and *Antimonium tartaricum* when considerable constitutional disturbance precedes the appearance of the eruption;—*Antimonium tartaricum* or *Rhus* when the eruption has appeared; —and *Sulphur* when the scabs are forming.

In cases, either distinct or confluent, which are complicated with affection of the chest (pleurisy in particular), *Bryonia*, and sometimes *Rhus*, followed by *Sulphur*. For those with affection of the brain, *Belladonna* or *Opium;* and those with typhoid fever, *Rhus* and *Arsenicum* chiefly, but sometimes also *Bryonia* and *Mercurius*.

When cough attends or follows the eruptive or the maturative stage, *Chamomilla*, *Bryonia*, *Tartarus*, or *Hepar s.* And when diarrhœa prevails, *Chamomilla* or *Mercurius*, &c.

To enter somewhat into details, it may be stated,

that, in the first stage of the affection, the main object to be accomplished is the subjugation of the fever when it exists in a rather intense form. The employment of *Aconitum* for this purpose, and for the prevention of local congestions and inflammations, is attended with the happiest results; since whilst it most effectually and speedily subdues overaction by diminishing the unnatural force and rapidity of the circulation, it does so without, in the slightest degree, depriving the patient of the strength which is required to carry him through this so frequently protracted, exhausting, and ever-loathsome disease. The indications here for *Aconitum* are those which have already been repeatedly given in various parts of this work, viz.: dry, hot skin, thirst, quickness and fulness of pulse.

Administration. Six globules may be dissolved in two tablespoonsfuls of water, and a dessert-spoonful of the solution given every six or eight hours, until the skin becomes moist, and the acceleration of pulse subsides, when the intervals between the doses may be lengthened, or another remedy selected, in accordance with the remaining symptoms. In confluent smallpox, occurring in plethoric children, it is sometimes necessary, in consequence of the continuance of the fever even after the appearance of the rash, to administer *Aconitum* in alternation with the remedy otherwise indicated; but more frequently it is only necessary to resort to *Aconitum* again during the secondary fever, which frequently sets in when the scabs are forming. (See *Confluent Smallpox.*)

In mild cases, with a little or no inflammatory fever, but considerable restlessness and excitement, COFFEA is of good service, and appears to exert some influence over the development of the eruption.

ADMINISTRATION. Six globules, in two tablespoonsful of water, a dessert-spoonful every six or eight hours. When considerable tightness and oppression of the chest, sometimes attended with nausea and vomiting, or even purging, are manifested before the appearance of the eruption, IPECACUANHA and ANTIMONIUM TARTARICUM may be substituted for *Coffea.*

ADMINISTRATION. Three globules of each remedy, alternately every six or eight hours in a dessert-spoonful of water, until signs of improvement appear or some other remedy becomes indicated. *Antim. tart.* is frequently very useful after, as well as before, the evolution of the eruption;—the existence of a hollow-sounding cough, with *loud mucous rattling* in the chest, is an additional indication for its employment. *Administration:*

Six globules, in two tablespoonsful of water, a dessert-spoonful every six or eight hours.

BRYONIA is also useful in promoting the development and assisting the natural course of the eruption; it is chiefly indicated when symptoms of considerable derangement of the digestive organs are present, such as bitter taste in the mouth, foulness of the tongue; or when there is headache, with aching pains in the limbs, increased by motion; constipation, and irritability of disposition; also, when there is complication with inflammation in the chest, with shooting or pricking pains, especially during inspiration.

RHUS is equally serviceable at this stage of the disease, and it is to be preferred to *Bryonia*, when the acute pains in the head, back, and loins are aggravated during a state of rest, and temporarily relieved by movement. It is further indicated when the fever assumes a low typhoid type.

ADMINISTRATION. In slight cases, two globules, in a teaspoonful of water, given every twelve hours, as the eruption continues to develop itself; in severe cases, six globules, to an ounce of water, a dessert-spoonful every six hours. Either of these remedies may be preceded or followed by ACONITE, should there be considerable fever with dry heat of the skin,—the medicine being administered as above ordered, until these symptoms abate.

Should neither *Bryonia* nor *Rhus* be indicated, *Tartarus emeticus* may be administered as above, at longer intervals (every twelve hours), while the disease is running its course, but more particularly during the distension of the pustules (should no other remedies be imperatively called for), and also towards the period of their drying up or bursting. As soon as the latter process has commenced, however, *Sulphur* may be resorted to.

ADMINISTRATION. Four globules, in the same number of dessert-spoonsful of water, a dessert-spoonful of the solution morning and evening.

When rheumatic pains, in the back and extremities, which become worse at night, and are somewhat relieved by movement, are complained of at this period, *Rhus* may be advantageously alternated with *Sulphur*.

ADMINISTRATION. Three globules of *Rhus*, alternately, with three of *Sulphur*, every twelve hours, until relief is obtained, or a change of symptoms occurs, requiring some other remedy. In favorable cases, nothing further is required but frequent and gentle sponging, and light, nourishing food, when the scabs are drying up, and falling off. When there is much irritation and restlessness, *Coffea,* and sometimes, though more rarely, *Aconitum,* may be alternated with *Sulphur.*

If *Antimonium tartaricum* and *Ipecacuanha* do not succeed in allaying the nausea and vomiting, and the patient complains of excessive thirst and dryness of the mouth, the tongue being at the same time very foul and dark, and the prostration of strength excessive, we may administer ARSENICUM, two globules, in a teaspoonful of water, and repeat the dose every two or three hours, if required; but the remedy must be discontinued as soon as decided benefit has resulted from its action.

In *confluent* smallpox, during the filling up of the pocks, which is the most serious period of the disease, a secondary or suppurative fever frequently sets in. Should this run high, the employment of ACONITUM, as already stated, will sometimes be necessary, either alone, or in alternation, if needful, with some other remedy which is indicated by coexisting symptoms not embraced by *Aconite. Sulphur*, *Mercurius*, *Chamomilla*, *Hepar s.*, *Belladonna*, *Opium*, *Arsenicum*, *Rhus*, *China*, *Carbo vegetabilis*, and *Acidum muriaticum*, are the medicines whieh are more frequently wanted at this stage of confluent smallpox; but as the treatment of the forms of disease which call for these remedies is, properly speaking, beyond the pale of domestic treatment, and as some of them are only required among adults, I shall confine myself to a few of the more common indications for each of the remedies just mentioned.

SULPHUR may be given in alternation with *Aconitum*, when this latter is insufficient to mitigate excessive febrile action.

MERCURIUS is, principally, indicated when there is inflammation of the eyes, soreness of the throat and nose, fetid breath (salivation), cough, hoarseness, tenderness of the stomach, excessive looseness of bowels, attended with incessant straining, and sometimes bloody stools.

CHAMOMILLA is frequently of much use in very young children, when there is predominating looseness of the bowels, with deep green stools, severe colic, tenderness of the belly, and difficult breathing (see art. *Diarrhœa*, should the looseness become excessive and not yield to *Merc.* or *Cham.*); also when there is much restlessness and whining, and a distressing nocturnal cough.

HEPAR SULPHURIS is to be preferred where hoarseness or an incessant, hoarse, croupy cough, with tenderness of the exterior of the throat, and a dry, hot skin, form the most striking symptoms.

BELLADONNA is sometimes required after *Chamomilla*, when that remedy produces only temporary relief; or it is to be preferred thereto, particularly in plethoric children, when the head becomes prominently affected,—evidenced by flushed countenance, fulness and throbbing of the vessels, red and inflamed eyes, intolerance of light, headache, delirium, thirst, heat of skin, excessive irritability of stomach, with nausea or vomiting on the slightest movement, delirium, prostration of strength, drowsiness, &c.

OPIUM may follow, or it may be selected in preference to *Belladonna*, when there is continuous lethargy, with open mouth, half-closed eyes, and snoring respiration; but also when there is violent delirium, with incessant movements of the hands, &c.

ARSENICUM is sometimes required in an earlier stage of the disease, before the appearance of the eruption, when *Ipecac.* and *Ant. tart.* are insufficient to allay the vomiting (or purging), and tightness of chest, which occasionally precede; but it is more especially required when, in confluent smallpox of a bad type, the attack of secondary fever is rapidly followed by extreme prostration, coldness of the limbs, great thirst, dryness of the mouth, with foul, brownish, or almost black-looking tongue, livid spots on the surface of the body, and other symptoms of typhus.

RHUS is also required in cases which assume a

typhoid character, attended with aching pains and paralytic weakness in the extremities, but not quite so much exhaustion as in the foregoing instance.

CINCHONA is serviceable when the debility arises from the depleting effects occasioned by diarrhœa or the drain of matter from the pustules.

CARBO V. may be resorted to when gangrene is apprehended; or when the pustules are thin and unhealthy, and the scabs or incrustations are of a dark brown color, and have a very fetid smell—provided *Arsenicum* does not correspond better to the other symptoms of the case. The alternate use of these two is sometimes attended with advantage.

A number of troublesome and even dangerous consequences often follow attacks of smallpox, such as boils, inflammation of the eyes, glandular swellings, and other scrofulous affections, requiring a more or less prolonged and careful treatment for their removal.

Before concluding, it may be added, that THUJA OCCIDENTALIS has very recently been employed on the Continent, with much success, although on a limited scale, in the treatment of smallpox; no fatal cases having occurred amongst the patients to whom it was administered, and no pock-marks having been left behind;—whilst several fatal cases, and still more disfigurations, occurred at the same time amongst the patients who were treated allopathically.* It has also been recommended as a preservative against the disease. Should it prove so, it will form an appreciable improvement upon Jenner's discovery; for, with due deference to the value of vaccination, it cannot be denied that there appears to be strong presumptive evidence of the fact, that the said process has, in some measure, contributed to the spread of scrofula.

Modified Smallpox is merely a mild description of the above, and, as we have before said, is the form the disease generally assumes when it attacks those who have been properly vaccinated. We must regulate our treatment according to the symptoms, being guided in the selection of the remedies by the indications before given.

Diet and Regimen. The diet should be regulated by the virulence of the attack; in all instances, the beverages ought to be cold, as a warm regimen, combined with neglect of the precautions before mentioned, may convert the mild into the

* According to the old mode of practice, i. e. by means of blood-letting, aperients, opiates, &c.

malignant form. While the fever runs high water or toast-water should alone be allowed; but when the affection is going off, mildly nutritious food, such as Hecker's farina, arrow-root, cocoa, and light animal broths, may be allowed. Stimulants are only to be tolerated in rare cases—almost never in the case of children; and it is sometimes necessary that the patient abstain, for a considerable time, from animal food. (See *Diet in Fever.*) The pustules may be anointed with oil of almonds, or gently sponged with tepid water, when they become hard; or dusted with pure starch when a thin, acrid, or otherwise unhealthy discharge runs from them. The hair of the head should be clipped, for the sake of the cleanliness and comfort of the patient; and the hands muffled, to prevent injury to the pustules from scratching.

It may be remarked that, after recovery from an attack of malignant smallpox, the patient's constitution often requires a thorough renovation, and that he should, therefore, be put under a course of medicine best calculated to attain that result.

Chicken-pock.

SYMPTOMS. A disease, bearing a considerable resemblance, in its external character, to smallpox, but differing in its duration, and symptomatically, being considerably milder, and but rarely becoming dangerous, except when it extends itself to the lungs or brain. The fever, however, occasionally runs high.

When this affection attacks an individual, and smallpox is epidemic, which is not unfrequently the case, it is often mistaken for that disorder; but it soon discovers its real character, by the rapidity with which the eruption declares itself: the pustules (in many instances closely resembling those of the smallpox) being generally fully matured by the third day, and the whole eruption disappearing at the end of the fourth or fifth without leaving any mark.

TREATMENT. Medical treatment is not often required,—attention to diet, inhibiting animal food for two or three days, and confinement to bed being generally sufficient. When much fever is present, we should check it by the administration of ACONITE, three globules, in three dessert-spoonsful of water, one every six hours; or COFFEA, three globules, in the same way, if there is simply extreme restlessness and anxiety.

CONSTITUTIONAL AFFECTIONS.

Scrofula affecting the Glands of the Neck.

The period at which these glands are most liable to become affected, is that betwixt the fifth year and the age of puberty. The first appearance of the glandular enlargement is often noticed during the existence of eruptions behind the ears or on the scalp, or as a consequence of scarlet fever or measles, the irritation of dentition, or during ordinary affections of the throat, A deranged state of the mucous membrane of the stomach and bowels, proceeding from improper food, and conjoined with impure air, forms a fruitful source, or, at all events, gives a powerful stimulus to the development of the disease, as it does of scrofula in general, particularly amongst the children of the poor. The glands, at the commencement, look like small, oval, or spherical tumours, which are moveable, soft, or possess some elasticity, and are situated upon the sides of the neck below the ears and under the chin. They frequently remain in this state for some time; but by degrees they become larger, harder, and more fixed; the skin over them, or over that gland which is furthest advanced acquires a purple redness; a process of softening then takes place, the tumour at the same time increasing in redness unattended with much pain. Finally, some part of the skin becomes of a paler color; and ere long a somewhat thin whitish-yellow fluid escapes through one or more small apertures. As the matter continues to ooze out, it becomes more and more watery, and is intermingled with small white flakes resembling the curd of milk. The swelling now gradually subsides, while the broken skin opens more, extending irregularly, and an obstinate ulcer, generally with flat smooth edges, is constituted. New tumours then form, and pursue the course described; and so the disease proceeds, some of the ulcers healing up wholly or partially during summer, and breaking open again in spring. Under favorable circumstances the disease is spontaneously cured in four or five years; all the ulcers healing up, but leaving some unsightly traces of their previous existence in the form of indelible scars.

TREATMENT. In a disease of this description, it may well be supposed that a long course of treatment is very generally required before any permanent benefit can be effected. When early attacked, or when no injudicious and hurtful treatment in the form of large and frequent doses of *Mercury, Iodine, Sulphur*, &c., has previously been pursued, a favorable impression, if not a radical cure, is often made by homœopathic medicines in a wonderfully short period. On the other hand, cases repeatedly occur which prove exceedingly obstinate, notwithstanding every advantage in the way of recovery. In all cases, however, there is less risk of the tumor becoming converted into an open sore, or, when that is unavoidable, there is usually much less subsequent disfiguration when the case has been appropriately treated, than when it has been allowed to pass through its different stages unchecked. The medicaments which are most frequently indicated in the homœopathic treatment of glandular swellings, are *Mercurius, Belladonna, Conium, Rhus, Natrum c., Phosphorus, Sulphur, Calcarea, Acidum nitricum, Lycopodium, Hepar sulphuris, Silicea, Dulcamara, Baryta, Thuja, Spongia, Carbo animalis, Clematis, Iodium, Bryonia, Pulsatilla, Chamomilla, Nux vomica, Lachesis, Arsenicum, &c.*

The selections of these must be regulated by a variety of circumstances, to attempt to detail which would materially encroach upon the intended limits of this little volume. I may, therefore, very briefly observe that in general cases *Mercurius, Sulphur, Calcarea,* and *Hepar sulphuris* are the remedies which I am in the habit of resorting to in the early stage of the affection whilst there is still no change in the color of the skin, and the glands are free from pain and not sensitive to the touch. In the absence of any special indications for any one of these in particular, they may be given, in the order specified, in the following manner: six globules of MERCURIUS in six dessert-spoonsful of water, a dessert-spoonful of the solution morning and evening. When finished, repeat the medicine as before. About a week afterwards proceed with SULPHUR in the same way: and so on with the others. If, however, a visible improvement becomes apparent during the employment of any one remedy in particular, a pause must be made, and no more medicine administered as long as the improvement continues; but if a cessation of amendment becomes evident, or if threatening signs of relapse supervene, that medicine which had effected the favorable change must again be had recourse to, unless contra-indicated by any fresh symptoms, and administered as above described.

In other cases, and particularly when the organs of digestion are in a deranged state, BRYONIA, NUX V., CHAMOMILLA, and PULSATILLA are required in the early stage. The two former, especially when, amongst other symptoms, there is foulness of tongue, or vivid redness of the tip and margins, with impaired or irregular appetite, and constipation; and the latter (*Cham.* and *Puls.*) when the said symptoms are more frequently associated with a relaxed condition of the bowels. In more advanced cases, somewhat more circumspection is usually required in the selection of the remedies. Considerable impediment is sometimes offered to the cure by a complicated state of matters arising from the injury done to the system at large by over doses of mercurial and other mineral preparations (calomel, &c.) If *Mercury* has evidently been injudiciously administered, ACIDUM NITRICUM becomes necessary, succeeded after an interval of a few days by HEPAR S. After which, CONIUM and AURUM are usually the most appropriate. The former when the glands are hard and somewhat sensitive to the touch—the latter when there is still more sensibility of the affected glands, with a good deal of general debility, and a tendancy to eruptions on various parts of the body. If *Iodine* has been given so as to affect the system injuriously, *Hepar s.*, *Phosphorus*, *Spongia*, and *Sulphur* are more or less required. When, on the other hand, the health does not appear to have suffered from injudicious allopathic treatment, *Dulcamara*, *Rhus*, *Belladonna*, *Natrum c.*, *Baryta*, *Lycopodium*, &c., are often of much efficacy at this stage. DULCAMARA is chiefly indicated when the tumour has attained a large size, and has become indurated; exposure to cold during a bleak, moist state of the atmosphere having apparently contributed to develop or aggravate the affection. RHUS is generally preferable to all other remedies when the gland is very hard, and much swollen, and when the skin over it is considerably reddened or inflamed. This remedy is often sufficient to disperse the swelling in a week or two. When it proves inadequate to accomplish this desirable end, *Belladonna*, *Mercurius*, *Bryonia*, *Phosphorus*, *Hepar*, &c. become requisite. When the redness is less marked than in the preceding instance, *Natrum c.* is often an effective remedy; or *Conium*, *Spongia*, *Clematis*, *Carbo v.*, and *Baryta*, either in the order named or otherwise, if special indications call for the employment of one more than another. LYCOPODIUM is frequently very serviceable when there is considerable pain and tension in the glands under the ear, and more especially when the enlargement extends in the direction of the angle of the jaw, and materially interferes with the act of mastication. *Dulcamara*, *Iodium*, and also *Rhus*, *Hepar s.*, and *Calcarea* are useful when a congeries of swollen glands extends under the chin like a chaplet.

When the skin over the swelling presents a livid or a purple color, *Lachesis* and *Carbo v.*, as also in a secondary degree, *Hepar s.* and *Aurum*, are sometimes the most appropriate. If softening has commenced, *Hepar* and *Silicea*, in alternation, should generally be given without delay, as they will either have the effect of promoting absorption even at this stage of the disease, or of forwarding the suppurative process,* if dispersion be impracticable. No local treatment is necessary; much harm is frequently done by frictions with oily, or greasy and stimulating substances. Warm fomentations are occasionally soothing when there is much pain and tension in the tumor. The employment of the knife is almost always objectionable, even when matter is formed and the tumor large; since absorption may often be accomplished by means of such remedies as *Hepar s.*, *Silicea*, and even *Rhus*, &c., after the establishment of suppuration,† as the author has repeatedly witnessed. When the skin is clearly on the point of giving way, a poultice may be applied, to render its bursting more easy, under the stimulus of the medicine. After the swelling (abscess) has burst, it may be covered with a poultice, if the discharge is copious; subsequently the part may be dressed with dry lint. The healing of the wound is occasionally very difficult

* The ripening of the abscess; the formation of matter.

† The formation of matter.

and tedious. The homœopathic medicines, which are commonly the most successful in promoting the closing up of the sore in a favorable manner, are *Arsenicum*, *Sulphur*, *Silicea*, *Acid. nitric.*, *Sepia*, and *Lycopodium*. (See 'Homœopathic Domestic Medicine' by the Author, art. ULCERS.)

DIET. Great attention should be paid to the diet in scrofulous affections of all kinds. The stomach ought on no account to be overloaded, as it so frequently is, with a superfluity of stimulating food, not to speak of drinks, such as wine, porter, &c. A sufficiency of light, nutritious food, including that of an animal kind, should be allowed.; but errors in diet, both as to quality and quantity, cannot be too carefully avoided. Daily exercise in the open air, and free ventilation of the apartment occupied by the child, are to be enjoined. A residence on the coast during the summer months is often beneficial.

Scrofulous Inflammation of the Eyes.

By the above title is here meant that form of inflammation of the eyes and eyelids which is of frequent occurrence in scrofulous children, and is commonly recognised by the following features:—In the first stage of the affection, there is only a slight degree of swelling and inflammation of the edges of the eyelids, and a constant tendency to their agglutination during sleep—which induces no little pain and inconvenience, every morning, during the act of removing the secretion which gives rise to the adherence. On turning down the lids, the lining membrane is observed to be redder than natural; but no other morbid appearance of sufficient moment to attract attention is as yet discernible. By degrees, however, an aggravated state of the foregoing condition becomes evident; the eye, at the same time becomes watery and over sensitive to light, and the blood-vessels of the white part become distended. As the inflammation advances, small pustules form on the edges of the eyelids, and also upon the ball of the eye. These subsequently terminate in ulceration, and are productive of excessive irritation. When the transparent portion of the ball of the eye (the cornea) is implicated in the inflammation, it is generally rendered dull throughout its texture; and, sometimes, a portion of it becomes apparently opaque; or total blindness results.

TREATMENT. In mild cases, or in the first stage of the complaint, *Pulsatilla*, *Mercurius*, *Sulphur*, and, sometimes, *Nux v.* and *Hepar s.* are the most useful.

PULSATILLA is, generally, the most appropriate

with which to commence, and more especially when the symptoms become aggravated in the afternoon and towards evening; also when the patient is fretful and very sensitive, being disposed to weep from the most trivial cause.

MERCURIUS is usually to be preferred when an exacerbation occurs in the evening and at night in bed.

SULPHUR, very commonly, acts beneficially after either of the preceding. When there are no characteristic indications for any one of these medicines in particular, they may be given in rotation in the order named.

ADMINISTRATION. Four globules in two dessert-spoonsful of water; one dessert-spoonful to be given in the morning and the other at bed time, or invertedly. Two to four days afterwards, if some improvement has taken place, repeat the remedy; but if no alteration has occurred, or if the inflammation threatens to increase, select another.

NUX V. is to be preferred to *Pulsatilla* when the pain, and other symptoms, are worst in the morning; also when the patient is excessively irritable, frequently breaking into fits of passion at the slightest contradiction. (*Chamomilla* is sometimes useful in the early stage, when *Nux v.* produces little or no amendment. The existence of diarrhœa is an additional indication for *Chamomilla*.) *Pulsatilla* and *Nux v.* are further indicated when the digestion is much deranged. HEPAR S. is always more or less useful when the patient has previously taken calomel repeatedly. At a more advanced stage of the complaint, *Belladonna*, *Mercurius corrosivus*, *Hepar s.*, *Euphrasia*, *Conium*, *Sulphur*, and *Arsenicum* are required.

BELLADONNA, when there is considerable redness of the ball of the eye, with extreme sensibility to light, and frequent discharge of tears; or when pustules and small ulcers have commenced to appear on the ball of the eye and on the margins of the lids. MERCURIUS CORROSIVUS is often of much service after, or in alternation with *Belladonna*, in some of the worst forms of the complaint, with ulceration of the edges of the eyelids, or of the transparent part of the eye, and incipient dullness of the latter texture. (*Hepar s.* is to be preferred to *Merc. c.*, if the patient has formerly suffered from the abuse of calomel or other mercurial preparations.)

EUPHRASIA is indicated under similar circumstances, as *Belladonna*, with perhaps a greater degree of pain and irritation, as well as more constant flow of tears and more extensive ulceration. SULPHUR is often useful in winding up the cure in this stage of the complaint also. ARSENIC.

is chiefly called for when the pain complained of is described as an intense burning; and is, moreover, often of much service when given alternately with *Euphrasia*, in obstinate cases of the complaint. RHUS is serviceable when there is redness and swelling around the affected eye, resembling erysipelas; or when this inflammation is conjoined with scrofulous eruptions (tetters) on the face. STAPHYSAGRIA is also of utility in the latter case.

ADMINISTRATION OF THESE REMEDIES. Six globules in four dessert-spoonsful of water; a dessert-spoonful of the solution every twelve hours. Two to four days afterwards, the same medicine may be repeated, or another selected according to the effects produced.* Sometimes it is necessary to give all the above remedies in rotation, before a cure can be accomplished. In less active forms of scrofulous inflammation of the eye, or in old and indolent cases, the same medicines as above noted, together with the following, are more or less frequently indicated—*Conium*, *Calcarea c.*, *Graphites*, *Sepia*, &c. In these cases, it is commonly necessary to allow an interval of a week or so between each remedy, when a series of medicaments are found requisite to effect a cure. When the transparent centre of the eye

* See rules for the administration and repetition of the dose.

begins to look filmy, *Pulsatilla*, *Sulphur*, and *Calcarea;* as also *Euphrasia*, *Conium*, and *Cannabis*, are the medicaments which are chiefly to be relied on.

DIET. The food should be light whilst the inflammation is active, and the pain severe. No local remedy is needful,* beyond a poultice of bread and cold water, contained in a muslin bag, and applied over the eye at night, when there is much irritation and redness,—together with the use of a broad, blue silk shade during the day, to protect the eyes from the direct rays of light.

Scrofulous Inflammation of the Ear.

Children of scrofulous constitution are very liable to inflammation of the lining membrane of the outer passage of the ear, accompanied by the formation of pustules, and discharge of thin, acrid, or otherwise unhealthy and often offensive matter. The affection is, frequently, conjoined with ulcerations of the external ear. In severe attacks, or in neglected cases, the inflammation may extend into the internal ear, implicating and destroying its structure, and consequently giving rise to irremediable deafness. More or less dangerous at all

* An eyewash, consisting of the same medicine which is administered internally, seems, occasionally, to facilitate recovery

times, the disease is particularly so when it spreads to the bones of the skull. The different symptoms which characterise the complaint will be gleaned from those which are mentioned after each remedy. In the acute form or stage, *Pulsatilla*, *Mercurius*, *Chamomilla*, and *Belladonna* are the principal remedies.

PULSATILLA is almost a specific in this complaint when early resorted to. Its leading indications are, severe aching, piercing, throbbing, or darting and burning pains in the interior of the ear, combined with heat, redness, and swelling of the external ear, and of the auditory tube; also when delirium occasionally occurs.

CHAMOMILLA. Aching, tearing pains, extending to the lobe,—sometimes alternated with a sharp stab as if a knife were thrust into the ear; dryness of the ear; excessive peevishness, and impatience under suffering even when not of the severest description. (*Chamomilla* is, properly speaking, better adapted to common earache, or rheumatism in the ear, proceeding from a chill; but it is occasionally useful in this affection when it occurs in very young and delicate children.)

MERCURIUS is chiefly required in less severe cases; or when the violence of the attack has been subdued by *Pulsatilla*. The symptoms which more especially denote its appropriateness, are aching, tearing pains extending to the cheeks, and frequently alternated or intermingled with painful jerks or dartings in the ear; aggravation at night, accompanied by profuse perspiration; slight discharge from the ear; burning heat and redness externally, with sensation of ice-like coldness internally.

Belladonna is required in the most serious forms of the complaint, particularly when the brain is involved, and the symptoms are as follows: darting, piercing. squeezing, pressive, aching pains in the ear, exacerbated by movement and from the slightest noise; extreme agitation; heat of the head, with distention and violent throbbing of the vessels; delirium; vomiting; coldness of the extremities. (See *Inflammation of the Brain.*) After the employment of one or more, if called for, of the above medicines, *Nux v.*, or *Sulphur*, and *Calcarea*, are sometimes required. *Nux v.* chiefly in cases where *Chamomilla*, has been employed. *Sulphur* and *Calcarea*, in general cases, against any remaining symptoms.

Administration of the remedies. Six globules in two tablespoonsful of water, a dessert-spoonful of the solution every three to six hours, according to the severity of the symptoms. As soon as improvement sets in, and in less acute cases, the intervals between the doses may be lengthened.*

In old standing cases, or in those of recent origin which have begun in a milder and more insidious form than the preceding, and have terminated in *running of the ears,*—*Pulsatilla*, *Mercurius*, *Sulphur*, *Lycopodium*, and *Conium* are almost always more or less useful; but *Calcarea*, *Causticum*, *Hepar sulphuris*, *Aurum*, *Carbo v.*, *Silicea*, *Acid. nitr.* and *Assafœtida*, &c. are also serviceable in protracted cases. When the discharge is fetid, *Carbo v.*, *Aurum*, *Hepar s.*, and *Causticum* are generally the more useful. If the discharge is accompanied by soreness behind the ear, *Conium*, *Sulphur*, *Lycopodium*, *Calcarea*, *Hepar s.*, *Silicea*, *Acid. nitr.*, *Petroleum*, &c. usually claim a preference. *Mercurius* and *Sulphur*, followed, if required, by *Belladonna*, *Lachesis*, *Silicea*, and *Calcarea*, are chiefly indicated when headache attends. When pain suddenly comes on in old standing cases: or when, in those of more recent origin, the pain becomes increased, and the patient complains of violent throbbing and buzzing in the ears, headache or tightness around the head, with deafness and some degree of fever,—*Hepar sulphuris*, *Lachesis*, and *Silicea* may be given in alternation every

* See rules for the administration and repetition of the dose.

four or five hours. A sudden suppression of the discharge is generally attended with serious consequences. If it has been caused by getting the feet wet, *Dulcamara* should immediately be administered, and succeeded by *Belladonna* if headache, with heat of skin and other signs of fever supervene. *Bryonia* may follow *Belladonna* if the headache continues. If glandular swellings are the result, *Mercurius*, *Belladonna*, and *Pulsatilla* are generally required. The selection of these will frequently be facilitated by the indications already given under these remedies at the commencement of this article. In cases of long standing a succession of medicines at intervals of eight or ten days is sometimes called for. So long, however, as one remedy appears to do good, it ought not to be changed. It is usually advisable, nevertheless, to discontinue the medicine when some amelioration has been effected, and only to return to it when further improvement ceases to be apparent. If, after a repetition of the medicine which had produced the amendment, the symptoms remain unaltered, another remedy should be administered.

In tedious cases, and in those which become associated with affection of the head, medical aid should be sought.

In simple *earache* arising from cold, and occur

ring in otherwise healthy children, *Belladonna*, *Mercurius*, *Pulsatilla*, *Chamomilla*, are the most serviceable medicines. They are indicated by nearly the same train of symptoms as mentioned beforehand.

When there is fever with fulness and acceleration of pulse, one or more doses (two globules) of *Aconitum* may be given. When the pain increases in intensity, and is attended with, or consists almost exclusively of a continuous and painful throbbing, sometimes accompanied by shivering, *Hepar s.* should be administered.

ADMINISTRATION of these. Six globules in two tablespoonsful of water, a dessert-spoonful every six or eight hours. In slight attacks, a single dose (of two to three globules) will be sufficient.

DIET. When the symptoms are severe, and attended with considerable fever, toast and water, barley water, or thin gruel, should only be allowed. (See *Diet in Fever*.)

In less violent attacks, although the appetite may be good, the food should be light for the first day or two. Exposure to currents of air, or to sudden changes of temperature, should always be avoided as much as possible when there is any predisposition to complaints of the ear.

Rickets.

This distressing disease, commonly begins to show itself about the tender age of from one to two years. It is generally preceded, for a longer or shorter period, by derangement of the general health, before any of its well-known characteristic features become developed. The following comprise the more common of these premonitory symptoms: pale and sickly countenance; dry, harsh skin; soft and flabby flesh, irregular appetite, sometimes with desire for indigestible or unnatural food; constipation or diarrhœa; general febrile excitement, fretfulness and languor. Subsequently, the head is observed to become preternaturally enlarged, and the forehead unusually prominent. The breast-bone projects; the ribs appear flattened; the belly is much distended; while the rest of the body, and the limbs in particular, are greatly emaciated: and the debility is extreme. As the disease advances, the muscles become more flaccid; the wrists and ankles become swollen; the legs, thighs, and arms distorted; and the spine partakes in the general deformity, by becoming shorter, and curved in various directions. Sometimes the distortion and deformity of the ribs and spine increase to such a degree as to bring on a fatal result, by impeding the performance of the lungs, and other important internal parts. When the disease is early attended to, and the more general exciting causes, such as defective nursing—damp, or wet, ill-ventilated dwellings—insufficient exercise out of doors—improper food—and uncleanliness, are capable of being removed, the chances of recovery are much increased; and the deformity is, frequently, materially, if not wholly, diminished as the patient grows up. Otherwise, if life be spared, it is liable to be rendered miserable by a state of almost continuous suffering.

TREATMENT. When there is an hereditary predisposition to this disease, too great attention cannot be paid to the first manifestations of ill-health. Great care should, at the same time, be taken to avoid undue pressure upon the chest and other parts. From the deficiency of earthy matter in the bones of a rickety child, they are wanting in the natural and requisite strength or firmness to support the weight of the frame. Consequently, when every precaution is not adopted, and the child is allowed, or rather compelled, by its heedless and culpable nurse or others, to use muscular exertion, deformity inevitably results. It will, therefore, be necessary to deal gently and cautiously with the child from the first day of its earthly existence. And while every care is observed to escape the mischief alluded to, by giving proper support to the back and loins on all occasions—keeping the child habitually on its back, and carrying it about in a little cot or tray constructed for the purpose, particularly if some of the symptoms of the disease have, even in the slightest degree, already become apparent—other means, having for their object the improvement of the general health, must be strictly followed. The child should be regularly sent into the open air, when the weather permits; its apartments ought to be well ventilated; its personal cleanliness should be constantly ensured; and wholesome and appropriate nourishment provided. When the health and strength are improving, but the limbs or other parts have become deformed to a greater or less extent, in defiance of every solicitude,—or as more frequently happens, from oft-repeated infractions of the rules laid down,—considerable benefit may yet be accomplished by judiciously-applied mechanical aid. At the head of the artificial contrivances for counteracting deformity, may be placed the gentle and cautious use of gymnastic exercises, as soon as the child is old enough to undergo them—and it is surprising how early they may be advantageously resorted to. Without these, all instruments are often futile—

not to say hurtful. But *in combination with them*, the objection to the temporaneous employment of an appropriate apparatus for the purpose of exercising compression, is, I opine, in certain cases removed. I allude, more especially, to the instance in which the legs have become very much bent, either in consequence of neglect or from its having been found impracticable to prevent a high-spirited child from constantly getting on his feet, before his delicate frame had become sufficiently invigorated by suitable treatment. I am free to admit, however, that instruments should always be rejected whenever, and wherever, they can possibly be dispensed with.

The Homœopathic treatment, required for the subjugation of the constitutional disturbance which ushers in the local peculiarities of the disease, is so analogous to what has been recommended in the chapter on *Infantile Remittent Fever*, that the reader is referred thereto.

If the local manifestations of the disease have supervened, *Calcarea* is a remedy of primary importance, more particularly when the moulds of the head are in an open condition, and the process of dentition is unduly protracted, or the teeth that are protruded have a tendency to premature decay. *Belladonna*, *Mercurius*, *Pulsatilla*, *Sulphur*, and *Silicea*, together with *Assafœtida*, *Phosphorus*, or

Acidum-phosphoricum, Acidum-nitricum, Petroleum and *Mezereum* are however, of equal importance with *Calcarea* in the established disease. It is sometimes necessary to resort to the whole of these, in rotation, in the order mentioned; giving two globules morning and evening for four or five days, and allowing, under ordinary circumstances, an interval of at least five or six days to elapse between the finishing of one remedy and the commencing of another. But the selection of the remedy ought to be regulated as strictly as can be, by the nature of the symptoms. (See *Infantile Remittent Fever*, where some of the general indications given for several of the above medicines, will be found equally applicable in this affection.) And if a decided improvement occurs after the administration of any special remedy, it ought not to be exchanged so long as it continues to do good.*

CUTANEOUS DISEASES.

Ringworm (*Herpetic or Vesicular*).

This affection is of frequent occurrence in children after the period of infancy. It has been considered contagious from the circumstance of

* See rules for the administration and repetition of the dose.

several children of one family, or at the same school, being sometimes attacked at the same time; but there is every reason to believe that this opinion is erroneous, from the fact of none of the other species of herpes* being communicable by contact. When not complicated with another disease, it is not attended with any general constitutional derangement. The disease is characterised by an eruption of small rings or circular bands, the vesicles only occupying the circumference; these are small, and have a red-colored base of greater or less intensity. About the third or fifth day the vesicles become turbid, and then discharge, when little brownish scabs form over them. The portions of skin within the circlets are usually healthy at first; but, for the most part, subsequently become rough, of a reddish hue, and scale off as the vesicular eruption dies away. The duration of the eruption frequently does not extend beyond a week or two; but when there is a series of consecutive rings on the face, neck, arms, and shoulders, as frequently happens in warm climates (where the affection, moreover, assumes a more serious and obstinate character), or during hot weather in this country, it is necessarily protracted considerably beyond this pe-

* *Herpes.* Clustered vesicles, which concrete into scabs.

riod. Furthermore, there are some children in whom the affection has a tendency to reappear every spring and summer.

TREATMENT. In the majority of cases, the affection yields readily under the action of *Sepia*, of which from two to three globules may be given in a little water, and the dose repeated on the fourth day, if required by any appearance of tardiness in the subsidence of the eruption, or should there be any indications of the formation of fresh rings.

In some obstinate cases, the alternate use of *Rhus* and *Sulph.* every four or five days is found necessary. In others, *Calcarea* and *Natrum* are needed. Where there is a liability to annual visitations of the eruption, the employment of *Sulphur* and *Sepia* in alternation at intervals of a week, often suffices to eradicate the constitutional tendency. All manner of household applications must be avoided. But when the irritation is considerable, before the specific influence of the homœopathic remedy has begun to tell, lint, moistened with cold water,—holding if requisite some of the medicine in solution,—and covered over with oiled silk, may be applied to the part.

DIET. See that recommended under SCALD HEAD.

Scald-Head. Ringworm of the Scalp. Pustular Ringworm.

This troublesome disease occurs, most commonly, about the sixth or seventh year of childhood; but it is liable to take place at an earlier, and also somewhat later period of life. In short, it may make its appearance any time between the age of about two years to that of puberty. It is not confined to the scalp, but also appears on the neck, trunk, and extremities; when confined to the trunk, it proves by no means so obstinate and rebellious a disease as when located in the hairy scalp.

It is of a highly contagious nature, being readily communicated among children who make use of the same comb and brush, or even towel, and is of long and uncertain continuance,—indeed there are few cutaneous affections which have more frequently baffled the unwearied efforts of practitioners than this; and it would have been well had *less* been attempted by those of the old school in the way of treatment; for in but too many instances the so-called *cure* has proved worse than the disease.

SYMPTOMS. The affection is characterised, at the commencement, by the appearance of isolated, red-colored, irregular, circular patches, on which appear numerous small yellowish points or pustules, which do not rise above the level of the skin, and are generally traversed in the centre by a hair. These pustules, which are much more thickly studded in the circumference than the centre of the circular patches, soon break and form thin scabs, which frequently unite with the adjacent patches, and assume an extensive and irregular appearance, but commonly retain a somewhat circular shape. The incrustations become thick and hard by accumulation, and are detached from time to time in small pieces, which bear a close resemblance to crumbling mortar. When the scabs have been removed or torn off, the surface which they had occupied looks red and glossy, but is studded with slightly elevated pimples, in some of which minute globules of matter subsequently become apparent.

By these repeated evolutions of the eruption, the incrustations become thicker, the areas of the primary patches extend, and new ones are formed, so that the corresponding edges become blended, and frequently the whole head thus becomes affected. As the patches or clusters extend, the hair covering them usually becomes lighter in color, and breaks off short; and as the process of scabbing is repeated, it is thrown out by the roots, and finally there is left only a narrow chaplet of hair round the head. If the hair-follicles are destroyed, the baldness remains permanent. The external characters of scald-head are liable to vary, more or less, from the above description in many cases; the variation proceeding, conjointly, from the constitution of the patient and the duration of the disease. Thus we have, firstly, the variety that has been technically denominated the *Porrigo lupinosa*, which is characterised by small, dry, circular scabs, of a yellowish-white color, having raised margins, and a central depression like that on the seeds of the lupine. The incrustations are deeply set in the skin, to which their edges are firmly adherent.

Secondly, the *Porrigo furfurans*. This variety commences with the eruption of small pustules, containing a straw-colored fluid, which soon discharge, dry, and form thin laminated crusts, with scale-like exfoliations. The affection is confined to the scalp, and is attended with considerable itching and soreness, although there is but slight excoriation; the hair partially falls off, and occasionally, becomes subsequently somewhat lighter in color.

Thirdly, the *Porrigo favosa*, distinguished by the eruption of large, soft, straw-colored pustules, generally somewhat flattened, possessing an irregular margin, and surrounded by a slight inflammatory redness. They are met with on other parts of the body as well as the scalp, and are accompanied by much itching. On breaking, these pustules discharge a viscid matter, which hardens into semi-transparent, greenish-yellow scales. The disease extends to the face, and eventually the ulceration spreads over the entire head, and, from the continued discharge, the hair and moist scabs become matted together. Pediculi are generated in large numbers, and aggravate the excessive irritation. The incrustations thicken into irregular masses, bearing some resemblance to a honeycomb. And the acrid exudation, from the ulcerated patches on the scalp, exhales an offensive and pungent vapor.

Fourthly, and lastly, the *Porrigo decalvans* which is chiefly characterised by patches of baldness.

Scald-head is very evidently a constitutional, and not a local affection. It is, moreover, invariably attended with a greater or less degree of constitutional disturbance, such as glandular swellings and indurations, deranged digestion, distended abdomen, paleness of the face, emaciation, &c.

Causes. The disease is chiefly propagated

by contagion, but appears to originate spontaneously in children of scrofulous, flabby, or feeble and emaciated habit, if they be ill-fed, ill-lodged, uncleanly, and deprived of a wholesome degree of exercise.

TREATMENT. It cannot be denied that, even under homœopathic treatment, the disease frequently proves extremely obstinate; but, in many cases, the difficulty experienced in effecting a cure, arises from the previous treatment which the patient has undergone: or from culpable conduct, on the part of the parents or others, in allowing the disorder to pursue its course, for a lengthened period, unchecked and utterly neglected, ere proper assistance is sought.

In general cases, while the patches exhibit an irritable and inflammatory aspect, *Rhus* will usually be found the most appropriate remedy; the head should at the same time be regularly and gently sponged with tepid water twice a day. Should a dry exfoliation or scaliness and scabbing then ensue, *Sulphur* may be had recourse to; but if, on the other hand, an offensive discharge break out, attended by violent itching, without much redness, *Staphysagria* may be administered, and then again *Rhus*.

The last-named, important remedy, is also useful in cases which are of some standing, and particularly when there is a copious discharge of a greenish color, accompanied by extensive formation of thick scabs; or when the entire scalp is covered with cup-shaped scabs, presenting a honey-combed appearance, and exhaling a most repulsive odor. If, notwithstanding the administration of these remedies, very little favorable progress is made; or if, on the contrary, the affection grows rather worse, the exudation becoming very acrimonious and consequently productive of an extension of the disease, or of the formation of ulcers, *Arsenicum* should be given; after the action of which, *Rhus* will frequently produce a satisfactory effect. These remedies may also be occasionally administered externally with good effect, by dissolving a few globules of the remedy selected in a little water, and applying the liquid once or twice a day to the affected parts.

When the foregoing means are insufficient to effect a cure, which sometimes happens in inveterate cases that have previously been subjected to a long course of injudicious allopathic treatment, and in neglected cases occurring in scrofulous and debilitated children, the following remedies may be used :—

Hepar s., when the eruption is not confined to

the head, but also appears upon the forehead, face, and neck; when, moreover, the eyes and eyelids become inflamed and weakened, and soreness or ulceration breaks out on or behind the ears. In the latter case *Baryta c.*, *Graphites*, and *Oleander* are also useful.

Dulcamara, when the glands of the throat and neck are enlarged and indurated (or *Bryonia*, when there is inflammation and tenderness of the said glands;) after which, *Staphysagria* may be administered, and then one or more of the remedies mentioned at the commencement, followed by *Baryta c.*

If these medicines prove ineffectual, *Sulphur*, *Graphites*, *Calcarea*, *Lycopodium*, *Phosphorus*, or *Oleander*, may answer the purpose required, and must be selected according to circumstances. In some cases, the alternate use of two or more medicaments will be found advantageous, such as *Sulphur* and *Calcarea*,—*Sulphur*, *Rhus*, and *Graphites*,—*Graphites* and *Lycopodium*,—*Graphites* and *Phosphorus*, and so on. A dry, inert, and scaly appearance of the eruption, chiefly requires *Calcarea*, or *Sulphur*, but also *Hepar s.*, *Phosphorus*, *Rhus*, *Arsenicum* or *Oleander*. A humid or moist-looking eruption: *Lycopodium* or *Staphysagria*, *Rhus*, *Arsenicum*, *Sulphur*, *Sepia;* and also *Baryta c.*, *Calcarea c.*, *Graphites*, *Cicuta virosa* and *Oleander*.

In *Porrigo decalvans* (with patches of baldness,) *Graphites*, *Phosphorus*, *Baryta*, *Lycopodium* and *Zincum*, are, commonly, the more serviceable; but *Sulphur*, *Calcarea*, *Silicea*, &c. and most of the other aforesaid remedies, may be found indicated in particular cases. When the digestive organs are in a deranged state, the intermediate employment of *Bryonia*, *Nux v.*, *Pulsatilla* is occasionally required, provided *Arsenicum*, *Sulphur*, *Calc.*, etc. are not amply sufficient to cope with this complication.

ADMINISTRATION OF THE MEDICINES. With regard to the administration of the medicines, it may be stated that, at the commencement of the disorder, a dose (three globules) may be given daily, or every second day, until symptoms of improvement make their appearance; the medicine must then be discontinued, and only renewed when the amelioration ceases, or the disorder threatens to extend itself. When no signs of improvement become perceptible, or when, on the contrary, the malady evidently seems to be getting gradually worse, notwithstanding the exhibition of two or three doses of a particular remedy, another must be selected, according to the indications.

In cases of old standing, the intervals between the exhibitions of the medicine must generally be lengthened, or a dose may be given daily for a week, and then a period of ten to twelve days, and even upwards, allowed to elapse before the medicine is repeated, or another remedy substituted.

Diet and Regimen. The diet should be light and nutritious. Fish and salt meat must be abstained from, and any article of food, even though generally considered wholesome, should, if found to disagree, be strictly avoided. Heating farinaceous food, such as oatmeal (in the form of porridge or stirabout, gruel, and soup,) maize, &c. is, generally, to be objected to. Undeviating attention to cleanliness must be observed throughout the entire course of the complaint, and regular exercise in the open air enjoined. The sleeping chamber should be airy, and not overcrowded. Lastly, a sufficiency of appropriate clothing ought to be worn, and the heat should be protected against damp. The hair ought, generally, to be removed early in the disease.

Milk-Crust.

This affection usually makes its appearance during the period of the first dentition. It commences in the form of numerous small, whitish, more or less confluent pustules, which appear in clusters upon a red ground. These generally show themselves, in the first instance, on the forehead and cheeks, but sometimes spread over the whole body. The ears rarely escape; and when the scalp becomes implicated, the glands at the nape of the neck swell, and sometimes end in suppuration. The lymph contained in the pustules soon becomes yellow, dark, or even sanguineous, and, on being discharged, forms into thin, greenish yellow crusts; those on the scalp bearing some similitude to the smeared yolk of a hard-boiled egg.

Frequently, there is considerable surrounding redness and swelling, with distressing itching, which renders the little patient excessively restless and fretful, and causes him to keep continually rubbing the affected parts, by which the discharge and crusts are repeatedly renewed, and increased in thickness, often to such extent that the whole face becomes covered as with a mask,—the eyes and nose alone remaining free. The eyes and eyelids, as also the glands beneath the ear, and, in exceptional cases, even those of the mesentery,* occasionally become inflamed, and sometimes emaciation supervenes.

TREATMENT. The following medicines have

* The membrane in the middle of the intestines, and by means of which they are secured to the spine.

been found serviceable in this affection: *Aconitum*, *Viola tricolor*, *Rhus*, *Sulphur*, *Calcarea*, *Lycopodium*, *Sassaparilla*, *Mezereum*, *Belladonna*, *Hepar sulphuris*, *Euphrasia*, *Staphysagria*, *&c.*

ACONITE should commence our treatment, when we find excessive restlessness and excitability produced by this affection, and when the skin around the parts is red, inflamed, and itching.

ADMINISTRATION. Two globules, in four teaspoonsful of water, a teaspoonful every four or five hours.

As soon as beneficial effects have resulted from the administration of the above remedy, we may follow it up with VIOLA TRICOLOR, which is often sufficient to effect a cure in the simple, uncomplicated form of the disease, particularly when the accompanying irritation is evidently worse at night, and when the urine has a peculiarly offensive odor.

ADMINISTRATION. Three globules, in four teaspoonsful of water, one night and morning. The prescription to be repeated in four days—or another remedy selected, if the affection threatens to extend, or otherwise become worse.*

RHUS TOXICODENDRON may succeed or supersede *Viola tricolor*, when the scalp is considerably af-

* See rules for the administration and repetition of the dose.

fected and thickly studded with incrustations, or when the surrounding inflammation is still severe, and the itching apparently excessive—from the frequency with which the child rubs and scratches the affected parts.

ADMINISTRATION. Same as *Viola tricolor.*

When *Rhus* is insufficient to complete the cure, *Calcarea* or *Lycopodium* are generally to be selected in preference to other remedies; the former more particularly when there is little or no discharge, the latter when there is considerable oozing (suppuration.)

In other cases, *Sulphur* is more appropriate after *Rhus,* but particularly when the eyelids are severely implicated. The alternate use of *Sulphur* and *Rhus,* in chronic cases of the above description, is attended with beneficial results.

MEZEREUM is often very efficacious when, from the bursting and discharge of the contents of the pustules, incrustations have formed, from which an acrid exudation flows and gives rise to a fresh eruption of vesicles wherever it comes in contact with the skin. (See also SCALD HEAD.)

ADMINISTRATION. Same as *Viola tricolor.*

Every possible attention should be paid to the diet; and acids or stimulants of every description strictly inhibited.

Chafing. Scalding. Excoriations.

This affection is of frequent occurrence in infants and young children. It displays itself most readily on all parts where opposite surfaces of the skin are in continual contact, or exposed to friction; consequently the groins, upper part of the thighs, and neighboring regions; as also the neck, and the space and angle behind the ears, are its usual sites. In severe cases, it sometimes spreads over the greater part of the surface of the body.

The more common form in which it appears is in red, irregular, inflammatory patches, occasionally attended with excessive itching, and the discharge, or oozing out, of a watery yellowish fluid.

In neglected cases, the skin becomes hard, chapped, and much excoriated. General fever rarely attends; but the child is rendered extremely peevish and restless when the local inflammation is severe and extensive.

TREATMENT. Against this affection, cleanliness is the best preventive, and often a sufficient remedy; however, we frequently find it proceed to such an extent as to require the aid of medicine for its removal.

CHAMOMILLA will be found speedily effective in most instances, and particularly in those which proceed from acidity, and are, consequently, attended with green-colored, sour-smelling, evacuations. But as the malady is frequently produced, and still more frequently aggravated, by mechanical friction, the alternate employment of *Arnica* and *Chamomilla* materially facilitates the cure, in the majority of cases.

ADMINISTRATION. Two globules of *Arnica* in the morning, and again at bed-time. Twenty-four hours afterwards, *Chamomilla* may be given in the same manner; and so on for the space of ten or twelve days.

For severe or neglected cases, which have spread over the greater part of the body, and are accompanied by troublesome excoriations, *Mercurius* is generally the most effective remedy.

ADMINISTRATION. Two globules every other day for a week. Four or five days afterwards, if no amendment has resulted, LYCOPODIUM may be administered in the same way.

In all obstinate cases, and in those which have been preceded by, or are associated with, a miliary eruption, SULPHUR should be had recourse to.

ADMINISTRATION. Same as *Mercurius*.

Sepia, *Calcarea,* and *Graphites* are sometimes required in inveterate cases, which do not yield to the above remedies. *Graphites* is more especially required when the chafing is chiefly confined to the space behind the ear.

DIET. The diet of spoon-fed infants and young children, who are troubled with this affection, ought to be strictly attended to. The stomach should never be overloaded; and stimulating food, or that which is liable to create acidity, ought to be withheld. When the discharge is considerable, starch powder may be dusted over the parts. Undeviating care should be bestowed upon the personal cleanliness of the child. The same caution is necessary as regards the cooking and feeding utensils used.

Hordeolum; or Stye.

This is an inflammatory action of one of the glands in the margin of the eye-lid, of the nature of a boil, and mostly makes its appearance near the inner angle of the eye.

REMEDIES. *Pulsatilla*, *Aurum metallicum*, *Staphysagria*, *Arsenicum*, and *Sulphur*.

PULSATILLA is considered almost specific in this disease, as it mostly disappears after taking a few doses of it.

ADMINISTRATION. Six globules three times a day.

Aurum metallicum, if the eyelids are red and swollen, with obstruction and ulceration of the nostrils.

Administration. Six globules night and morning.

Staphysagria, if they are of frequent recurrence, and leave a tendency to fresh inflammation, or if indurations and hardness of the eyelid remain.

Administration. Six globules night and morning.

Arsenicum, scrofulous inflammation of the eyes, with œdematous swelling of the lids; dryness of the margin of the lids.

Administration. Six globules night and morning.

Sulphur, itching and inflammation of the eyelids; swelling of the lids, with pimples on them, and dryness.

Administration. Six globules night and morning.

Bold Hives, Nettle Rash; or Urticaria.

This is a very common eruptive disease of children, and is known by large, red, and diffused patches, or wheals of various sizes and irregular shapes, resembling the stings of nettles; or in streaks. The elevations generally are of a pale, but occasionally of a bright red color, white in the centre. Sometimes the eruption is paler than the surrounding skin. It is accompanied with burning and troublesome itching, especially when the patient gets warm in bed, causing continual scratching, and is mostly preceded by gastric disturbance: such as nausea and vomiting, restlessness, languor, thirst, want of appetite, and coated tongue, with more or less febrile excitement.

After the eruption has made its appearance, the gastric disturbance and febrile excitement gradually disappear, and nothing is left but the itching caused by the eruption.

This disease is frequently brought on by errors in diet, indigestion, or a faulty state of the skin and its secretion. In those who have a constitutional predisposition to the disease, it may be excited by a particular article of food, as shell-fish, almonds, honey, mushrooms, cucumbers, and acid fruits.

REMEDIES. *Aconite*, *Dulcamara*, *Pulsatilla*, *Rhus toxicodendron*, *Bryonia*, *Belladonna*, *Hepar sulphur*, *Arsenicum*, *Calcarea carbonica*, *Nux vomica*, *Sulphur*, and *Urtica urens*.

ACONITE, if with the eruption there is much fever; hard, accelerated pulse; dry and hot skin; much thirst; coated tongue, with restlessness and anxiety.

ADMINISTRATION. Four globules every two or three hours, according to the state of the case.

DULCAMARA, if the patient has been exposed to damp and wet weather; has fever; bitter taste in the mouth; diarrhœa, and coated tongue, with itching and burning after scratching.

ADMINISTRATION. Four globules every four hours.

PULSATILLA, if the attack has been brought on by fat or indigestible food; or is accompanied with looseness of the bowels. Pulsatilla is particularly adapted to persons of an even temperament and quiet disposition, and especially females and children.

ADMINISTRATION. Four globules three times a day.

RHUS TOXICODENDRON is adapted to many cases of this disorder, especially where it arises from a peculiarity of the constitution; or if the eruption is caused by some particular kind of food, and scratching increases the irritation.

ADMINISTRATION. Six globules twice a day.

Bryonia, if the eruption has been suddenly suppressed, and is attended with difficulty of breathing and oppression of the chest.

Administration. Four globules three times a day.

Belladonna, if with the eruption there is congestion to the head, with red face, giddiness and headache.

Administration. Three globules four times a day.

Hepar sulphur will be useful if the eruption is attended with catarrhal symptoms, as cold in the head, with coryza, affecting only one side.

Administration. Six globules night and morning.

Nux vomica, if the eruption is excited by the use of stimulants; or where there is much gastric derangement, constipation, indigestion, &c.

Administration. Six globules night and morning.

Sulphur, if the disease has been suppressed, will be found very serviceable in restoring the eruption to the surface.

Administration. Four globules three times a day until the eruption is brought out again.

Urtica urens is found very useful in many cases, if the eruption has a pale and hard appearance, and causes a great deal of scratching.

Administration. Six globules every two or three hours.

Prickly Heat; or Heat Spots.

Infants and children are often attacked in warm weather with an eruption of small vesicles, about the size of a pin's head, which sometimes fill with a thin, watery fluid; at other times they are red and inflamed, and attended with more or less fever, which makes the child very irritable, and causes it continually to scratch the parts affected. The duration of this disease is very uncertain, and apt to disappear in cool weather, and return again when it becomes warm.

If it does not interfere too much with the child's comfort, better let it alone. In aggravated cases we may resort to one of the following

Remedies. *Aconite*, *Chamomilla*, *Bryonia*, *Rhus toxicodendron*, and *Sulphur*.

Aconite, if the eruption is accompanied with much fever, dry, hot skin, and restlessness.

Administration. Four globules three times a day.

Chamomilla, if Aconite is not sufficient, and there is still great restlessness.

ADMINISTRATION. The same as given of Aconite.

BRYONIA, if the eruption is suppressed, accompanied with much restlessness, and the patient is excited and cannot bear to be moved.

ADMINISTRATION. Four globules every three hours.

SULPHUR will mostly relieve a tendency to this affection, or if the eruption manifests a disposition to spread.

ADMINISTRATION. Six globules every night.

Vaccination.

This is a purely homœopathic means of preventing one of the most loathsome diseases to which the human system is liable—the small-pox. Vaccination, alone, has probably, within the last fifty years—since its general introduction—saved more human life than all other remedial means put together have done, in twice that length of time.

It will answer well to vaccinate a child at almost any age, but probably about the sixth month is the best time, as the child is as easy nursed at that age as any other, and is less liable to get the pustule broken, from accidental causes or its own scratching, than when older.

It is a matter of great importance to obtain the virus from a healthy child of healthy parents, as few removes from the matter obtained from the cow as possible. The child selected should be free from scrofulous taint and all other hereditary diseases, especially cutaneous diseases.

The proper place to insert the matter is on the outer portion of the left arm, about half-way between the elbow and the shoulder.

To prepare the matter, take a portion of the scab and rub it up with a drop of clean water with the point of a lancet on a piece of glass or other hard and smooth substance, until it attains the consistency of cream. Then take a portion of the matter thus prepared on the point of the lancet, and insert it beneath the cuticle, by making three or four slight punctures close together; then apply more matter, and allow it to become dry without being wiped off.

If the operation is successful, on the fourth or fifth day a small red pimple is observable, which the next day becomes a little vesicle, and increases in size until it reaches about the quarter of an inch in diameter. On the seventh day the areola is formed, which goes on increasing until the ninth or tenth day, when it is about an inch and a half in diameter. The lymph contained in the vesicle is at first clear, then milky, afterward yellow, and finally dries into a mahogany brown scab, indented near the middle, with a hardened point in the centre. The constitutional symptoms usually appear about the seventh day, and consist of a little fever and restlessness, with some soreness in the axilla of the vaccinated arm—they last from twelve to eighteen hours. The scab falls off about the seventeenth day, leaving a cicatrix, with a number of small pointed pits in its inclosure.

The vaccine disease is so mild in its course, that medical treatment is seldom necessary. If the fever should be considerable, a dose or two of Aconite or Belladonna will be sufficient to remove all the unpleasant symptoms.

The best means of preventing the development of eruptions which sometimes follow vaccination, is to administer a dose of homœopathic sulphur on the evening of the eighth day.

Asphyxia, or apparent Death of New-born Infants.

This condition of new-born children is generally caused by the winding of the cord around the neck; by long detention of the head in the pelvis; by tedious labors; the accumulation of mucus in the mouth and throat; sudden change of temperature before respiration is fully established, &c.

REMEDIES. *Tartar emetic, Aconite China* and *Opium.*

TARTAR EMETIC may be given where there are no signs of life, slight pulsations of the cord, or if the face is purple and swollen.

ADMINISTRATION. Dissolve six globules in four teaspoonsful of water, and of this solution give six drops every few minutes, until there are signs of life.

ACONITE, when life is restored, and when the face has previously been of a bluish color.

ADMINISTRATION. Two globules every ten or fifteen minutes, until complete restoration has taken place.

CHINA, for similar symptoms, as for Aconite, except where the face has been pale.

ADMINISTRATION. The same as of Aconite.

OPIUM may be used if Tartar emetic fails to produce any beneficial effect in fifteen or twenty minutes, especially if the face has a bluish appearance.

ADMINISTRATION. The same as of Aconite.

Lock-Jaw of Infants.

This serious disease is almost exclusively confined to tropical climates, and happens only in the first days of infantile life. The child cries, and in vain attempts to nurse, the milk chokes it, and is ejected. On examination, the masseter muscles are found to be so rigid, that the lower jaw cannot be depressed; the jaws gradually close, the abdomen swells, the stiffness extends to the whole frame, and in two or three days the little sufferer is relieved by death. It is generally caused by foul atmosphere, taking cold, improper food, and local irritation from mechanical causes.

REMEDIES. *Arnica, Belladonna, Chamomilla, Mercurius vivus*, and *Lachesis*.

ARNICA, if it has been caused by mechanical injuries, irritation about the umbilicus, &c.

ADMINISTRATION. Three globules every four hours, at the same time, linen cloths wet with a solution, made of ten drops of the tincture of Arnica to a wineglassful of water, may be applied locally.

BELLADONNA, where it cannot be assigned to any particular cause, and the child cannot swallow.

ADMINISTRATION. Three globules every hour.

CHAMOMILLA, if it has been brought on by a sudden chill or fright.

ADMINISTRATION. Four globules every two hours.

MERCURIUS may be given, if Belladonna has failed to give relief.

ADMINISTRATION. The same as Belladonna.

LACHESIS, if it is caused by a bad state of the mother's milk.

ADMINISTRATION. Four globules every three hours.

Hiccough, or Singultus.

This is a common and mostly unimportant affection, and may generally be left altogether to nature. But if it should become troublesome, so as to prevent sleep, two or three globules of Ignatia or Pulsatilla put on the tongue will relieve it.

Sniffles.

Infants are often attacked with a kind of catarrh, or obstruction of the nose, which prevents them from breathing whilst they are suckling.

REMEDIES. *Nux vomica, Sambucus*, and *Chamomilla.*

NUX VOMICA, where there is oppressive dullness of the head, continual heat and dryness of the nose, or fluent coryza in the day-time, and dry coryza at night.

ADMINISTRATION. Four globules dissolved in a

wineglass of water, and a teaspoonful to be given three times a day, and if no relief is obtained in twenty-four hours, give the next mentioned remedy.

SAMBUCUS, if there is stoppage of the nose, with accumulation of thick, tenacious mucus.

ADMINISTRATION. The same as directed for Nux vomica.

CHAMOMILLA will be found very useful, if there is a watery discharge from the nose, or if the nostrils are sore and ulcerated.

ADMINISTRATION. Three globules every four hours until better.

Retention of Urine.

Young infants are frequently the subjects of this complaint. Dissolve six pellets of Aconite in a wineglassful of water, and give the child a portion of it every two or three hours until relief is obtained. Should this fail, give Nux vomica or Pulsatilla in the same way.

Profuse Urination.

Occasionally young children have frequent and profuse emissions of colorless and inodorous urine. They are apt to be pale and fretful during its continuance.

REMEDIES. *Phosphoric acid*, or *Silicea*.

PHOSPHORIC ACID, irresistible desire to urinate; enuresis, with cutting and burning; frequent micturition; urine fetid.

ADMINISTRATION. Three globules, morning, noon, and night.

SILICEA, desire to urinate, with copious emission, especially at night, with smarting in the urethra.

ADMINSTRATION. Three globules at night, for two successive nights.

Nocturnal Urination.

Constant "wetting the bed," in a majority of instances, is the result of disease, although in a few cases it may be owing to the indulgence in filthy habits. Whipping is a remedy that is frequently applied, but I never knew it to cure a single case.

REMEDIES. *Sepia*, *Silicea*, and *Cina*.

SEPIA, continual desire to urinate; pressure on the bladder, with frequent discharges of urine; spasms of the neck of the bladder.

ADMINISTRATION. Three globules at night, for several nights in succession, and if no improvement take place, consult the next remedy.

SILICEA, micturition every night; desire to urinate, with pressure upon the bladder; yellow sediment like sand in the urine.

ADMINISTRATION. Six globules at night for several nights in succession.

CINA, if there is suspicion that worms are the cause, and there is involuntary emission of urine, which becomes turbid immediately after being passed.

ADMINISTRATION. The same as directed for Silicea.

Crying of Infants.

An infant is not always in pain when it cries. This is the language by which it makes known its wants. It may be hungry or need changing. Young infants should never be obliged to lie in one position longer than an hour or two at a time. They should be placed on the side to sleep, and turned over occasionally.

Although the above be true, we are not to think that children never have pain when they cry. An experienced ear can generally perceive a difference in the tone, and in that way determine whether the child have pain or not. If a child continue to cry and will not be pacified, the cause should be diligently sought for—a pin may be pricking it, or its clothes may be too tight, or it may have pain somewhere.

REMEDIES. *Belladonna*, *Aconite*, *Coffea*, and *Chamomilla.*

BELLADONNA, if the child continues to cry for a long time without any apparent cause, or starts out of its sleep and cries.

ADMINISTRATION. Dissolve six globules in half a tumblerful of water, and give a teaspoonful every one, two, or three hours, according to circumstances.

ACONITE, if there be much uneasiness, accompanied with dry heat.

ADMINISTRATION. The same as directed for Belladonna.

COFFEA, if the child appears to be nervous and very restless, with heat, and tossing about.

ADMINISTRATION. Three globules every hour until it is better

CHAMOMILLA, when the child cries, and is restless, with frequent startings, or there is reason to believe it has earache or headace, and cries when it is moved.

ADMINISTRATION. The same as directed for Belladonna.

Atrophy.

This affection is caused by the system not receiving a sufficient supply of nourishment from the food taken, for the subsistence and development of the organism. In other words, defective nutrition.

REMEDIES. *Calcarea carbonica*, *Arsenicum*, *Belladonna*, *China*, *Nux vomica*, *Rhus toxicodendron*, and *Sulphur*.

CALCAREA CARBONICA, where there is emaciation; voracious appetite; enlargement of the glands of the mesentery; general weakness: clay-colored discharges from the bowels; softness of the flesh; and excitability of the nervous system.

ADMINISTRATION. Six globules twice a day.

ARSENICUM, dry and parchment-like skin; vomiting of food; frequent desire to drink; but little at a time; restlessness; sleep interrupted by starting and jerking; greenish or brown stools; passage of undigested food; night-sweats, &c.

ADMINISTRATION. Six globules three times a day.

BELLADONNA, cough, with rattling of mucus in the throat; swelling of the glands of the neck; colic, with involuntary stools; suited to children with precocity of intellect.

ADMINISTRATION. Six globules three times a day.

CHINA, emaciation; enlarged and tympanitic abdomen; night sweats; diarrhœa, with discharges of undigested food; pale face; disturbed sleep, &c.

ADMINISTRATION. Six globules three times a day.

NUX VOMICA, yellow, bloated face; constipation of the bowels; large and distended abdomen, with much flatulency; and desire to eat, with vomiting of food.

ADMINISTRATION. Six globules twice a day.

RHUS TOXICODENDRON, great debility, with constant desire to lie down; hard and distended abdomen; slimy or bloody diarrhœa.

ADMINISTRATION. Four globules three times a day.

SULPHUR, in the majority of cases, where there is swelling of the inquinal glands; hard and distended abdomen; rattling of mucus in the throat; diarrhœa or constipation; complexion pale, with sunken eyes.

ADMINISTRATION. Six globules twice a day.

Prolapsus Ani.

The descent of the rectum, or the "body coming down," as it is termed in domestic language, is generally consequent upon some other disease. It is apt to follow upon long continued diarrhœa, or an acute attack of dysentery; protracted costiveness also may give rise to it, or it may depend on a state of relaxation of the system, merely.

When the bowel is protruded, it can easily be reduced, by laying the child across the lap, and making pressure on the protruded part with a piece of fine linen cloth, anointed with fresh lard.

When it is but an attendant upon another disease, of course that disease must be removed before the prolapsus can be cured. But when it stands out as a disease by itself, the following remedies will frequently cure it:

REMEDIES. *Ignatia*, *Nux vomica*, *Bryonia*, and *Podophyllum pelt.*

IGNATIA, desire for stool, with protrusion of the rectum; sharp pain in the rectum after stool; violent itching of the anus.

ADMINISTRATION. Three globules three times a day until better.

NUX VOMICA, constipation, as if from contraction and constriction of the bowels of infants, especially from the use of coffee; frequent and ineffectual urging to stool.

Administration. Four globules night and morning until better.

Bryonia, constipation; stool hard and dry, or, as if burnt, with protrusion of the rectum; long, lasting burning at the rectum after stool.

Administration. The same as given for Nux vomica.

Podophyllum pelt. for the same symptoms, and to be given in the same way as directed for Ignatia.

Leucorrhœa of Children.

Little girls, from a little neglect and some other incidental causes, are liable to a discharge of whitish mucus from the vagina, somewhat similar to the leucorrhœa of adults. Frequent ablutions with luke-warm water will generally remove it in a short time; but if it should not, give six globules of Calcarea carbonica, two nights in succession, and continue the washings.

ADMINISTRATION AND REPETITIONS OF THE MEDICINES.

In the body of the work, special directions have been given for the dose and the mode in which it may be administered in the different diseases treated of; and although it is almost impossible to give any fixed rule that will serve in all cases, much more depending upon the discrimination of the administrator, and a careful observance of the symptoms than routine, the author, nevertheless, proposes, in this place, to offer a few general observations on the subject of the administration and repetition of the medicines:—

In severe *acute* diseases, or such as are attended with violent symptoms, and run a short course, we must carefully watch the symptoms, and, if no perceptible alteration become apparent within a couple of hours or so, we may usually conclude that the remedy administered is not the appropriate one. In *subacute* affections a somewhat longer interval must be allowed for the manifestation of medicinal action. Whilst in those of a chronic* description, no alteration of any kind may,

* Of long continuance. The term is used in opposition to that of *acute*.

generally speaking, be anticipated earlier than two to four days, at the soonest, after the first employment of the medicament; but these rules are liable to exceptions. Care ought always to be taken not to change the remedy prematurely, particularly when the case under treatment is not of an urgent nature, and too much stress cannot be laid upon the necessity of carefully watching the effects of each dose, as, in addition to the temporary aggravation of the symptoms which sometimes sets in, a development of medicinal effects occasionally takes place, particularly after frequent repetition of different remedies in susceptible patients; by a want of attention to this important point, we may incur confusion, and may be unconsciously treating a medicinal disturbance of our own creation. Such, unhappily, but too frequently occurs in all allopathic practice, and in a much more serious form. We must also guard against falling into the opposite extreme—allowing the disease to gain head unchecked.

If a *medicinal aggravation** take place, followed by

* *Very marked* medicinal aggravations are of comparatively rare occurrence; nevertheless, as they are occasionally very prominently manifested, particularly in highly nervous and susceptible habits, we shall here give the leading and most common distinctive points of difference between the medicinal aggravation (or exacerbation of symptoms produced by the medicine) and that of the disease. The *medicinal aggravation* comes on *suddenly*, and without previous amelioration; the aggravation of the disease more *gradually*, and frequently *following* an amelioration. Moreover, in the former several of the *medicinal* symptoms, some of which we may find under the *indications* for the remedy, and not *before* remarked, declare themselves. The pulse is also a discriminative guide, particularly in fevers

amelioration, we must let the medicine continue its action, until the amelioration appears to cease, and the disease again makes head; if new symptoms set in, we must then have immediate recourse to the medicine thereby indicated. Should, however, no perceptible *medicinal aggravation* take place, but *amelioration* follow, we may safely await its approach to a termination, ere we again administer. In cases of high inflammatory action, the dose has sometimes to be repeated every two hours, every hour, or even more frequently. If any symptoms of importance remain, from the remedy first selected having afforded only partial relief, we must have recourse to some other medicine, which seems best fitted to meet them—*but refrain from changing the remedy as long as benefit results from its employment.*

In *chronic* and *subacute,* as well as in acute forms of disease, when a very striking improvement takes place, it will generally be found advantageous to cease to administer the medicine as long as the improvement continues, and only to repeat as soon as the slightest symptoms of activity in the morbid phenomena reappear. But when a sudden or marked improvement, of comparatively short duration, follows the first dose of a remedy, and, on repeating the dose, the symptoms of the complaint increase instead of subsiding, as they did in the

and inflammation. Thus when it becomes less frequent, or when, at all events, it does not increase in frequency, on the accession of aggravation, the exacerbation is to be attributed to *medicinal influence;* but, when the reverse is the case, the aggravation of symptoms must be considered to depend upon the progression of the disease.

first instance, it is to be understood that the medicine does not answer, and that another must accordingly be had recourse to, in the selection of which it will be necessary to choose one which corresponds in its indications to the remedy first prescribed.

Slight diseases are often removed by a single dose of a well-chosen medicine, but more severe and deeply-seated disorders require a frequent repetition.

In severe acute affections, we may often repeat the *same medicine in the same dose, at regular intervals, as long as it does good;* but this rule has many exceptions, and the directions already given should always be borne in mind.

In chronic cases, by a long-continued administration of the same medicine, the patient often becomes less susceptible to its impression; in such instances if the improvement remain stationary, or progress slowly, we may give, at suitable intervals, some other remedy or remedies, of as nearly analogous medicinal properties to that first administered as possible, and then return to the original remedy, if needful; if, on the other hand, decided amelioration follows each administration, we should allow a longer interval to elapse before repeating, by which means the system gradually recovers itself, and the susceptibility of medicinal influence remains unimpaired until the cure is completed.

In rare cases, this susceptibility increases, particularly when the medicine has been frequently repeated, and given in solution; in such instances—provided the remedy still appears to be appropriate—the medicine should be given dry, and the *intervals* between the exhibition *lengthened.* When the beneficial effect of a medicine is interrupted by an attack of cold, diarrhœa, &c., some other medicine must be given for the new affection, on the removal of which, the medicine which was previously acting favorably may be recurred to.

Remarks. In the selection of the remedy, it is not necessary that *all* the symptoms noted in this work should be present; at the same time care must be taken that there are no symptoms uncovered by the medicine, or more strongly indicating another. When a medicine produces only temporary improvement, or when some degree of improvement has been effected, but on the repetition of the same medicine no farther amendment is brought about, another remedy which corresponds to the first, or which embraces the symptoms if they have become altered in character, ought to be selected.

The homœopathic remedies are best adapted for domestic use in the form of globules of sugar of milk, saturated with the tinctures of the diluted medicaments, for, in addition to the convenience arising from the facility with which they can thus be dispensed, they are, moreover, less readily deteriorated by keeping, and will remain unimpaired for many years if kept in well-stoppled bottles, and not allowed to be constantly handled by the curious.

When medicines require to be sent to any distance, or when it is desired to furnish any one with a dose of a particular remedy to be taken only when rendered necessary, it is customary to bruise down the globules in a small quantity of sugar of milk, and thus make up the dose in the form of a small powder.

If we wish to give a remedy in divided doses, this is most conveniently fulfilled by dissolving the globules in *distilled* water, *pure* cold water, or water which has been previously *boiled* or filtered. The wineglass, tumbler, or phial in which the medicine is to be mixed, should be scrupulously clean, and whenever a change is made in the medicine, if the same vessel is employed, it ought to be *carefully washed,* first with scalding, and subsequently with cold water, before it is again used. When a phial is preferred, the cork or stopper must also be washed. Hahnemann recommended that the phial should first be rinsed with pure spirits of wine, and then exposed to a rather high temperature by being placed near the fire for some time. If the medicine is retained in an open vessel, it should be covered over with a saucer, or some other utensil of the sort, to prevent evaporation. When two medicaments are to be administered alternately, there ought to be a clean spoon for each mixture, and care should be taken to keep them separate.

DILUTIONS. The terms *high*, *middle* and *low*, are given to the different dilutions or attenuations. By the *first* epithet is generally understood the eighteenth, twenty-fourth, and thirtieth (although the attenuations have recently been carried much higher); by the *second*, the ninth, twelfth, and fifteenth; and by the *third*, the first, third, and sixth. The strength of these is *relative;* for although the *low* attenuations contain more particles of the *original* medicinal substance, and are commonly found the more effective in acute diseases, they are, upon the whole, less so in those of a chronic nature, and do not maintain their action on the system for so long a period as the higher ones. For domestic purposes, the author would recommend the *middle* attenuations to those who wish a very small case containing only one attenuation of each medicine, from the circumstance that they are perhaps less liable to cause those temporary medicinal exacerbations which are occasionally manifested in extremely susceptible persons; but as it is frequently of advantage to change the attenuation (by commencing, for instance, with the sixth, and then resorting to the twelfth, on giving a second course of the medicine), a case or box containing both the lower and the middle attenuations, or one number of each of the attenuations, viz.: the third or the sixth, the twelfth or fifteenth, and the thirtieth, would be found more extensively useful. Homœopathists prescribe only one remedy at a time; but in some complicated cases, considerable advantage is occasionally to be derived from the alternate employment of two remedies, viz.: either when they seem equally well indicated, and it is difficult to make a selection, or, and more especially, when each remedy possesses certain properties which are wanting in the other, and the *sum* of both is required in the case under treatment. It is only in such instances that this procedure is admissible however.

When it is requisite to keep a medicine in solution for some days, a few drops of proof spirit may be added to the water, in order to preserve it from decomposition.

In conclusion, it is necessary to state that the medicines should be taken fasting, and food or drink, as also excessive bodily or mental exertion, abstained from for half an hour to an hour afterwards. The homœopathic remedies should be kept in a clean, dry, dark place, free from odors. Every description of allopathic medicine, patent or domestic, is prohibited; likewise bleedings, blisters, medicated fomentations, perfumery, and everything containing camphor.

INDEX.

THE END.